PORTABLE GRINDHOUSE

THE LOST ART OF THE VHS BOX

FBI

Jacques Boyreau

WATCH WHAT YOU WANT WHEN YOU WANT HOME VIDEO

COLOR/200 pgs.

GW00673183

WATCH WHAT YOU W

HOME VIDEO

WHEN YOU WANT

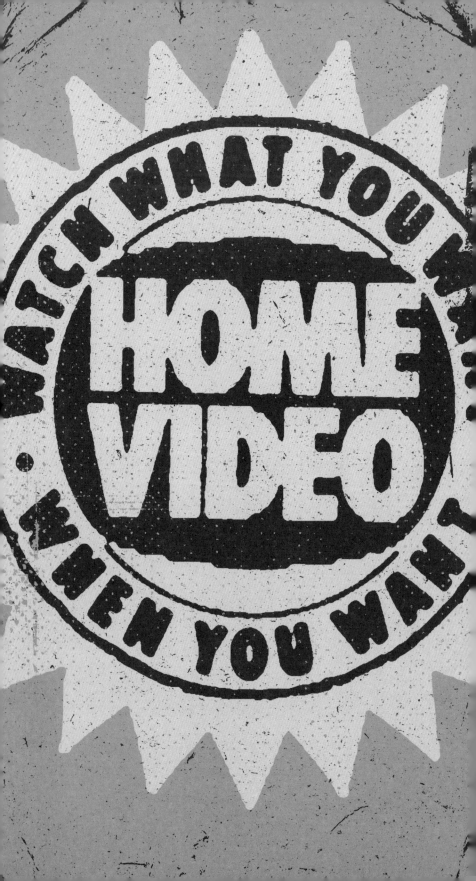

PORTABLE GRINDHOUSE

JAQUES BOYREAU

The people next door have a new machine in their family room that records TV.

"These tapes last one hour each. We have *The Wizard of Oz*."

"You have *The Wizard of Oz*?"

"Yes. On three tapes. With commercials. Look how this thing ejects—"

SSHHH-K-DANNGGG!

ACT TWO

A shop selling uncut movies on pre-recorded tape just opened. It is on the same street as the Chinese restaurant. Every time we chow, I ask, May we go into the movie store? The movies are on shelves under glass in fancy boxes...and the exciting feeling I get — as if leaning into a row of handguns and they are blowing me away. The video proprietor is the 'tan type' with hot silver hair and golf pro threads. The tapes are unbelievably expensive. Eighty dollars apiece. But I just keep coming and looking. One night the owner and my mom chit-chat. He says he'll copy any movie for $40.00.

The first one I want is *Enter The Dragon*. Every few weeks, we buy another: *Dirty Harry, The Godfather 1 & 2, Death Wish, The Wild Bunch*. He puts our copies in brown cases with punch-letter label strips. Then he is gone. Or rather, the FBI takes him away. And Tricky-Dick with the Florida-vibe does time.

Minnesota Fats, our neighborhood pool table store, has a new "We Have Video" banner in their window. I get off the bus and go in. Minnesota Fats is now stocked with Atari cartridges, synthesizers, hand-gadgets, and more locked-up VHS. I like looking at Warner Home Video boxes the most.

Holy box.

There. *A Clockwork Orange*...must have just come out. I am in the showroom with tall vitrines filled with VHS and Betamax, and billiards tables and home-neon stuff, and there are no sales people. The register is at the back with someone behind, acting ho-hum. But past that, down a short hall, another space —closet-like, darker lit— has activity. I enter. Inside this room is a pretty girl standing behind a counter. Two full walls are lined in exact shelving with dense rows of video in homogenous black cases. I ask about them.

She says, "They're for rent."

Original tapes, separated from their box, cheaply rentable. This is a moment.

TIME: 1980*s*
ACT FOUR

The store on the corner glows. The street is liquor and cigarettes and cop cars and Shazam! motherfuckers. You go into the portable grindhouse and grab one or more tapes for the night. The decals on the boxes —pasties that mark genre and inventory methods— are a fascinating kind of graffiti, scars that show what these videos do to survive. Videos are like hookers. You pay and take it back to the room and stick it in and let it happen and rewind it and return the booty— don't want late fees.

First, a skim of history.

The oldest color broadcast video known to exist is "An Evening With Fred Astaire" from 1958. In the 1960s Sony introduced open reel video recorders under the U-Matic system. The device was bulky. VHS made compacting possible with a parallel load design. U-format and Betamax used one load pole around the drumhead. VHS used two poles to pull the tape into an M-shape.

VCR stands for Video Cassette Recorder. VHS does not stand for Video Home System. It means Vertical Helical Scan, indicating that VHS works as a helical scan capture of a frequency-modulated luminance, which is then stored as a black-and-white signal, with a down-converted 'color-under' chroma signal. The first VHS machine was sold by JVC (aka Victor Company of Japan) in 1977 for $1060.00. VHS dueled with the superior Betamax for years for market control; other technologies that went mano with VHS included Video 2000 by Philips and Grundig, and V-Cord by Sanyo.7. The longest recorded time reached by Betamax was 5 hours on an ultra-thin L-830 cassette. VHS reached 10.6 hours on an SLP/EP T-210 cassette. In addition to its longer recording time, VHS's win over Betamax is assignable to a 'design goal' of making its Standard Play of 120 minutes fit the running time of most Hollywood movies.

For the record, the VHS cassette is a 7 3/8" wide, 4" deep, 1" thick (187mm X 103mm X 25mm) plastic clamshell held together with 5 Phillips head screws; and the robo-mod VHS logo is a typeface called "Lee," created in 1972 by Leo Weisz for Visual Graphics Corporation.

There you have some boilerplate about what VHS is. What it really meant and could mean for the future is a whole other matter, involving ideology.

The curt take on VHS is that it is a dead format, a quaint and sham way to watch a movie. Regardless, to date, there are quantities of VHS titles not available on DVD, and that may never be. But, beyond itemizing the available, I want to talk about the synergy that VHS and film enjoyed. More than any technical feud, the chasm between VHS and digital is that VHS does not threaten the traditional movie experience of seeing film projected as film. On one hand, digital offers to restore film, but also to discredit it through unneeded "improvements." There is a point where digital restoration becomes inner theft, if, having taken control of the stuff —the movie— it poisons the well, i.e. the movie theater. I am referring to the rise of digital theaters, which I see as a final straw in an aberrant Oedipal kill-off of the film experience. Really, the core issue is a fight over light. How do you want delivery on your light? What bulb is your signal? When movie theaters switched from carbon arc to Xenon lamphouses in the 1970s, the change was based on efficiency and longer usage, but aesthetically, though the Xenon light was bright, the fire had cooled. There is something alive and combustive and oneiric in the beam of a carbon arc. I want to call this quality "phlogiston," which is the magic, mythic element thought to exist in all things that burn. Certain voyeurs like me dig that touch of fire and what it does to film grain. Digital luminance lacks a kick, misses organic vigor —

the light does not spill, the wave is not undulant, the stream loses consciousness.

But what about all those digital lines of resolution? That's some real interesting bullshit. Extended Definition Beta, using metal tape, approached a resolution of 500 lines. Blu-ray outputs 720-1080 lines. VHS: 250 lines. So, analog video demonstrably wimps out, hmm? But a movie is not a frame and a frame-to-frame comparison of lines ignores the influence of time and the unfolding of hundreds of thousands of frames, into an 'unenumerable' sensation. For example, I typically notice how awesome digital projection looks at the beginning of a movie, but by the end, I am non-penetrated, weirdly tired...feel like I got a plastic bag on my head with a little hole to breathe through. With film, the opposite happens. At the start, got to admit film doesn't look techno-vivid, but time is on its side, and the machine and the flicker and the beat form a light that is special, that you can breathe, because it breathes with you...and sustains the brain in a dream or a nightmare or phlogiston. A film-sourced movie echoes a definition of analog as being "a continuous stream of waveforms." Saying digital is like film is like saying a speculum exam is like sex because they both involve entering the vagina.

Basically VHS is good to cinema. VHS is a part of film, a Samaritan-format, not a digital changeling out to usurp. While VHS and theaters competed for revenue, the value of film per se saw no dip; in fact, VHS exposed the 'long tail' of cinema...its archival largesse. At a personal level, video handed cinema to people, and took to the street via mom-and-pop video depots, not to mention every city's special store with monster inventory. You'd be in these places like you were in a demagogic library made for avenging nerds, punk-intellectuals, and romantic-deviants. You drifted, in the aisles, picking at boxes, scoping, digging bins, trying to keep track, agog at incongruous juxtapositions. You could be dithered by the box auras, your taste in movies —your filtration and rationality— were now victims of the postmodern clusterfuck. The silent delirium of cruising stacks on racks reminds one of Dali's remark, "I look at all women." I look at all VHS boxes!

Or Nathaniel Hawthorne, presaging VHS, writes, "those upquivering flashes of the spirit, to which minds in an abnormal state are liable." Translation: That box looks extra awesome!

What VHS created was the ability to hold a movie in your hand and feel its power. Film consumption is not film possession. A movie is a running out, a mechanized going-until-gone, and that great fleetingness subconsciously stokes a desire to possess this thing, and that's what video really accomplished: it turned movies into things, into sentimental totems in which VHS binds a clinging to the whole of a movie, where movie-magic is purloined by tape and by box —through the hand that possesses, through the box whose graphic stimulates, and finally the fetish that metonymically thinks: the VHS = THE Movie. Posters could advertise, slightly fetishize a movie; credit sequences could identify participants; but with conspicuous street cred and hustler-friendly mercantilism, VHS box-art 'became' the iconic equivalent of the movie. Like Merlin trapped in a tree, VHS shapes movie mojo into video juju — but without the box's voodoo, forget about it!

On par with the jukebox, disco, and neon, VHS reformatted the world's product-intake and conquered TV in the same way TV conquered comic books in the 1950s. Yet circularly, Portable Grindhouse-type VHS boxes contributed to the comics scene's reanimation, in the sense that video stores acted as sleazy libraries where judging a 'book' by its cover was de rigueur. By siding with artifice on the box, and by exploiting the hinge between adolescence and adulthood, VHS reestablished a style of hype without qualm, a staple of the comic book 'face.'

On a meta-level, Portable Grindhouse is SuperTrash. The philosophy on parade here is a synergized enigma made of art and trash —but which is which? Whichever's which, Portable Grindhouse speaks to our conflicts of interests, and coaxes co-dependencies between the piece of shit and the master(piece).

"The revenge of analog...has a nice ring"
It pays to know that VHS will never not be cool. It has a look that is very Homoousion with Film — i.e. "made of the same stuff." The digital world lacks much in the ways of tenderness. There is something supererogatory about the digital signal, reminds one of steroids and anorexia and neo-conservatism — anxieties of insatiable control. Of course "control" is often...useful. We'll find out eventually how invincible digital turns out to be, but when I need cinema and do not have film on the screen, I know some video tapes and boxes that will connect me. It points to the possibility that the 2001 monolith is a VHS.

– Jacques Boyreau
August, 2009

PORTABLE
GRINDHOUƧE
IƧ DEDICATED
TO KOLCHACK.

I thank Jimbo Blanchard for
turning me onto Gary Groth.
I thank Jacob Covey for his idealism.
Charlotte for her mock shots.
Rip-O-Matic for sharing the love.
Piggy Op for a few bucks.
And Marcel's sweaty ghost.

Editor: Jacques Boyreau
Editorial Liaison: Gary Groth
Art Director/Designer: Jacob Covey
Production Assistance: Paul Baresh
Associate Publisher: Eric Reynolds
Publishers: Gary Groth & Kim Thompson

Portable Grindhouse is copyright © 2009 Fantagraphics Books. The introduction is
copyright © 2009 Jacques Boyreau. All rights reserved. Permission to quote for
reviews must be obtained from the publisher or the author. Back cover image
from the box art for "Virtual Combat" ©1995 Amritraj/Stevens Entertainment.

Distributed in the U.S. by W.W. Norton and Company, Inc. (212-354-5500)
Distributed in Canada by the Canadian Manda Group (416-516-0911)
Distributed in the UK by Turnaround Distribution (208-829-3009)
Distributed to comics stores by Diamond Comics Distributors (800-452-6642)

Fantagraphics Books, Inc. 7563 Lake City Way, Seattle, WA 98115
Visit fantagraphics.com for more books to rend your eyes.

Printed in Singapore. ISBN: 978-1-56097-969-2

Crims⬤n

THE COLOR OF TERROR.

A film by **JEAN FORTUNY**
Starring **PAUL NASH, SYLVIA SOLAR, OLIVER MATTHEWS**
EVELYN PALMER, RICHARD ANDERSON, YUL SANDERS
Directed by **JEAN FORTUNY**

 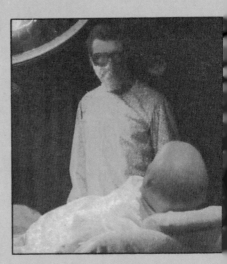

Gangster Jack Surnett is shot in the head by police in a gun battle. When a surgeon declares that only a brain transplant can save Surnett, the criminal's men go in search of another gangster who is biologically similar.

The victim is found and executed, and finally his severed head is grafted to Surnett's body. But the operation is hardly a success... Surnett becomes a murdering maniac, sowing terror as he stains the countryside CRIMSON.

Running Time: 90 minutes

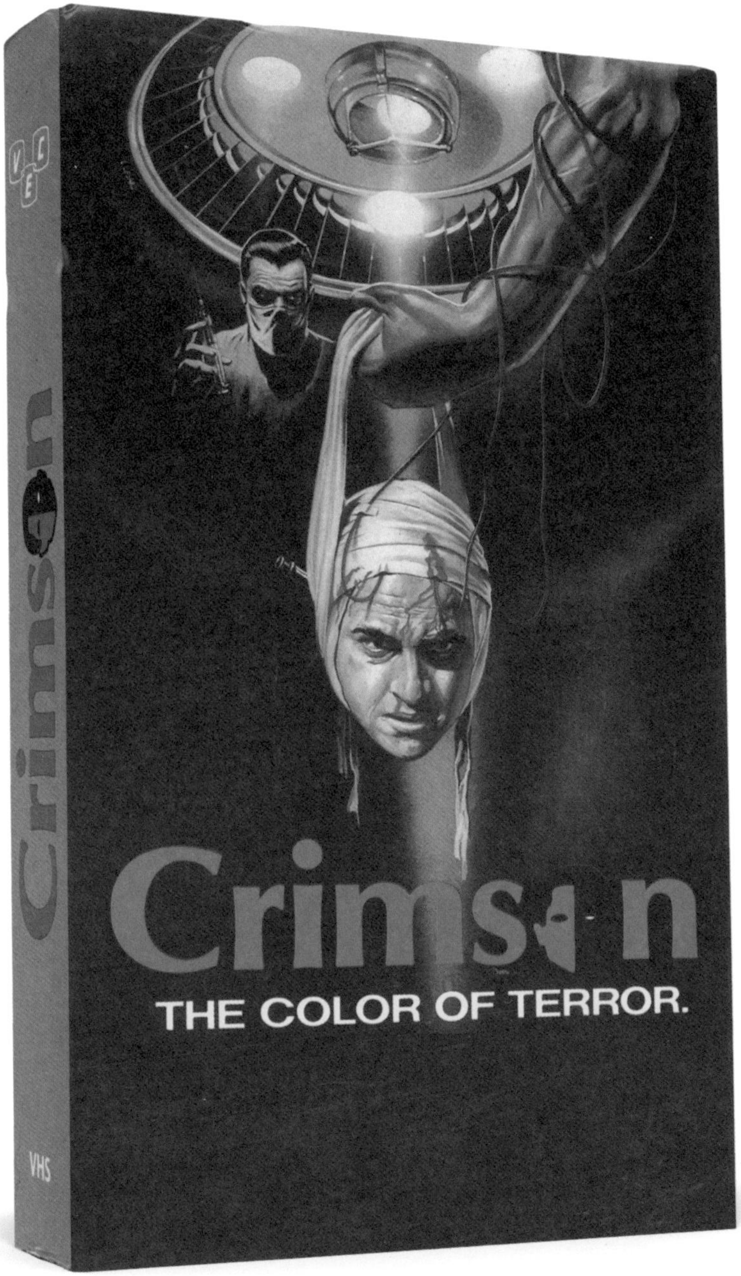
VEC
Crimson
Crimson
THE COLOR OF TERROR.
VHS

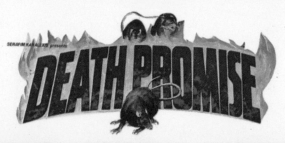

SERAFIM KARALEXIS presents

DEATH PROMISE

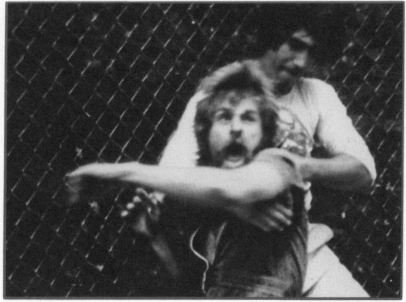

A STORY OF BLOODY REVENGE...

When the tenants band together to save their homes, the landlord resorts to any means possible to evict them...even the murder of an old man who had been their leader. The son, vowing revenge, makes a DEATH PROMISE.

Don't miss the film's explosive conclusion!!

RUNNING TIME: Approx. 96 Min.

R — RESTRICTED — UNDER 17 REQUIRES ACCOMPANYING PARENT OR ADULT GUARDIAN

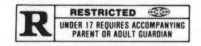

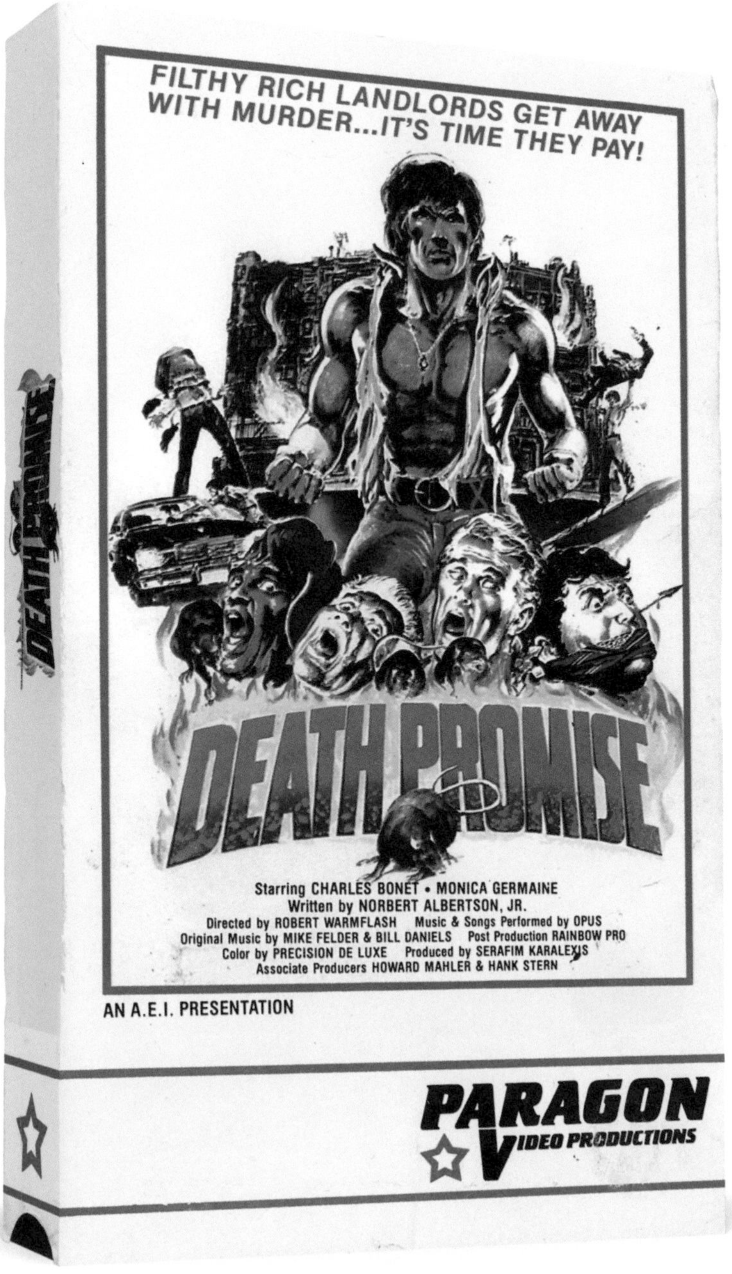
FILTHY RICH LANDLORDS GET AWAY WITH MURDER...IT'S TIME THEY PAY!
DEATH PROMISE
Starring CHARLES BONET • MONICA GERMAINE
Written by NORBERT ALBERTSON, JR.
Directed by ROBERT WARMFLASH Music & Songs Performed by OPUS
Original Music by MIKE FELDER & BILL DANIELS Post Production RAINBOW PRO
Color by PRECISION DE LUXE Produced by SERAFIM KARALEXIS
Associate Producers HOWARD MAHLER & HANK STERN
AN A.E.I. PRESENTATION
PARAGON VIDEO PRODUCTIONS
DEATH PROMISE

THE LEGEND OF THE...
WOLF WOMAN

See Daniella's Reincarnation!

Directed by: R. D. Silver
Starring: Anne Borel & Fred Stafford

On the night of the full moon, deep within a forest, a beautiful young woman starts a rhythmic, ritualistic dance into a circle of fire . . . As she reaches a frenzied climax, she collapses on the ground, writhing and groaning as her pure skin and lovely features assume the ugliness of a wild animal. She leaves a trail of bloody killings across the country-side as she runs for her life. Can love be the cure for this terrifying transformation or will the beautiful Daniella continue to return to her werewolf image.

#6208, 70 mins., Color, Rated R, Released in 1977

UNITED
HOME VIDEO

Distributed by
United Entertainment, Inc.
6535 E. Skelly Drive
Tulsa, Ok 74145
918-622-6460

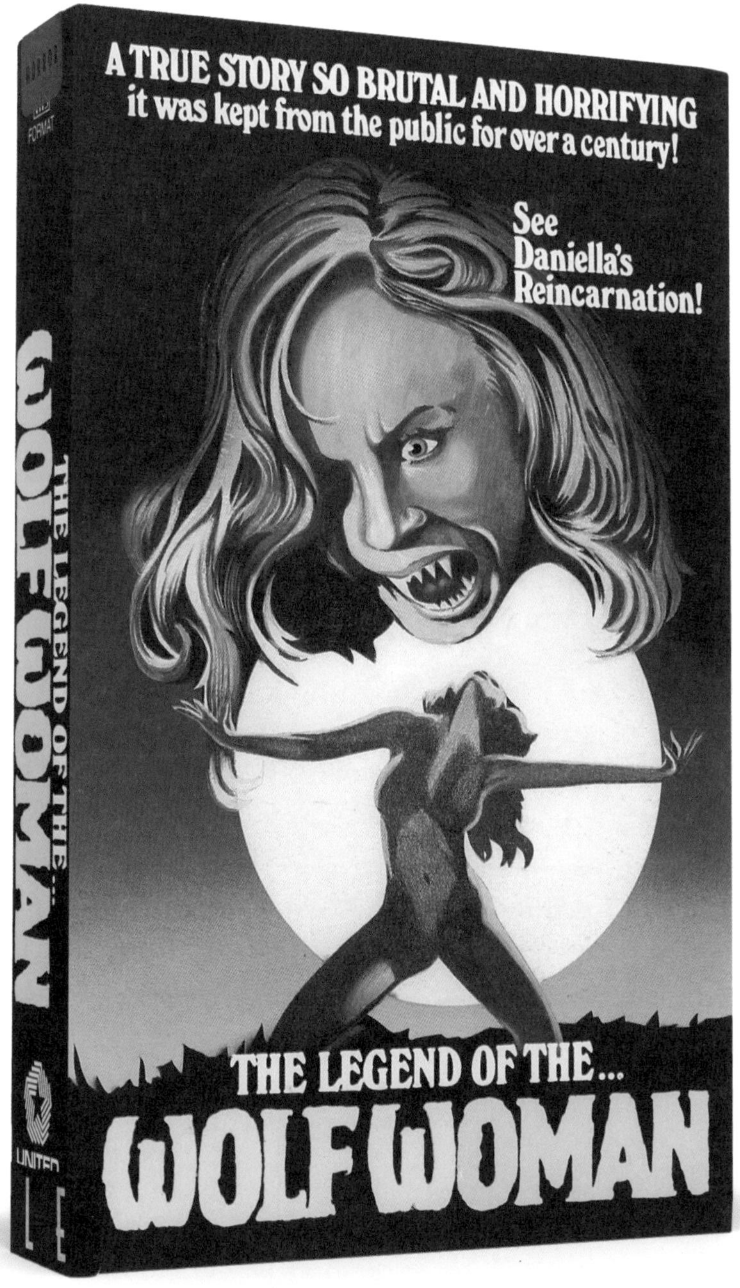
A TRUE STORY SO BRUTAL AND HORRIFYING
it was kept from the public for over a century!
See
Daniella's
Reincarnation!
THE LEGEND OF THE...
WOLF WOMAN
THE LEGEND OF THE...
WOLF WOMAN
FORMAT
UNITED

Some of the other fine
videocassette programs available are:

The Sound of Music / M*A*S*H / Patton
The French Connection / The African Queen
A Touch of Class / The Graduate
Carnal Knowledge / Tora! Tora! Tora!
Hello, Dolly! / The King & I
The Sailor Who Fell From Grace With The Sea
The Longest Day / Von Ryan's Express
The Lion in Winter / Mighty Mouse
Cleopatra / The Day The Earth Stood Still
Blue Hawaii / Those Magnificent Men in Their
Flying Machines / The Hot Rock
Beneath the Planet of the Apes / The Desert Fox
Fantastic Voyage / The Hustler
The Sand Pebbles / Valley of the Dolls
Heckle & Jeckle / C.C. & Company
Deputy Dawg / Rabbit Test
The Paper Chase / The Making of Star Wars
Doctor Dolittle / The Bible
Hercules / Girls, Girls, Girls
The Agony and the Ecstasy
The Day of the Dolphin / Soldier Blue
Hells Angels on Wheels
Voyage to the Bottom of the Sea / King Creole
The Poseidon Adventure / Butch Cassidy and
the Sundance Kid / In Praise of Older Women
The Duchess and the Dirtwater Fox
The Towering Inferno / Dirty Mary, Crazy Larry
The Blue Max / Planet of the Apes
The Omen / Silver Streak / The Producers
The Adventures of Sherlock Holmes Smarter Brother
The Seduction of Mimi / The Diary of Anne Frank
. . . and many more.

VHS Videocassette Format

T.M.

For complete information, write to:

Magnetic Video Corporation
Industrial Park
Farmington Hills, MI 48024

©
1980

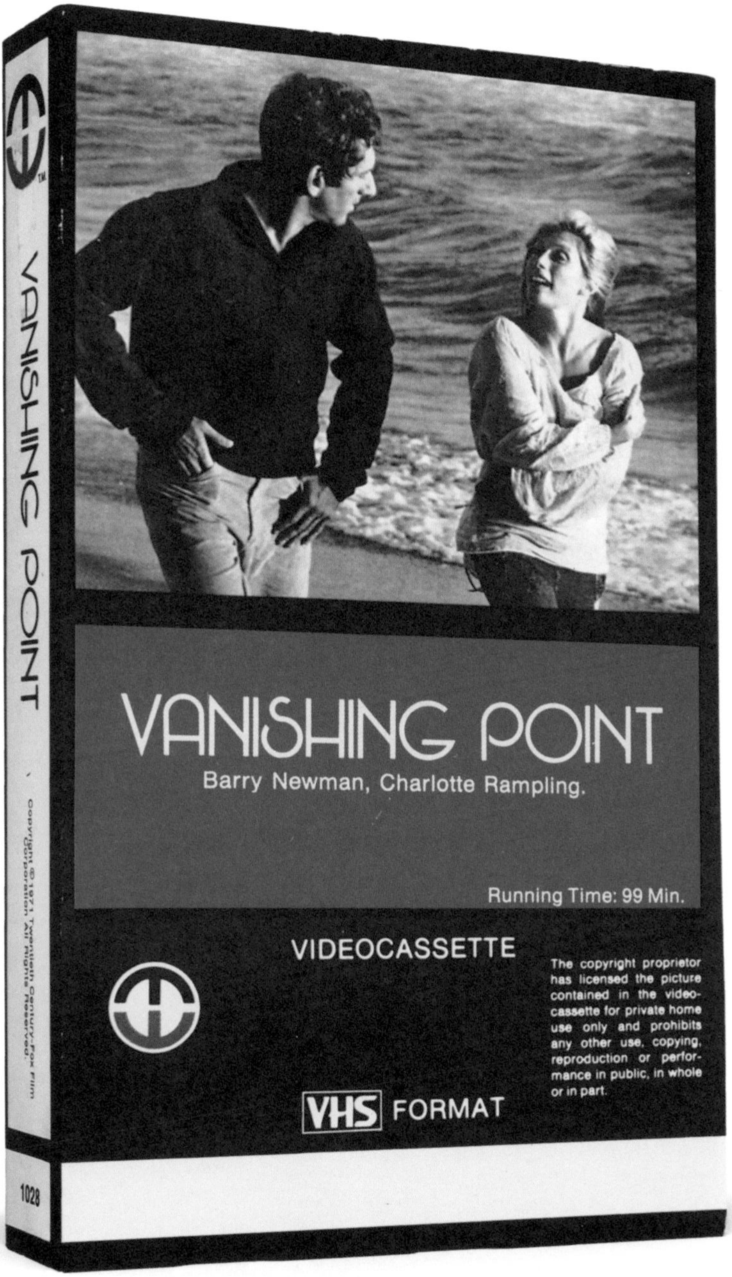

VANISHING POINT
Copyright © 1971 Twentieth Century-Fox Film Corporation All Rights Reserved.
1028
VANISHING POINT
Barry Newman, Charlotte Rampling.
Running Time: 99 Min.
VIDEOCASSETTE
The copyright proprietor has licensed the picture contained in the video-cassette for private home use only and prohibits any other use, copying, reproduction or performance in public, in whole or in part.
VHS FORMAT

BLOOD FEAST

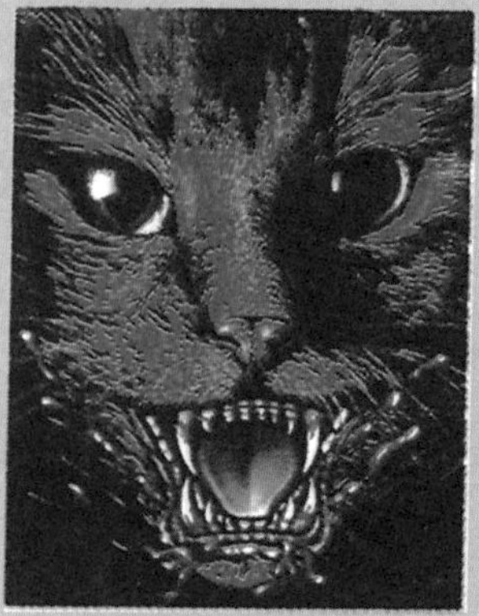

A helicopter hovers over the city The pilot is Hugo, seeking beautiful women to add to his grisly collection of pretty maids...bottle beheaded and all in a row.

He's suave, he's seductive, and certifiably insane. This playboy's mansion doesn't have a bunny, but instead, a cellar-full of living, lunging, hungry cats, screaming for scraps of human flesh.

Hugo's hulking butler is Drago, with an eye for the ladie himself. After trying to get one girl's attention with garden shears, Drago ends up as din-din, thrown into a forest of flashing fangs!

Anjanett Comer, a lovely lady who's husband travels too much, has become Hugo's most difficult conquest. Lulle by a candle-warmed cognac, she agrees to see Hugo's cadaverous collection, and then runs for her life, as the countless cats break free to become a carnivorous, flash-flood of terror!

Catalog #1023
83 Minutes
Color

PRINTED IN CANADA

R RESTRICTED
UNDER 17 REQUIRES ACCOMPANYING PARENT OR ADULT GUARDIAN

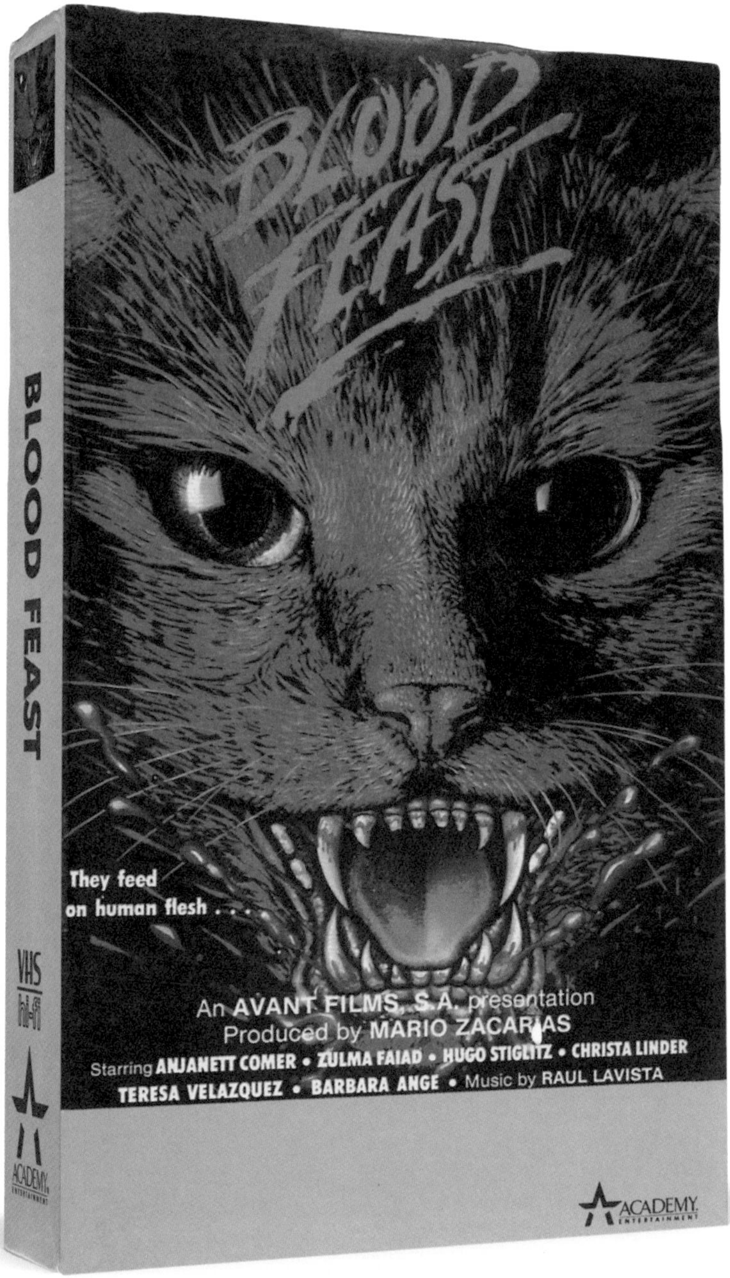
BLOOD FEAST
BLOOD FEAST
They feed on human flesh . . .
An AVANT FILMS, S.A. presentation
Produced by MARIO ZACARIAS
Starring ANJANETT COMER • ZULMA FAIAD • HUGO STIGLITZ • CHRISTA LINDER
TERESA VELAZQUEZ • BARBARA ANGE • Music by RAUL LAVISTA
VHS hi-fi
ACADEMY ENTERTAINMENT
ACADEMY ENTERTAINMENT

the WITCHING

IS HE FATHER...MOTHER...FRIEND... WARLOCK...OR INSANE?

Orson Welles is Cato, a sinister man who owns the strange town of Lilith, along with its only in-dustry, a toy factory, and all of the people in it... Mr. Cato permits most any and all indulgences to "his people" except for children — until his eight year old son, who died many years ago, lives once again.

RUNNING TIME: Approx. 87 minutes

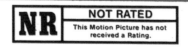

NR | **NOT RATED**
This Motion Picture has not received a Rating.

©1983 PARAGON • LAS VEGAS, NEVADA

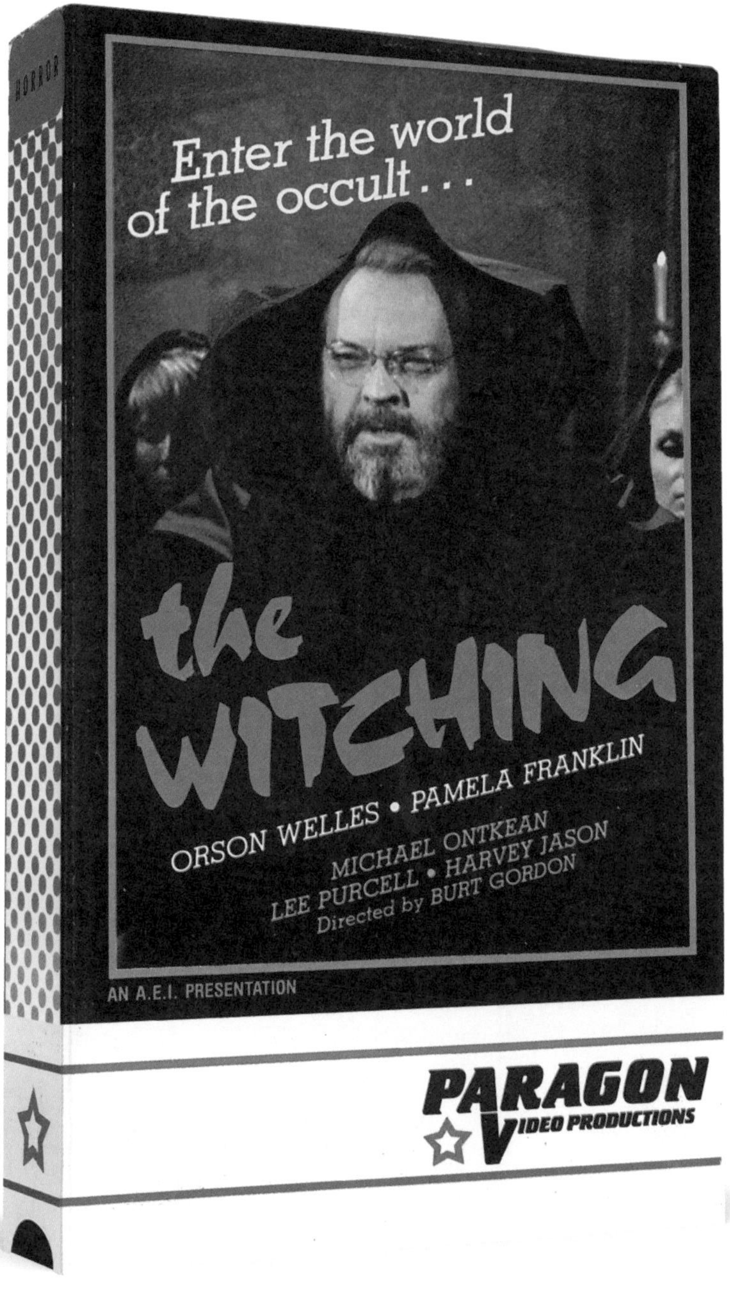
HORROR
Enter the world
of the occult . . .
the
WITCHING
ORSON WELLES • PAMELA FRANKLIN
MICHAEL ONTKEAN
LEE PURCELL • HARVEY JASON
Directed by BURT GORDON
AN A.E.I. PRESENTATION
PARAGON
VIDEO PRODUCTIONS

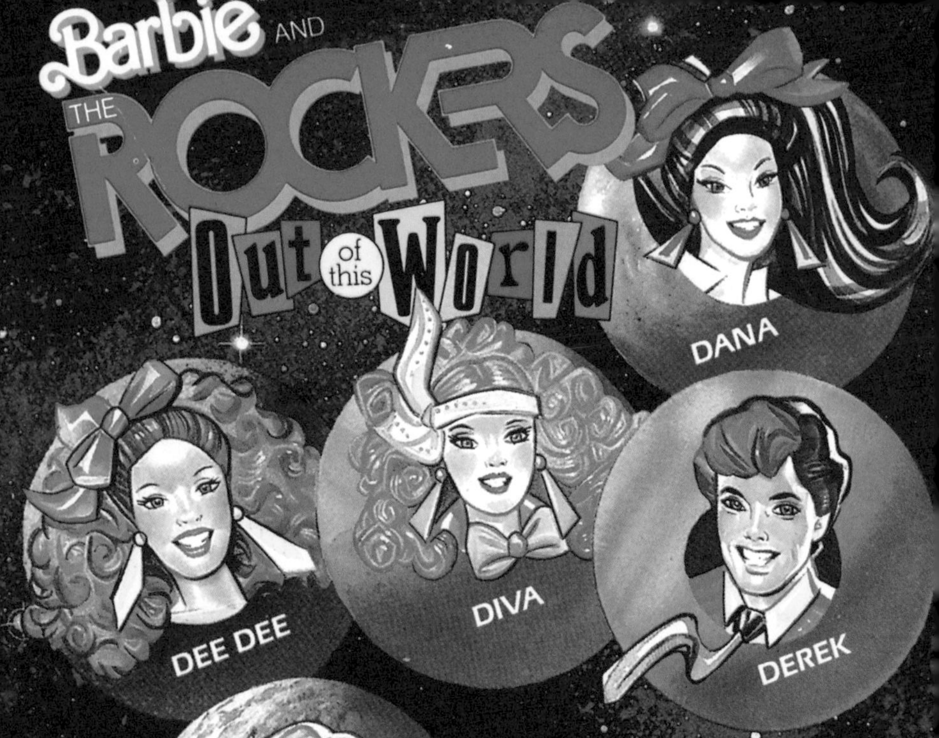

Barbie AND
THE ROCKERS
Out of this World
DANA
DEE DEE
DIVA
DEREK

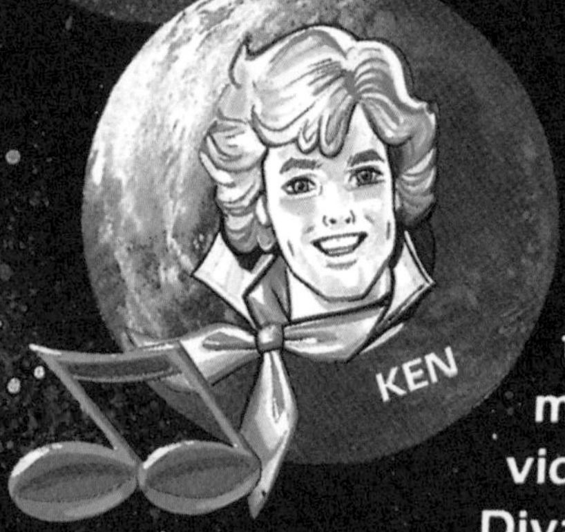

KEN

Hi, I'm Barbie™. My band The Rockers™, and I, are taking off for excitement in our very first video! Ken™, Dana™, Diva™, Dee Dee™, Derek™ and I are going where no band has gone before . . . into space! Now our music is rocking the outer limits because we've launched into an adventure that's totally "Out Of This World." So strap yourself in for action, because the countdown to fun has begun!

Love,
Barbie™

Color/Approx. Running Time 25 Min.

HI-TOPS™ VIDEO

BARBIE AND THE ROCKERS in OUT OF THIS WORLD
All songs performed by Barbie and The Rockers
Music produced by Mike Piccirillo
Executive Producers Haim Saban and Andy Heyward
Produced by Robby London and Ellen Levy   Directed by Bernard Deyries

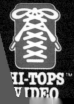

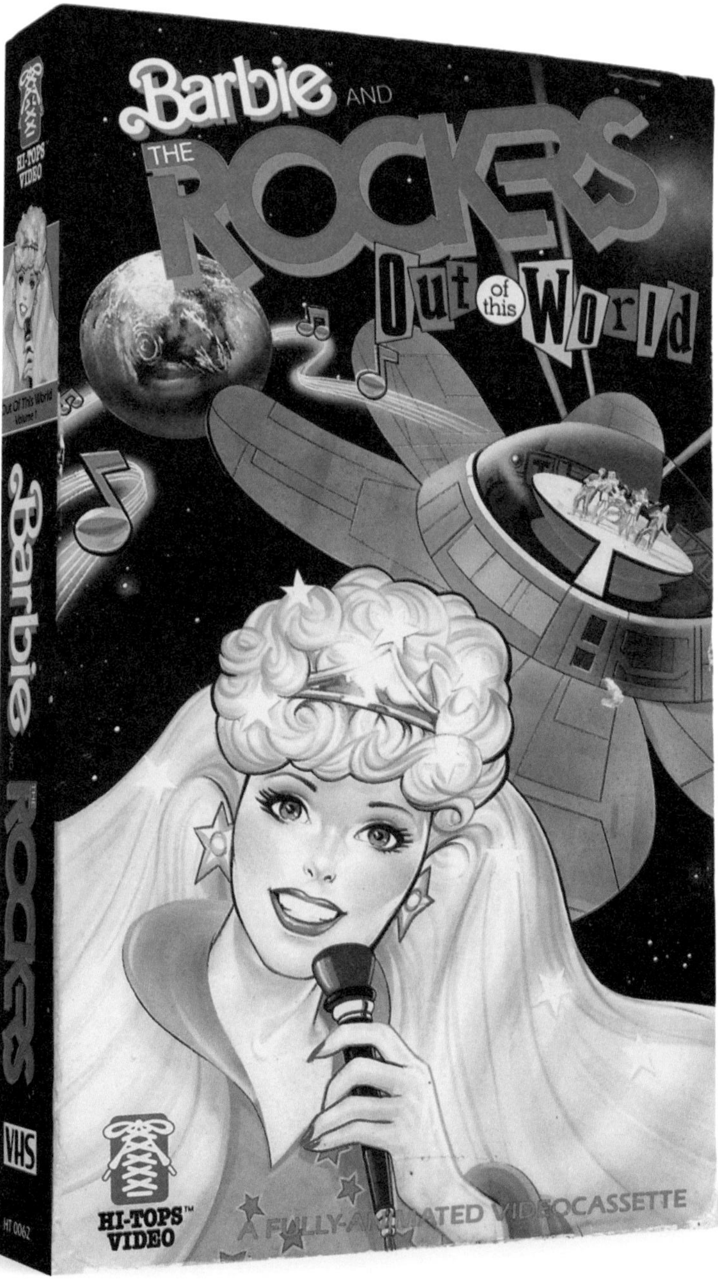
Barbie AND
THE ROCKERS
Out of this World
HI-TOPS VIDEO
A FULLY-ANIMATED VIDEOCASSETTE
VHS
HT 0062

CAMP MOTION PICTURES PRESENTS
a little zach production of

Video Violence

...When renting is not enough!!

VIDEO VIOLENCE is the ultimate in horror, gore and campy humor, with a crazy cast of characters and a 'twist ending'.

Instead of the usual psychopathic maniac unleashed on a normal unsuspecting town, we have a normal, unsuspecting couple completely immersed in a town of psychopathic maniacs.

A transplanted New York couple open a video store in a small country town. One day Steve, our hero, discovers an unmarked tape among the morning's rental returns. When watching it for a clue to who the renter might be, he witnesses the violent, bloody, mutilation of the town's postmaster.

'Is it real or is it a gag?'

'Should he try to find the owner of the tape-a possible deranged killer?'

'Could this really happen in his town?'

'Could this happen in your town???'

Don't miss the shocking conclusion!!!

RUNNING TIME APPROX: 90 MINUTES
IN FULL COLOR
STARRING
ART NEILL, JACKIE NEILL, UKI WILLIAM TODDIE, BART SUMNE LISA COHEN

WRITTEN BY
GARY COHEN AND PAUL KAYE

PRODUCED BY
RAY CLARK

DIRECTED BY
GARY COHEN

ORIGINAL MUSIC BY
GORDON OVSIEW

EXECUTIVE PRODUCERS
SALVATORE RICHICHI and JAMES GOI

DISTRIBUTED BY

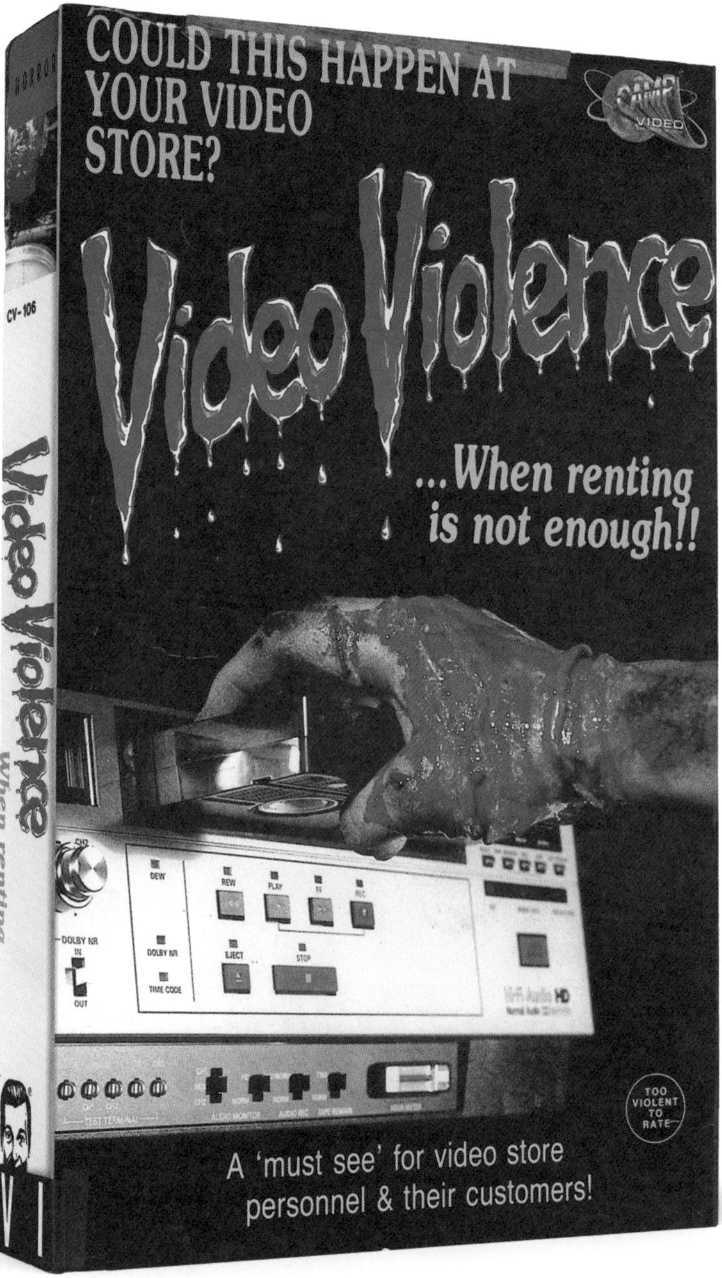
COULD THIS HAPPEN AT
YOUR VIDEO
STORE?
Video Violence
...When renting
is not enough!!
DEW
REW
PLAY
REC
DOLBY NR
IN
OUT
DOLBY NR
TIME CODE
EJECT
STOP
TOO
VIOLENT
TO
RATE
A 'must see' for video store
personnel & their customers!
HORROR
CV-106
Video Violence
When renting

1990: THE BRONX WARRIORS

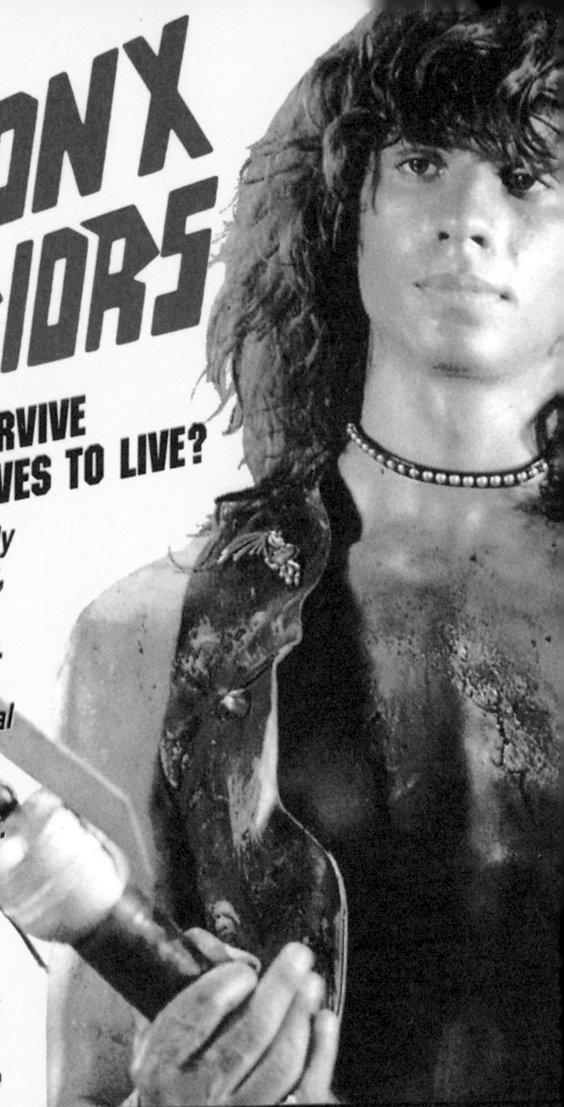

WHO WILL SURVIVE WHEN NO ONE DESERVES TO LIVE?

When the Bronx is officially declared a High Risk District, The Authorities give up any attempts to enforce The Law. From that moment on, The Riders reign—but their mortal enemies, The Zombies, The Tigers and The Scavengers, do not go easy into the night.

They are all the scum of the earth, your worst nightmare come true. Their names speak volumes of violence: Hammer, Ogre, Hot Dog, Ice, and Trash. For them killing is second nature and death has no meaning.

Theirs is a war of brutality with a unique prize: To the victor goes the Bronx.

Running Time: 84 Minutes

Cat. # 911

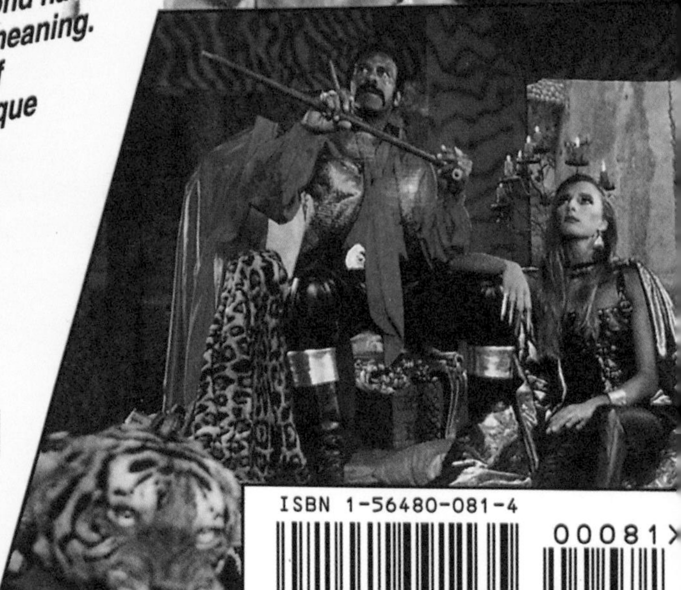

R RESTRICTED

Distributed by
BEST FILM & VIDEO CORP.
Great Neck, NY 11021

ISBN 1-56480-081-4

00081

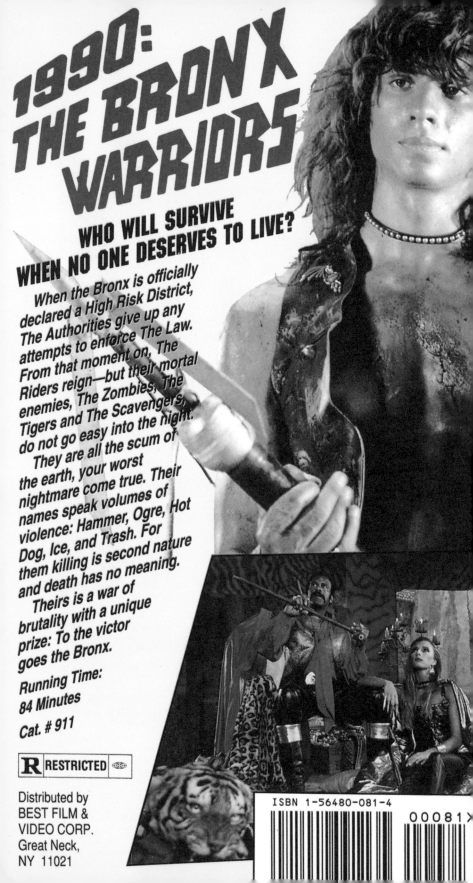

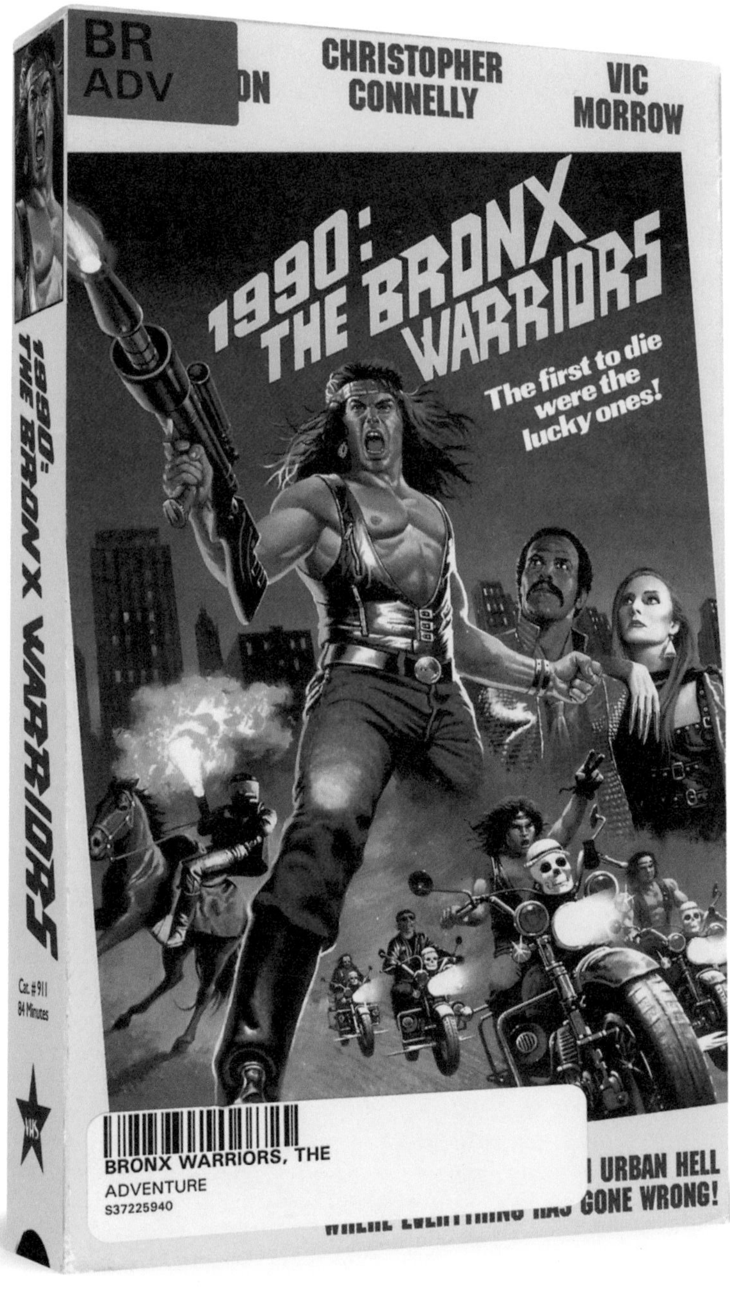
BR
ADV
CHRISTOPHER
CONNELLY
VIC
MORROW
1990:
THE BRONX
WARRIORS
The first to die
were the
lucky ones!
1990:
THE BRONX WARRIORS
Cat. #911
84 Minutes
BRONX WARRIORS, THE
ADVENTURE
S37225940
URBAN HELL
GONE WRONG!

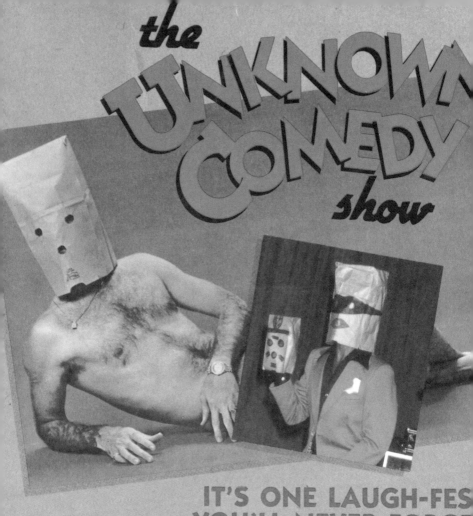

the UNKNOWN COMEDY show

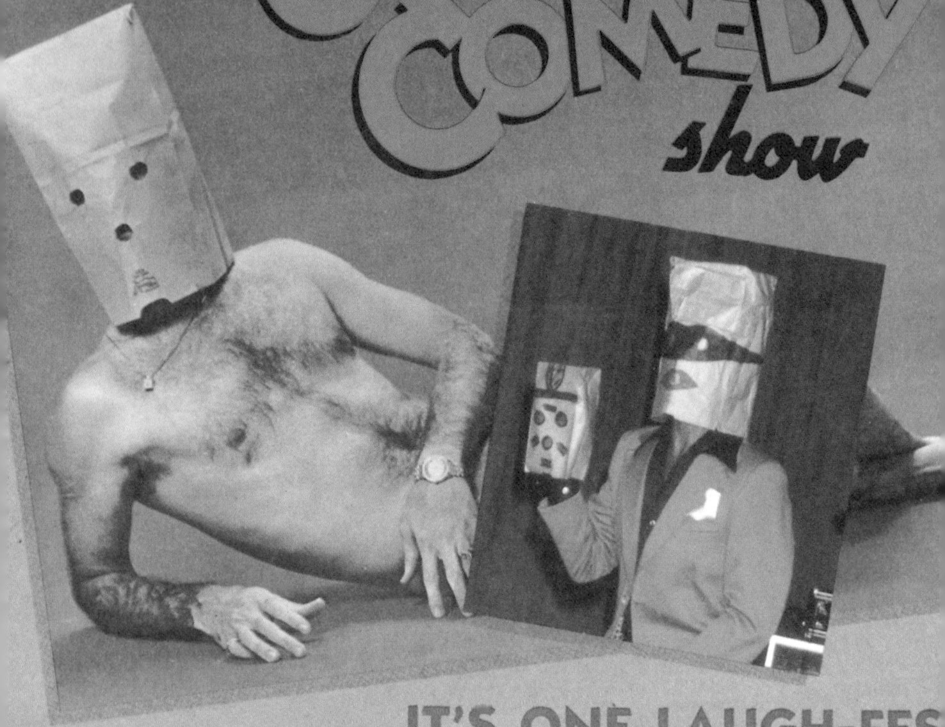

IT'S ONE LAUGH-FES
YOU'LL NEVER FORGE

Starring

THE UNKNOWN COMIC, MURRAY LANGS
JOHNNY DARK, JAMES MARCEL

From the risque to the raunchy, THE UNKNOWN COMEDY SHOW w
e kept under wraps for long! Prepare yourself for the crazed antics
Unknown Comic'' (that masked marauder of nonstop one-liners).
no surprise that the cat (and everything else) gets let out of the bag
wacky no-holds-barred comedy revue. Generously stretching the lin
good taste, three young stand-up comedians run through their outra
onologs, do some clever impressions and have a delightful time tea
udience. There's even an amazing juggler named James Marcel who
to handle three buzzing chainsaws at the same time! Also on hand
spoofs of TV shows, commercials and an ''unknown beauty pageant
Benny Hill would heartily endorse. It's a program of inspired luna
that'll have you bouncing off the wall—with laughter.

APPROXIMATE RUNNING TIME: 60 MINUTES

PRODUCED BY **BILL OSCO** AND **MURRAY LANGSTON**

U.S.A. HOME VIDEO / A DIVISION OF INTERNATIONAL VIDEO ENTERTAINMENT, IN

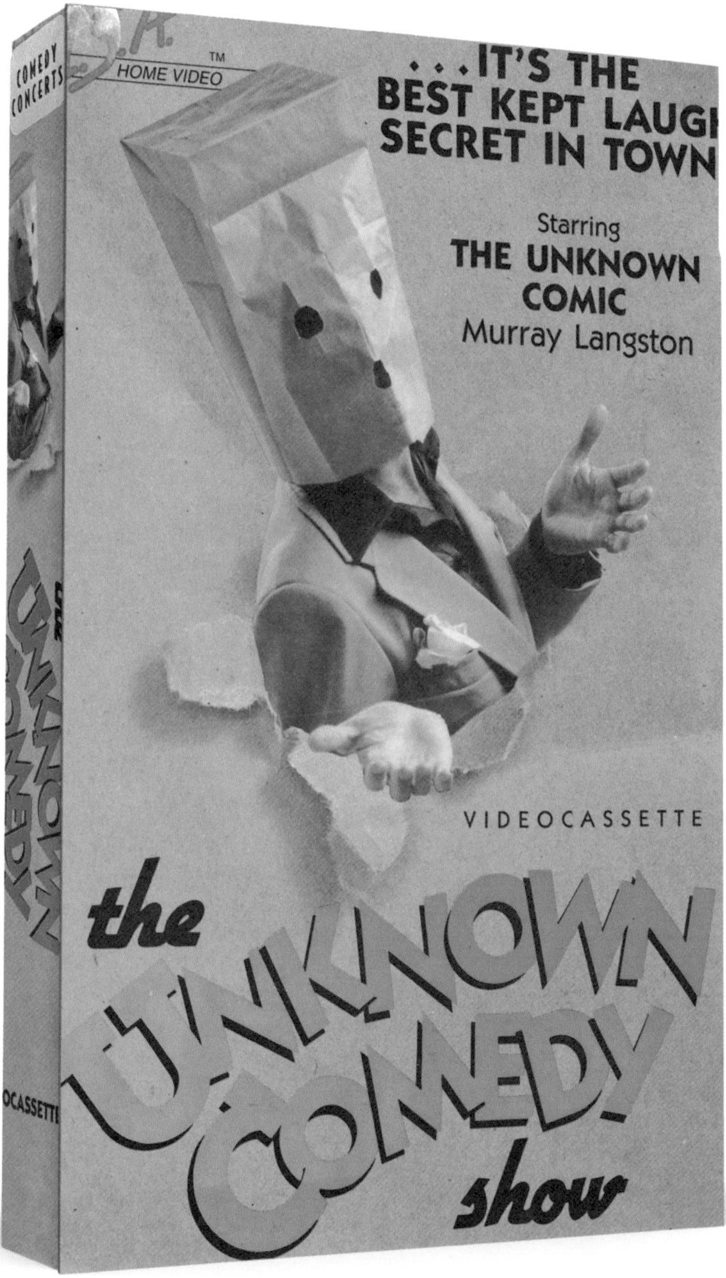
COMEDY CONCERTS
HOME VIDEO
...IT'S THE BEST KEPT LAUGH SECRET IN TOWN
Starring
THE UNKNOWN COMIC
Murray Langston
VIDEOCASSETTE
the UNKNOWN COMEDY show

"UNRELENTING..."

A TRULY ORIGINAL HAUNTED HOUSE THRILLER.
—*TOBE HOOPER, DIRECTOR OF*
'POLTERGEIST'

"TERRIFYING..."

ONE OF THE MOST FRIGHTENING FILMS I HAVE EVER SEEN.
—*KIM HENKEL, AUTHOR OF*
'TEXAS CHAINSAW MASSACRE'

Beautiful Liza has inherited a dilapidated New Orleans hotel she hopes to turn into a bed and breakfas inn...if she ever gets it opened First the painter falls to his death...then the plumber gets roto-rootered...while the interior decorator gets a "new look" from a tarantula stampede. Even the maid is terrifyingly tidied-up (Liza's got servant problems!). What's the cause? The hotel sits on one of the SEVEN DOORS OF DEATH! And the day these Gates-of-Hell are open, zombies will walk the earth. Get set for a gorey gumbo of gut-churning grotesqueries! Definitely not for the squeamish.

RATED R

7 DOORS OF DEATH

A FULL-LENGTH FEATURE FILM
APPROX. RUN. TIME: 80 MIN.

ThrillerVideo™

THRILLERVIDEO / A DIVISION OF
INTERNATIONAL VIDEO ENTERTAINMENT, INC.
AN NCB ENTERTAINMENT GROUP COMPANY

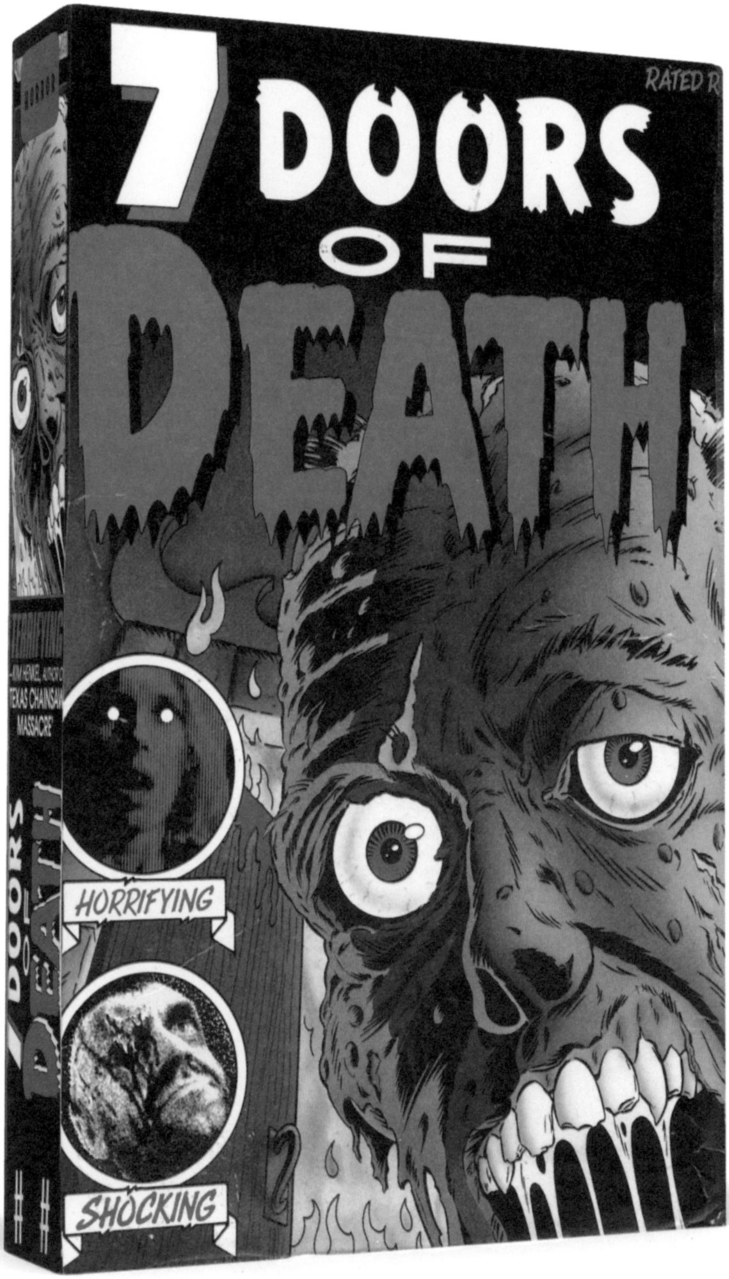
7 DOORS OF DEATH
RATED R
HORRIFYING
SHOCKING

The Making of:

THE TERMINATOR

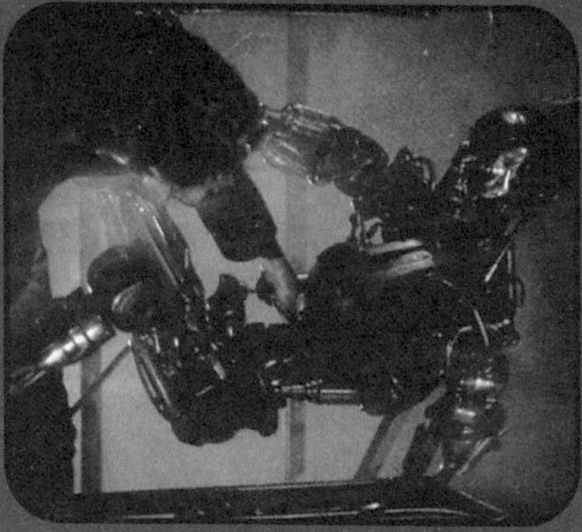

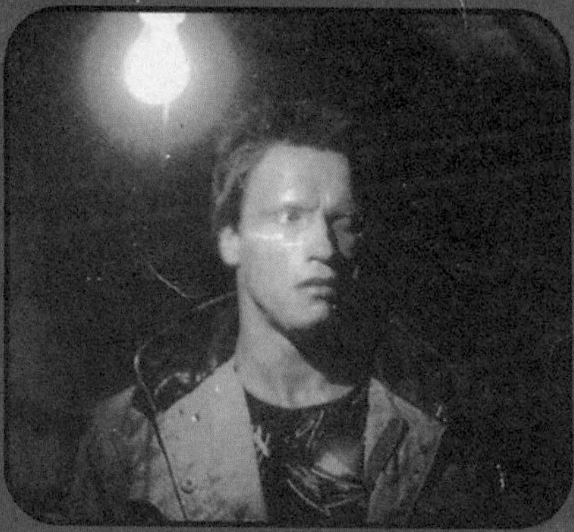

MISSING IN ACTION 2

THE BEGINNING

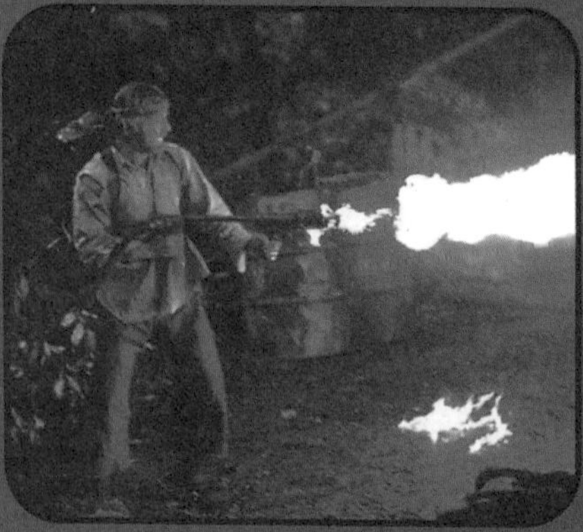

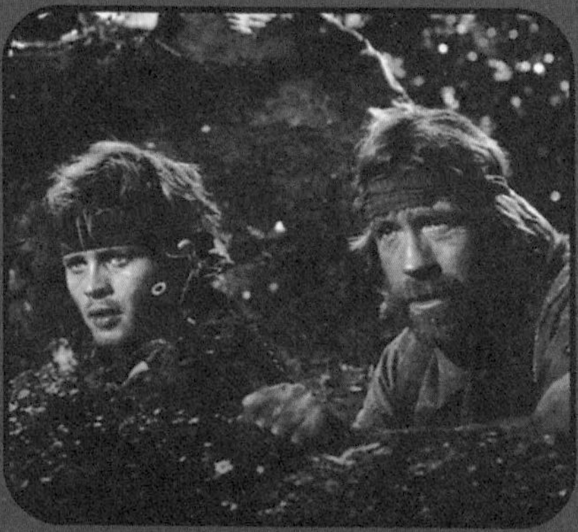

Spectacular explosions...Crazed Killer cyborgs...Deadly martial arts duels. All this and more awaits you in this special behind-the-scenes look at two of the year's most action-packed box-office sensations!

On the set of THE TERMINATOR you'll witness the ingenious wizardry utilized to create the terrifying story of a futuristic killing machine on the loose in a present-day metropolis. Make-up master Stan Winston's intricately designed mechanical Terminator heads and menacing steel skeleton-machine are among the never-before-seen creations you'll see in action. And a carefully choreographed chase involving gunshots, explosions, dangerous car stunts, and a hydraulic windshield-smashing Terminator arm is a sequence in fantasy film making you won't forget.

Then the crew of MISSING IN ACTION 2—THE BEGINNING takes you to a deserted island in the West Indies where they recreate the horrors of a North Vietnamese POW camp in savage detail. In addition to other breathtaking physical and pyrotechnic illusions, you'll see director Lance Hool, star Chuck Norris, and expert stuntmen meticulously set up a deadly martial arts fight sequence. Then they'll show you how they skillfully plan and rig a climactic conflagration that virtually destroys the camp!

Packed with in-depth interviews and thrilling action both before and behind the camera, this is a must-see for afficionados of movie magic everywhere!

VMT 3000, 1984, COLOR
60 minutes approx. running time.

VIDMARK ENTERTAINMENT

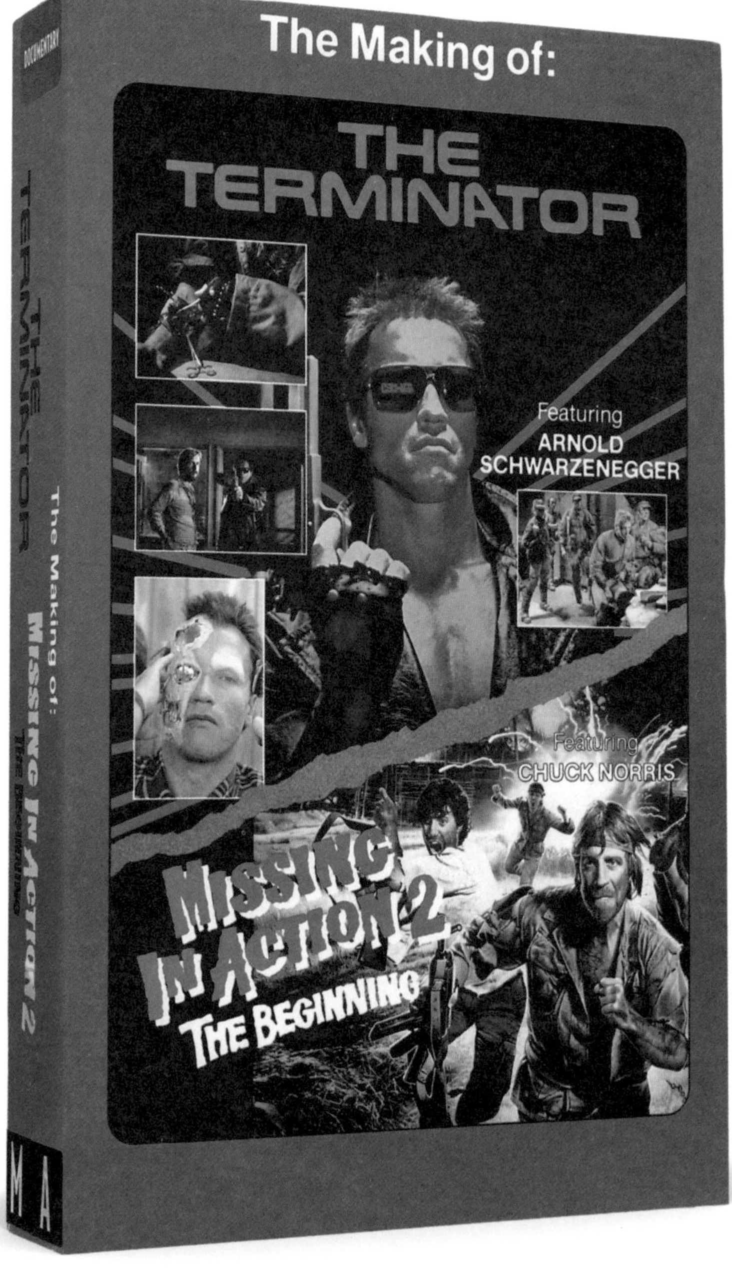
The Making of:
THE TERMINATOR
Featuring
ARNOLD
SCHWARZENEGGER
Featuring
CHUCK NORRIS
MISSING IN ACTION 2
THE BEGINNING
DOCUMENTARY
THE TERMINATOR
The Making of:
MISSING IN ACTION 2
M A

ALIEN MASSACRE

A bloody and vicious war ravages the galaxy. A father and daughter scientific team are brutally attacked by an alien craft containing a band of bloodthirsty mutants who attack and force the scientists to flee into a twisted time warp. To escape in one piece is almost impossible as their hideous captors try for revenge using methods of torture unheard of in the civilized world.

LON CHANEY / JOHN CARRADINE
Produced and Directed by
DAVID HEWITT

COLOR   77 MINS   R1028
1984   RATED R

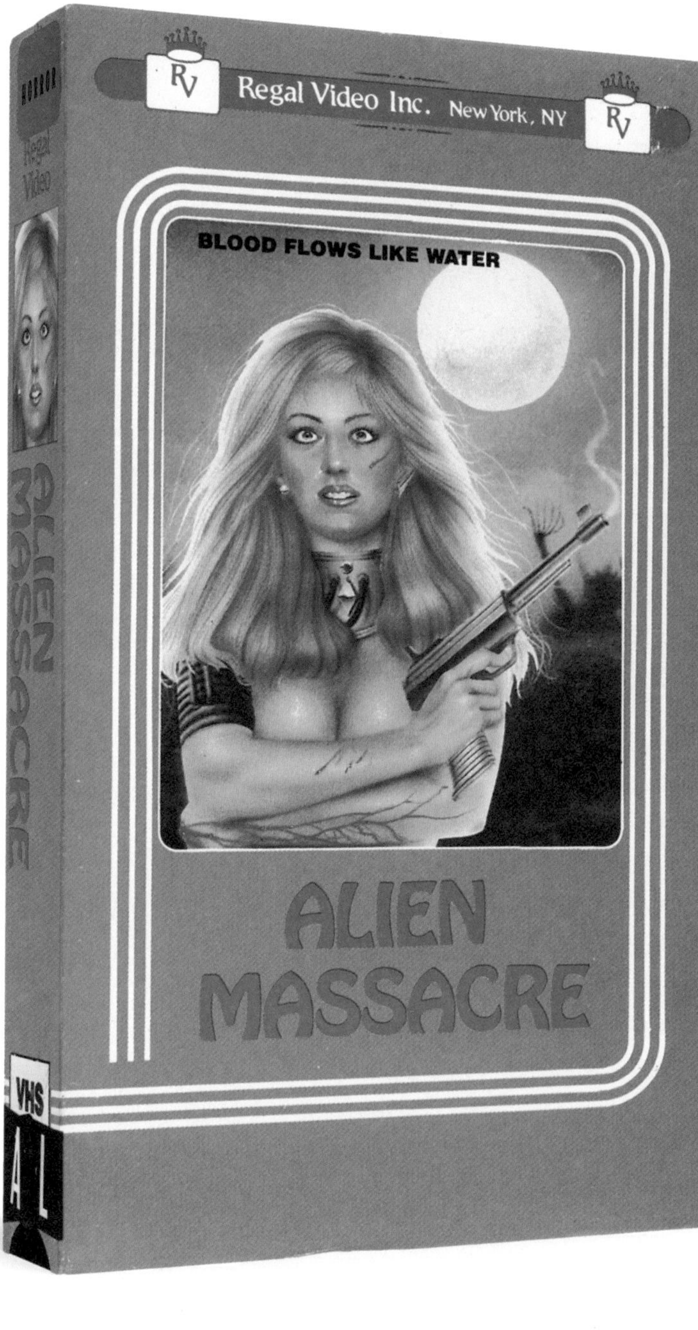
HORROR
Regal Video
ALIEN MASSACRE
VHS
A L
Regal Video Inc. New York, NY
RV
RV
BLOOD FLOWS LIKE WATER
ALIEN MASSACRE

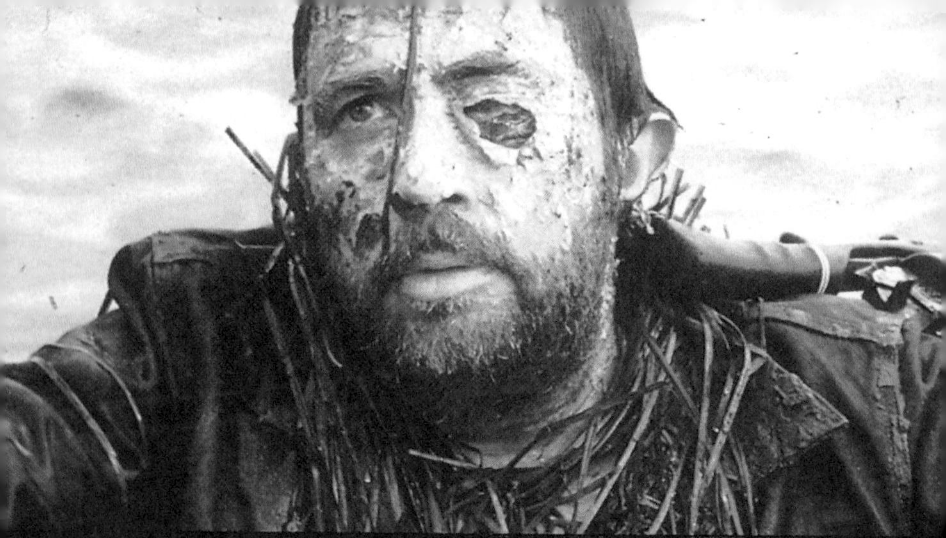

Every year 10,000 tourists visit Ocean Beach. This summer, Ocean Beach has attracted SOMETHING ELSE!

An all-star cast, including Academy Award winners HENRY FONDA and SHELLEY WINTERS, JOHN HUSTON, BO HOPKINS and CLAUDE AKINS, take part in this terrific thriller about an undersea force deadlier than any shark.

FONDA portrays the president of a company drilling a underwater tunnel in a California bay, using illegal radio sound waves to speed his project. After several mysterious deaths in the area, reported by newspaperman HUSTON, a marine scientist (HOPKINS) is called in to investigate. Wha he finds may mean the end of them all: a mammoth, raging octopus, whose tentacles are the touch of death!

The story reaches its fateful climax on the day of the annual youth sailboat regatta, as authorities try to return the youths to port...and the huge, ferocious beast vents his wrath on the young sailors. The marine scientist and his trained killer whales are the only hope left, as they prepare fo a titanic undersea encounter!

VESTRON VIDEO

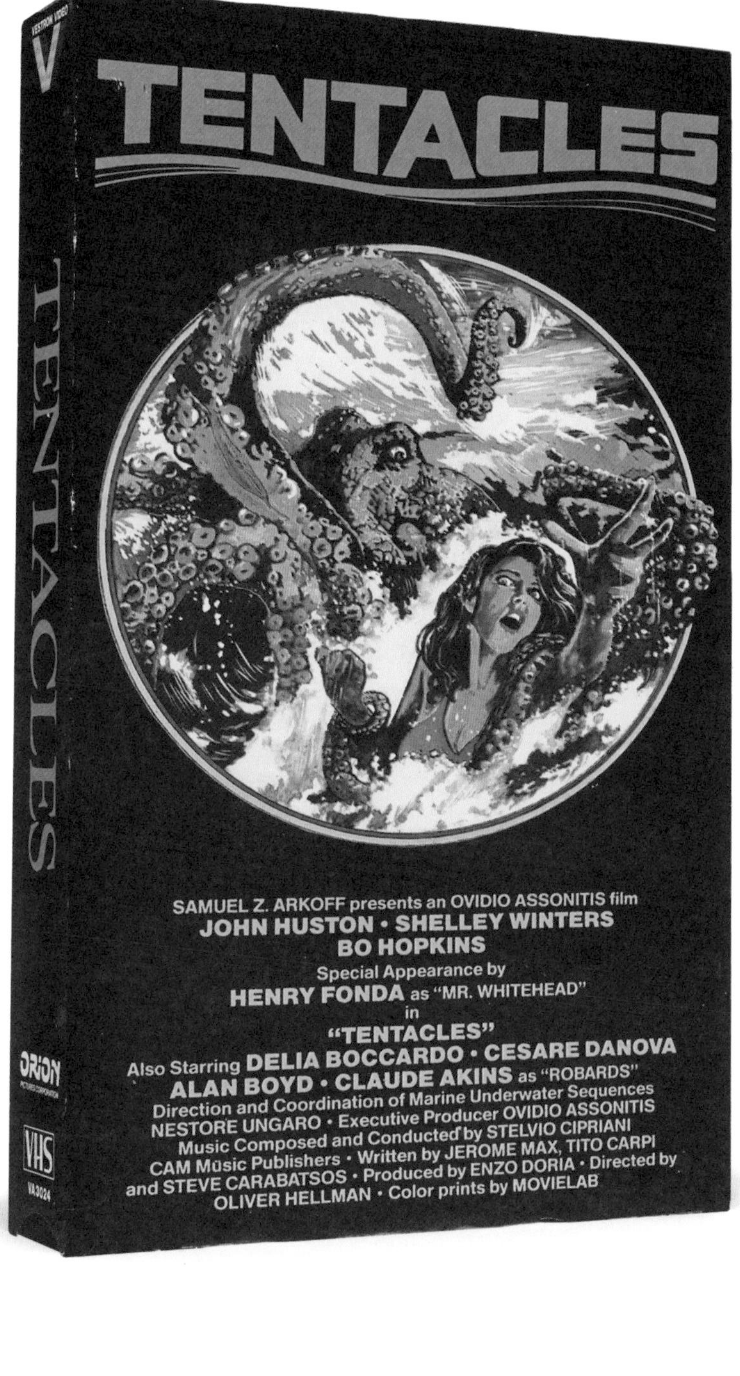
VESTRON VIDEO
V
TENTACLES
ORION
VHS
VA3024
TENTACLES
SAMUEL Z. ARKOFF presents an OVIDIO ASSONITIS film
JOHN HUSTON • SHELLEY WINTERS
BO HOPKINS
Special Appearance by
HENRY FONDA as "MR. WHITEHEAD"
in
"TENTACLES"
Also Starring DELIA BOCCARDO • CESARE DANOVA
ALAN BOYD • CLAUDE AKINS as "ROBARDS"
Direction and Coordination of Marine Underwater Sequences
NESTORE UNGARO • Executive Producer OVIDIO ASSONITIS
Music Composed and Conducted by STELVIO CIPRIANI
CAM Music Publishers • Written by JEROME MAX, TITO CARPI
and STEVE CARABATSOS • Produced by ENZO DORIA • Directed by
OLIVER HELLMAN • Color prints by MOVIELAB

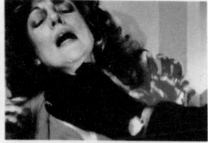

Starring **CAMERON MITCHELL PAMELYN FERDIN
WESLEY EURE NICHOLAS BEAUVY**
Directed by **DENNIS DONNELLY**
Produced by **TONY DIDIO**
Written by **ROBERT EASTER** and **ANN KINDBERG**

All the elements of a classic horror story are here!

Cameron Mitchell stars as the owner of the apartment building that becomes the site of the grisly action. Three attractive female residents of the building, all second-floor tenants, are found dead — victims of an appalling multiple murder. All three seem to have met their deaths via the use of one or another type of instrument common to the well-equipped handyman.

With no other clues, police are baffled and before any action can be taken, another young resident is attacked — this time to be brutally raped before meeting a gruesome death by use of a nailgun! The action shifts as a teenaged girl suddenly disappears. Her mother and brother are naturally frantic, considering the events of the past 24 hours, but police feel there is no connection and this attitude spurs the brother to take matters into his own hands by investigating on his own.

The twists and turns of plot and subplot will keep the viewer on the edge of his/her seat as clues revealing even more madness and mayhem are unveiled, finally resulting in a chilling surprise climax! You won't soon forget **THE TOOLBOX MURDERS!**

#10154, 93 minutes, Color, R

UNITED
HOME VIDEO

©1987 United Entertainment, Inc.

R | **RESTRICTED**
Under 17 requires accompanying Parent or Adult Guardian

PRINTED IN U.S.A.

#10154
VHS
THE TOOLBOX MURDERS
TOOL BOX MURDERS, THE
BIT BY BIT...BY BIT
HE CARVED
A NIGHTMARE!
"...the film (TOOL BOX MURDERS) generates some genuinely scary moments. One of the 10 scariest movies on video cassette."
—Stephen King
THE
TOOLBOX
MURDERS

**I baptize thee with the blood of Satan.
Now deliver upon to me a soul.**

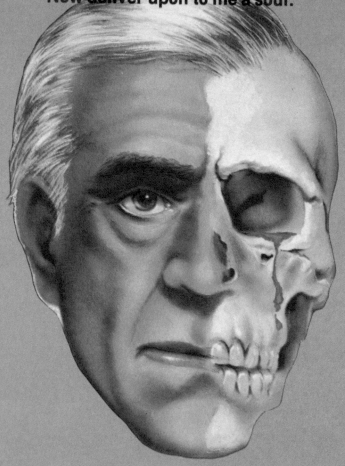

The crevice of the volcano is very deep. Scientists are searching for a form of underground life that according to theory still exists. This life is a result of the transformation of a substance at very high temperatures over thousands of years.

Once the underground life is located, it is then transported and kept in a chamber. Beautiful women are the victims of a tormented scientist. Hair raising scenes of merciless mental torture that paralyze the heart and senses! The only way this form of life can survive is by transfusions of a human being in extreme terror. When the terror freezes the blood, the scientist lives his experiments.

RUNNING TIME: 88 MINUTES

Distributed by: UNICORN VIDEO, INC.

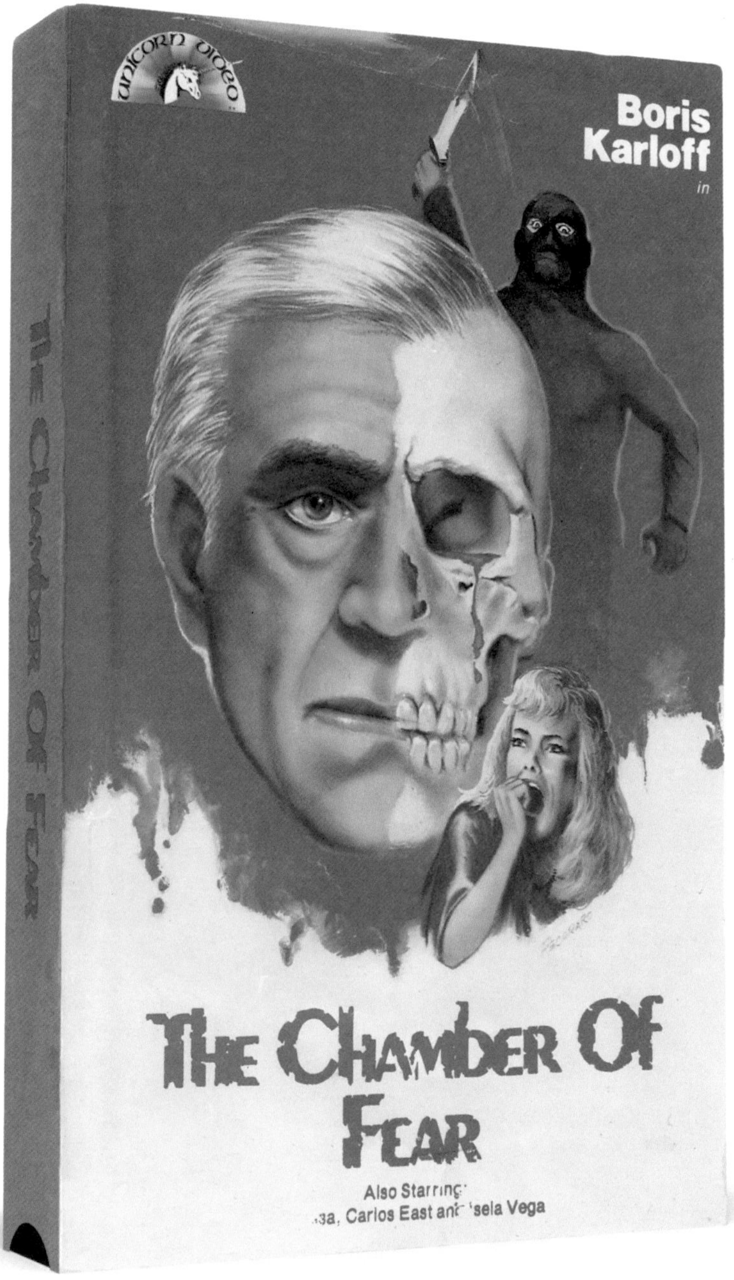
Unicorn Video
Boris
Karloff
in
The Chamber Of Fear
Also Starring
Carlos East and
sela Vega
The Chamber Of Fear

ATTACK OF THE SWAMP CREATURE

Starring

FRANK CROWELL

"How'd ya like to buy a choice piece of property at Elvira's Everglades Estates! Well, if you'd buy that...ATTACK OF THE SWAMP CREATURE might also be in order. There have been many bizarre reactions to this "demonic Esther Williams" flick (pe sonally, when I saw it I felt like swimming upstream and spawn ing!) Anyway, it takes place in Florida where this mad scienti transforms himself into this swamp creature which terrorizes small town. (I guess Godzilla was too busy to help out.) Believe n kids, you'll be oozing with laughter at this muddy fiasco. So set sail for the soggiest unpleasant dreams ever."

A FULL-LENGTH FEATURE FILM
APPROXIMATE
RUNNING TIME: 96 MINUTES

Starring FRANK CROWELL and PATRICIA ALLISON

ELVIRA FAN CLUB P.O. BOX 38246
HOLLYWOOD,CA 90038

THRILLERVIDEO™

THRILLERVIDEO / A DIVISION OF

PHOTOS BY ... ZE BA

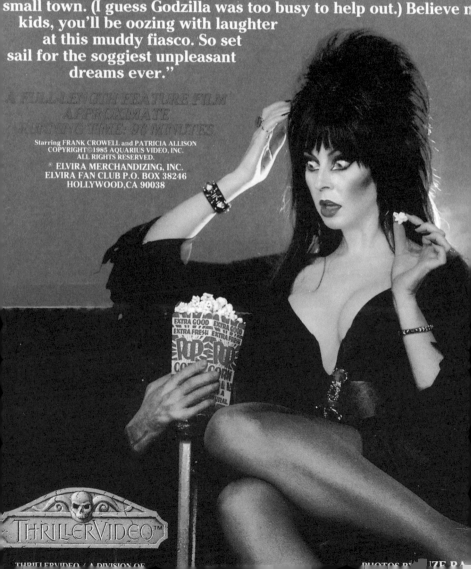

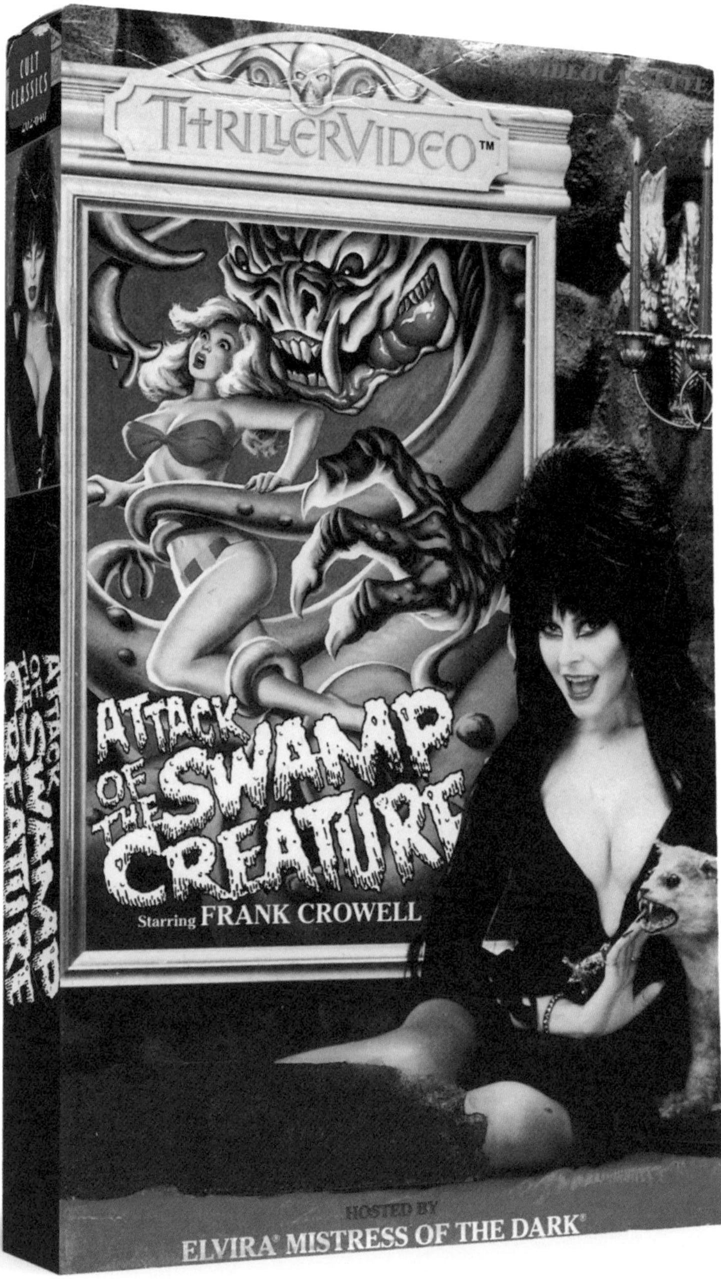
CULT CLASSICS
THRILLERVIDEO™
ATTACK OF THE SWAMP CREATURE
Starring FRANK CROWELL
HOSTED BY
ELVIRA® MISTRESS OF THE DARK®
ATTACK OF THE SWAMP CREATURE

BEAKS
THE MOVIE

It's a world where the birds have gone berserk! Even a canary can't be trusted! In this unintentionally hilarious sci-fi yuckfest, a glamorous (and terminally pouty) TV reporter (Michelle Johnson) and her horny (and terminally vain) camerman/boyfriend (Chris Atkins) travel the globe investigating vicious attacks by our fine-feathered friends. Unbelievable antics ensue as these "talons of terror" wreak havoc... and hilarity! The climax, where a flock of "killer pigeons" attack a train load of tourists, is especially "choice." Movies don't get much better than this! It's not for the birds...it's for nonstop laughs.

A FULL-LENGTH FEATURE
UNSUITABLE FOR AUDIENCES UNDER 17
APPROX. RUN. TIME: 86 MIN.

IVE INTERNATIONAL VIDEO ENTERTAINMENT INC.

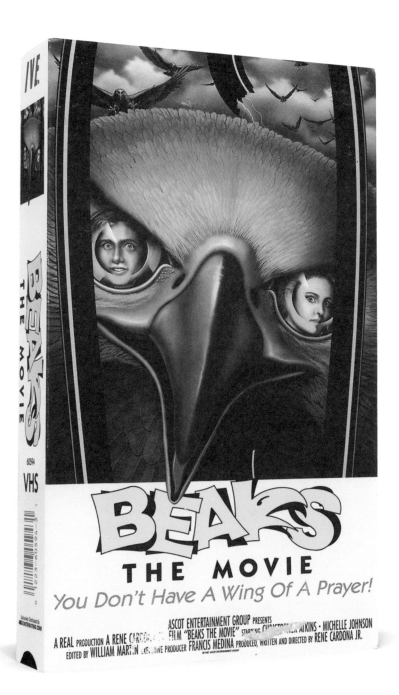

BEAKS THE MOVIE

THE MOVIE

You Don't Have A Wing Of A Prayer!

ASCOT ENTERTAINMENT GROUP PRESENTS
A REAL PRODUCTION A RENE CARDONA JR. FILM "BEAKS THE MOVIE" STARRING CHRISTOPHER ATKINS · MICHELLE JOHNSON
EDITED BY WILLIAM MARTIN EXECUTIVE PRODUCER FRANCIS MEDINA PRODUCED, WRITTEN AND DIRECTED BY RENE CARDONA JR.

STREETS OF FIRE

Color/1 Hr. 33 Mins./ PG

Closed captioned by the National Captioning Institute. Used with permission.

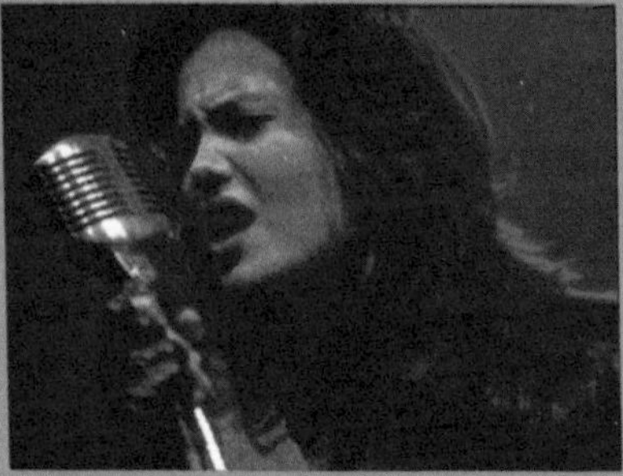
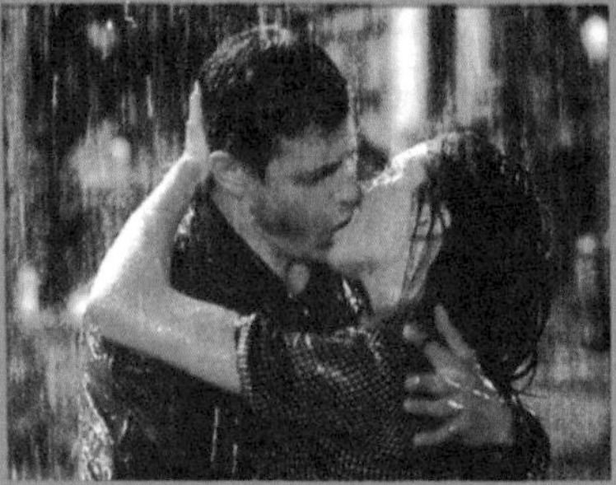

Streets of Fire is a movie unlike any ever seen before — a rock and roll fable in which songs are as essential to the film as the action sequences. Michael Paré stars as Tom Cody, handsome, heroic soldier of fortune who returns to his old neighborhood to rescue his gorgeous ex-girlfriend, rock star Ellen Aim (Diane Lane) from the clutches of the evil motorcycle gang that kidnaps her. Together with Ellen's manager, Billy Fish (Rick Moranis) and Tom's two-fisted, beer guzzling sidekick McCoy (Amy Madigan) they set off into a timeless world of smoke, neon, rain-splattered streets, hot cars and deadly enemies to bring Ellen back. In the words of Director Walter Hill of *48 Hours* fame, " . . . Leader of the Pack steals the Queen of the Hop and Soldier Boy comes home to do something about it." All to the sounds of today's top rock stars.

A HILL · GORDON · SILVER PRODUCTION "STREETS OF FIRE" MICHAEL PARÉ · DIANE LANE · RICK MORANIS · AMY MADIGAN MUSICAL SCORE BY RY COODER SPECIAL MUSICAL MATERIAL SUPERVISED BY JIMMY IOVINE DIRECTOR OF PHOTOGRAPHY ANDREW LASZLO A.S.C. EXECUTIVE PRODUCER GENE LEVY WRITTEN BY WALTER HILL & LARRY GROSS PRODUCED BY LAWRENCE GORDON AND JOEL SILVER DIRECTED BY WALTER HILL

A UNIVERSAL · RKO PICTURE

This Videocassette has been recorded in stereo with Dolby "B" type noise reduction and is compatible for monaural playback with all VHS equipment.

During playback set Dolby "B" N.R. switch to the on position.

MCA HOME VIDEO

70 UNIVERSAL CITY PLAZA, UNIVERSAL CITY, CA 91608

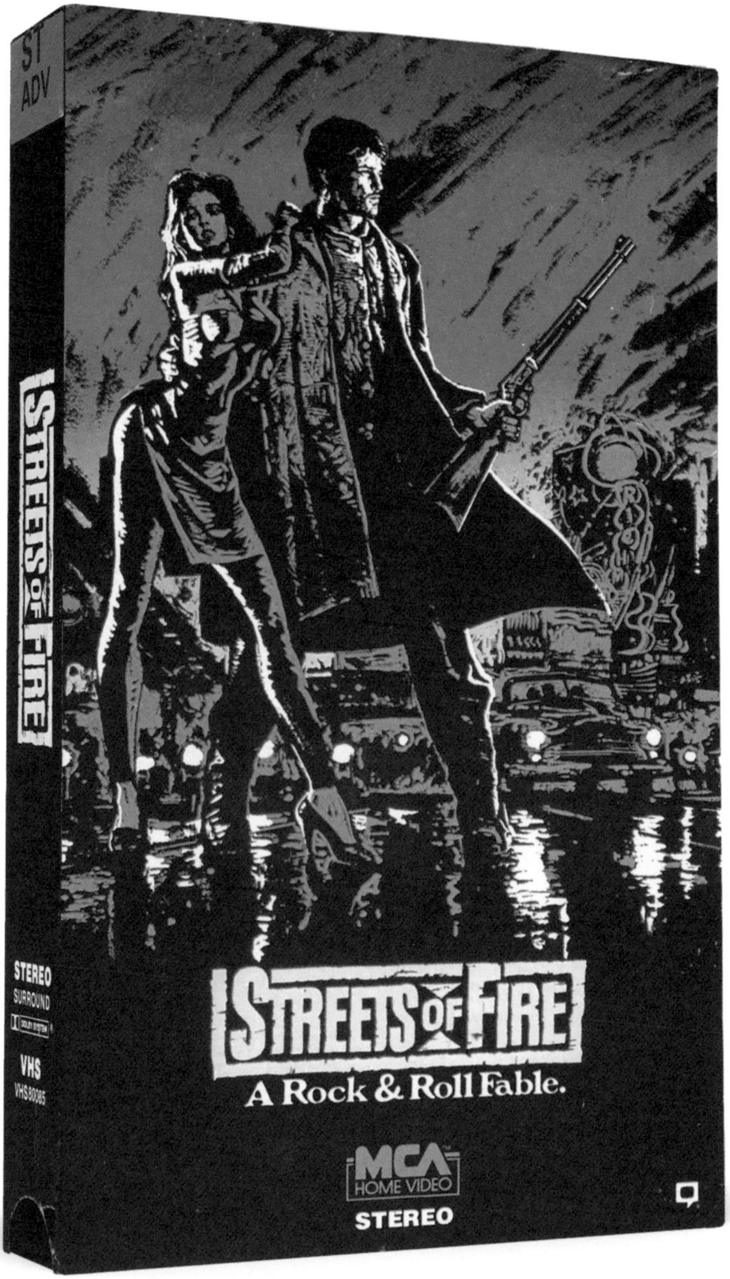
ST
ADV
STREETS OF FIRE
STEREO
SURROUND
VHS
STREETS OF FIRE
A Rock & Roll Fable.
MCA
HOME VIDEO
STEREO

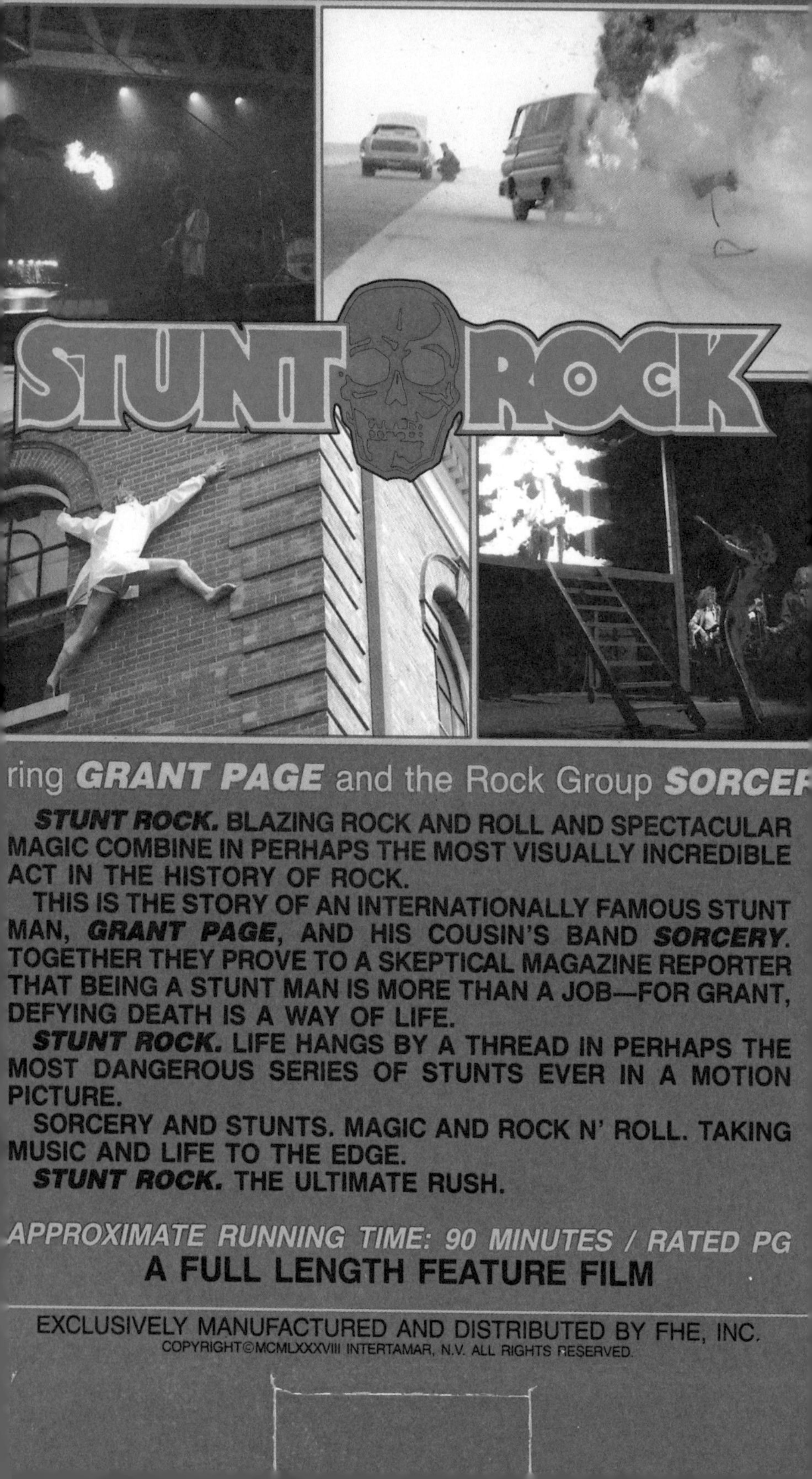
STUNT ROCK

ring ***GRANT PAGE*** and the Rock Group ***SORCER***

STUNT ROCK. BLAZING ROCK AND ROLL AND SPECTACULAR MAGIC COMBINE IN PERHAPS THE MOST VISUALLY INCREDIBLE ACT IN THE HISTORY OF ROCK.

THIS IS THE STORY OF AN INTERNATIONALLY FAMOUS STUNT MAN, ***GRANT PAGE***, AND HIS COUSIN'S BAND ***SORCERY***. TOGETHER THEY PROVE TO A SKEPTICAL MAGAZINE REPORTER THAT BEING A STUNT MAN IS MORE THAN A JOB—FOR GRANT, DEFYING DEATH IS A WAY OF LIFE.

STUNT ROCK. LIFE HANGS BY A THREAD IN PERHAPS THE MOST DANGEROUS SERIES OF STUNTS EVER IN A MOTION PICTURE.

SORCERY AND STUNTS. MAGIC AND ROCK N' ROLL. TAKING MUSIC AND LIFE TO THE EDGE.

STUNT ROCK. THE ULTIMATE RUSH.

APPROXIMATE RUNNING TIME: 90 MINUTES / RATED PG

A FULL LENGTH FEATURE FILM

EXCLUSIVELY MANUFACTURED AND DISTRIBUTED BY FHE, INC.

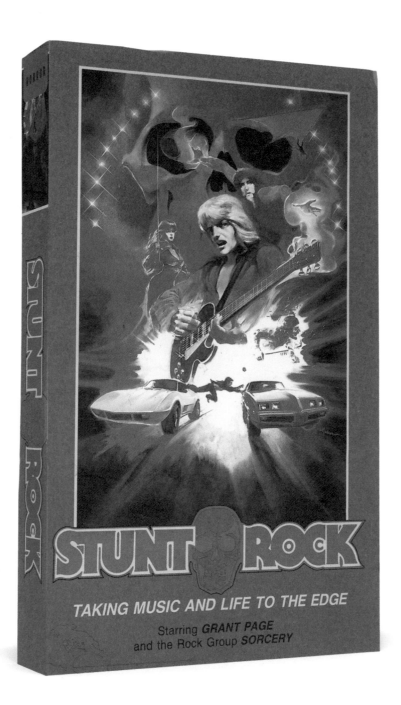

STUNT ROCK

TAKING MUSIC AND LIFE TO THE EDGE

Starring **GRANT PAGE**
and the Rock Group **SORCERY**

THE ASPHYX

We all have the spirit of both life and death trapped within us. The Asphyx is the very essence of death locked deep within our souls. A scientist (Robert Stephens) inadvertently photographs the Asphyx during a public hanging. He then becomes obsessed with the possibility of obtaining immortality through the capture and confinement of the Asphyx. The results of his experiments prove to be disastrous and chillingly eternal.

STARRING

ROBERT STEPHENS · ROBERT POWELL

DIRECTOR OF PHOTOGRAPHY

FREDDIE YOUNG B.S.G.

Oscar Winning Director of Photography
LAWRENCE OF ARABIA · DR. ZHIVAGO · RYAN'S DAUGHTER

RUNNING TIME 96 MINUTES—COLOR—RATED PG

MAGNUM
Entertainment

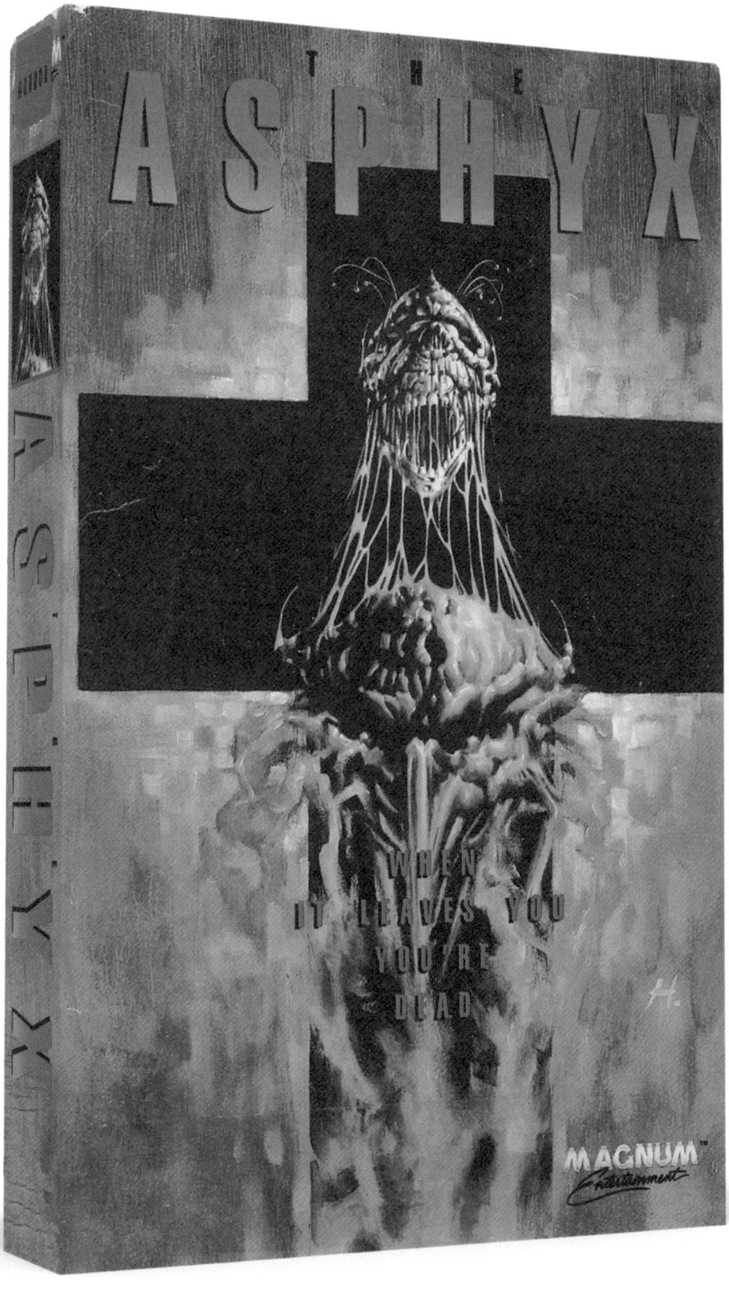
THE
ASPHYX
WHEN
IT LEAVES YOU
YOU'RE
DEAD
MAGNUM
Entertainment

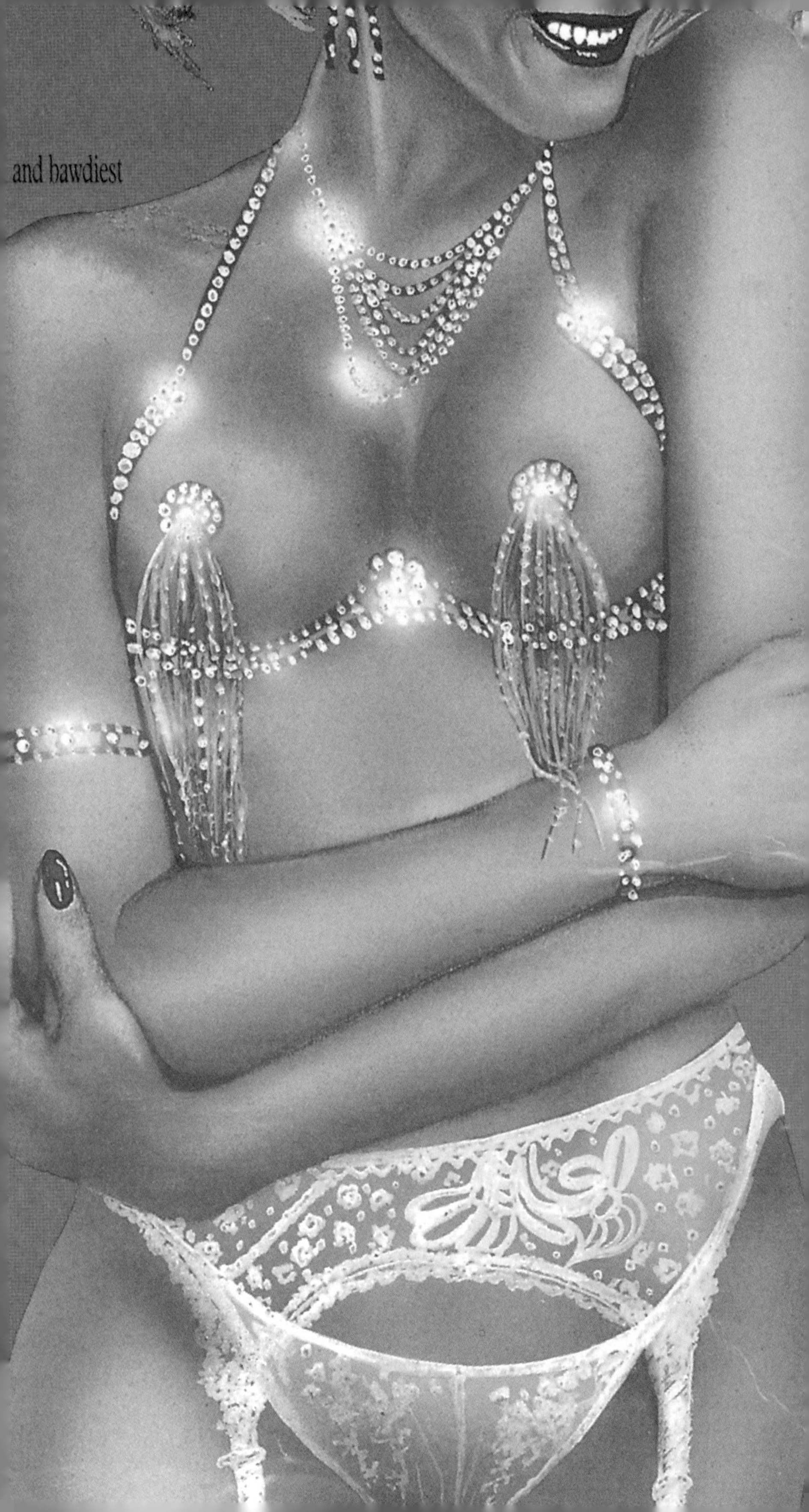
and bawdiest

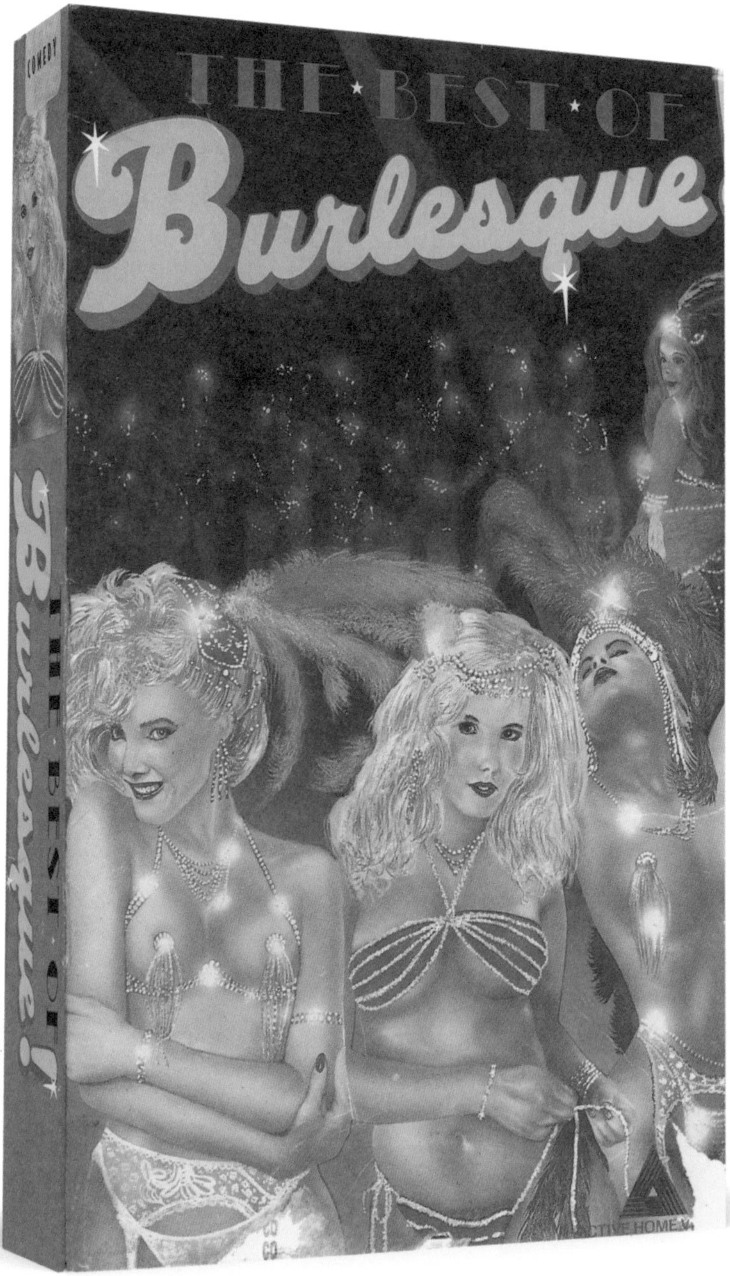
COMEDY
THE BEST OF
Burlesque
THE BEST OF
Burlesque!

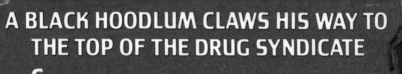

A BLACK HOODLUM CLAWS HIS WAY TO THE TOP OF THE DRUG SYNDICATE

Control the drugs. the dudes and the cops. and you control the whole damn neighborhood. J.J.. a black gangster who grew up the hard way on the mean streets. wants to rule the ghetto. With the help of the local militant guerillas. J.J. takes on the white dope peddlers who have been exploiting the neighborhood. In a violent wave of confrontations. dealers and hustlers are driven out until Tony Berton. white Mafia kingpin. gets angry. When a huge shipment of dope arrives. J.J.'s urban army intercepts it — and Berton's hoods are waiting. A bloody ambush erupts into an explosive struggle for the streets.

RUNNING TIME 100 MINUTES   COLOR   RATED R

STARRING

JIMMY WITHERSPOON ▪ ROD PERRY
DIRECTED BY JOHN EVANS

nemation Industries
MAGNUM ENTERTAINMENT
IN U.S.A.

MAGNUM™
Entertainment

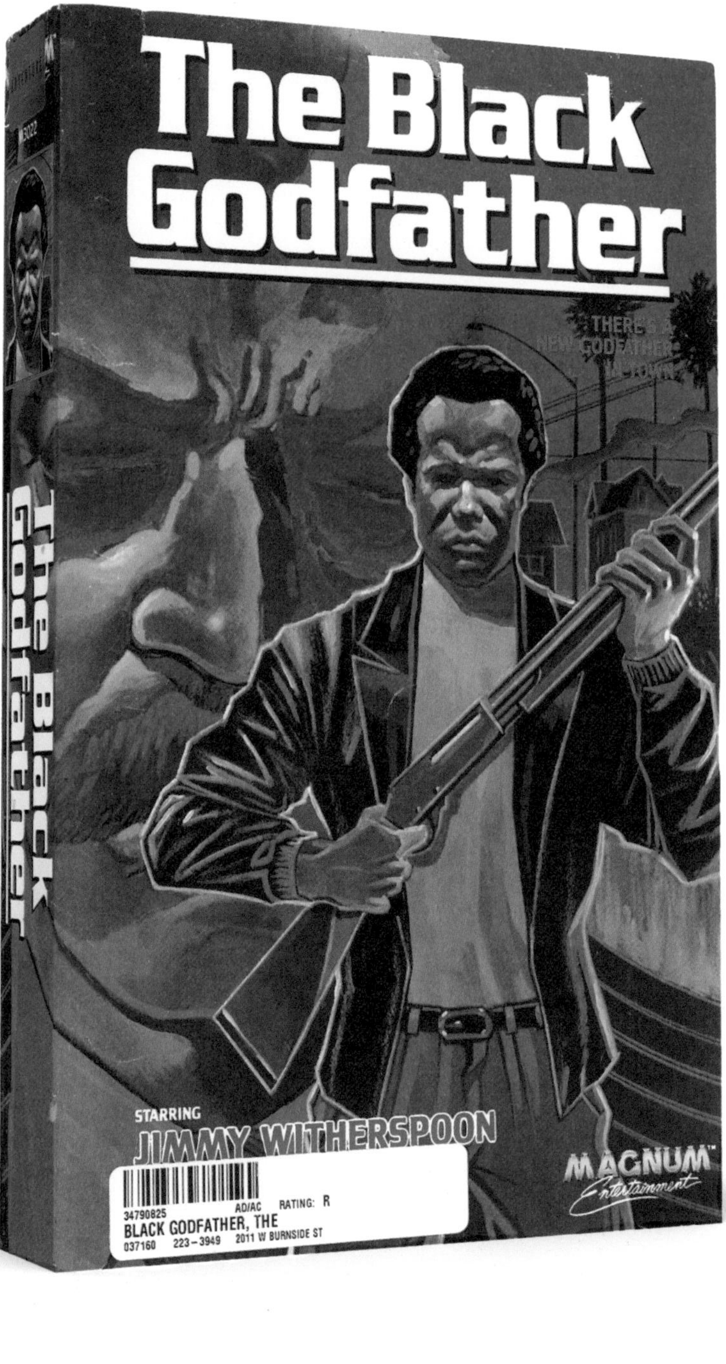
The Black Godfather
THERE'S A NEW GODFATHER IN TOWN
STARRING
JIMMY WITHERSPOON
MAGNUM
Entertainment
34790825 AD/AC RATING: R
BLACK GODFATHER, THE
037160 223-3949 2011 W BURNSIDE ST
The Black Godfather

Enemy troops leave senseless destruction and suffering in their wake turning everything into a bloody battlefield. Thousands of innocent civilians are killed and hundreds of thousands made homeless.

A group of undercover soldiers behind the lines are committed trying to infiltrate and sabotage enemy defenses.

The American High Command immediately starts operation "Gambit" to storm the enemy occupied zone and repress the aggressors.

Thus, eight highly trained human fighting machines are recruited and parachuted behind enemy lines to blow up and destroy their defenses.

SPECIAL FORCE

MOGUL COMMUNICATIONS PRESENTS AN

AL BRADLEY FILM

"SPECIAL FORCE"

STARRING PETER LEE LAWRENCE · GUY MADISON

ERIKA BLANC · TONY NORTON

PRODUCED BY RITODEO INTERNATIONAL

DIRECTED BY AL BRADLEY

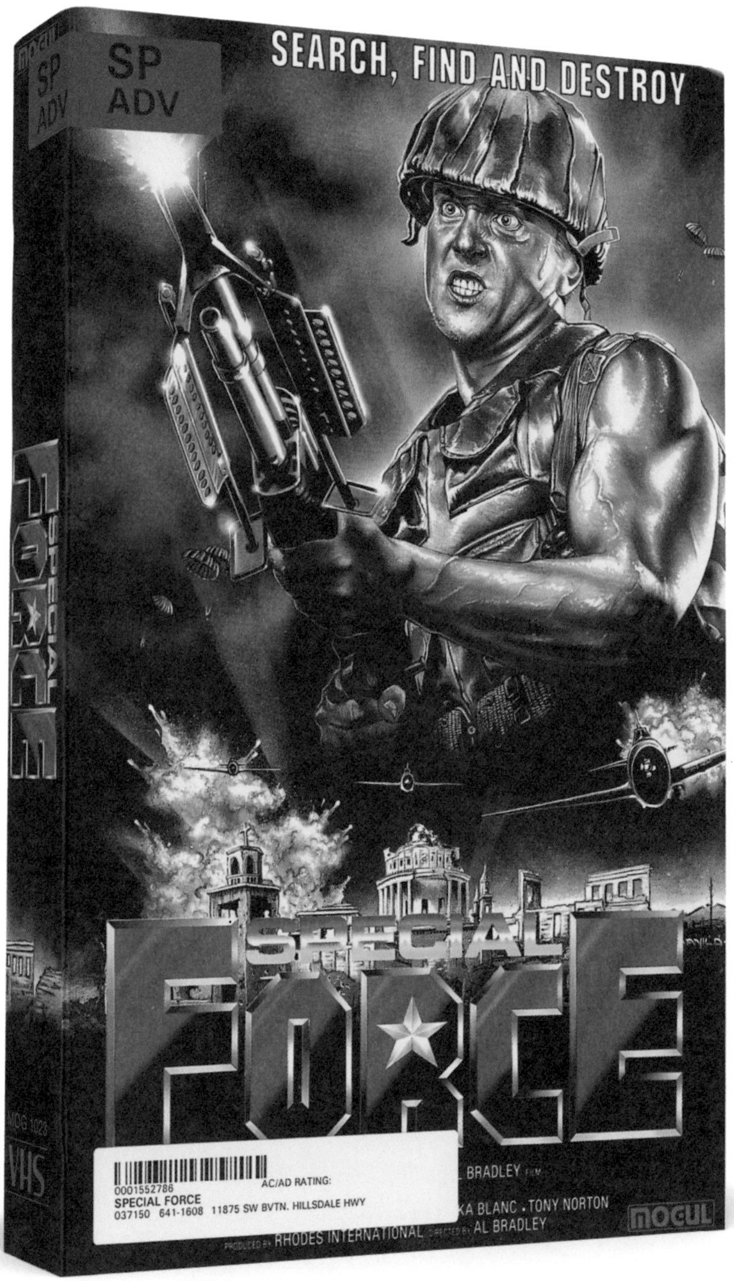
MOCUL
SP
ADV
SP
ADV
SEARCH, FIND AND DESTROY
SPECIAL FORCE
SPECIAL
FORCE
MOG 1023
VHS
0001552786
AC/AD RATING:
SPECIAL FORCE
037150 641-1608 11875 SW BVTN. HILLSDALE HWY
BRADLEY FILM
KA BLANC . TONY NORTON
PRODUCED BY RHODES INTERNATIONAL DIRECTED BY AL BRADLEY
MOCUL

BLACK MAGIC
Terror

**Starring Suzanna as the Queen.
Also starring W.D. Mochtar and Alan Nuary.
Directed by L. Sudjio.**

In this horrifying tale, the darkest witchcraft is
woven to create terrifying demons who attack the body,
mind and spirit of its victims.
Evoking these evil spells is the Queen of Black Magic
whose anger is matched only by her powers,
her passion matched only by her hate.

Color/85 Minutes

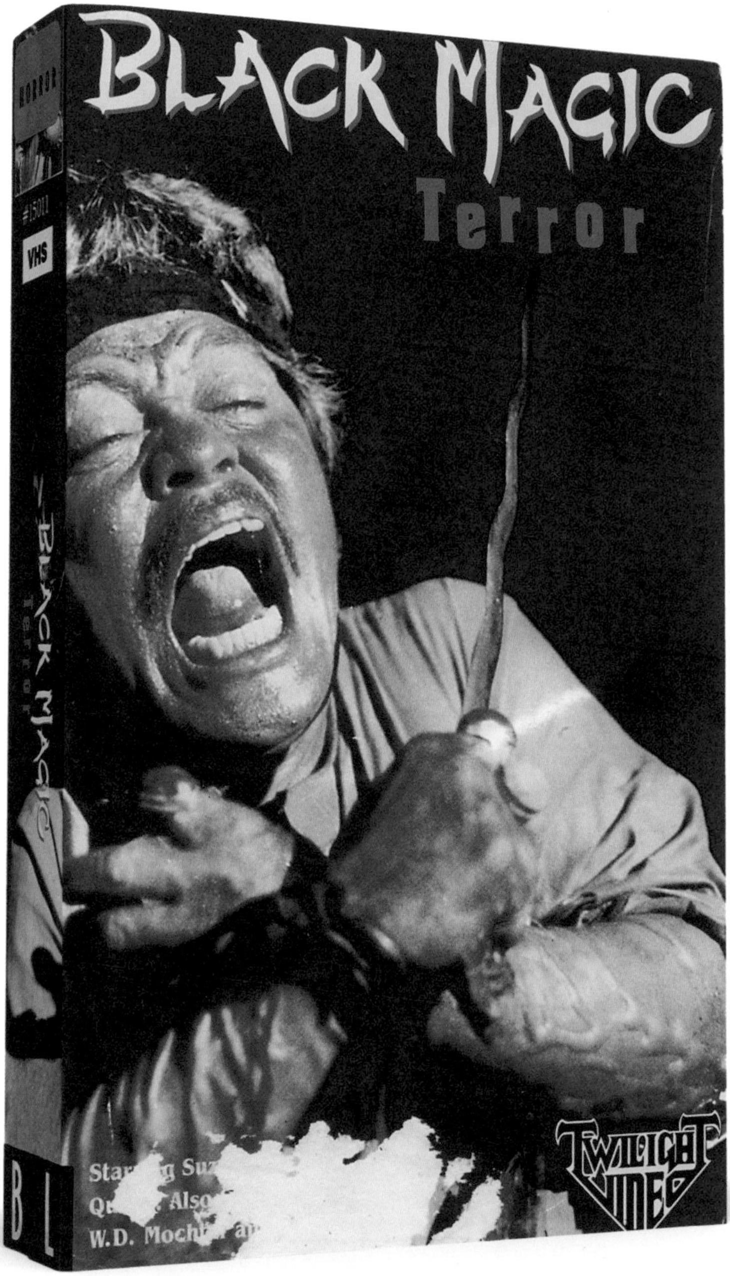
BLACK MAGIC
Terror
HORROR
#15011
VHS
BLACK MAGIC
Terror
BL
TWILIGHT

THEIR DEATHS CAME CENTURIES AGO. BUT THE TERROR LIVES ON.

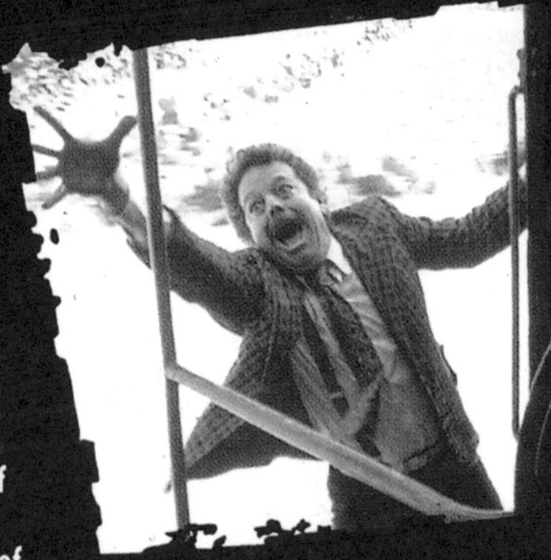

Bored with her nowhere career, young Karen takes the open road to anywhere . . . and comes upon what may be her personal dead end: a Mexican village shrouded by the curse of *Blood Screams.*

The story opens hundreds of years ago. An order of priests knows the whereabouts of gold hoarded by Cordova, a renegade defiant of the laws of God and man. To protect his secret, Cordova murders the priests, laughing as their "blood screams" pierce the night. Now, as Karen arrives, new cries are heard from the old monastery. Spectral denizens of the dark inhabit dreams. And a local coven works demonically to resurrect the ancient evil.

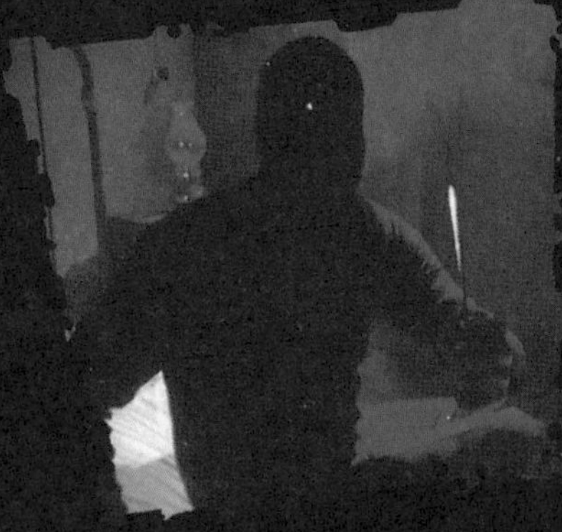

Forty-year screen veteran Russ Tamblyn (*tom thumb, West Side Story, The Haunting*) co-stars as a traveling magician named Frank. Frank is a chip off the ol' logging town, a character who brings to mind Tamblyn's wonderfully bizarre Dr. Jacoby in *Twin Peaks.*

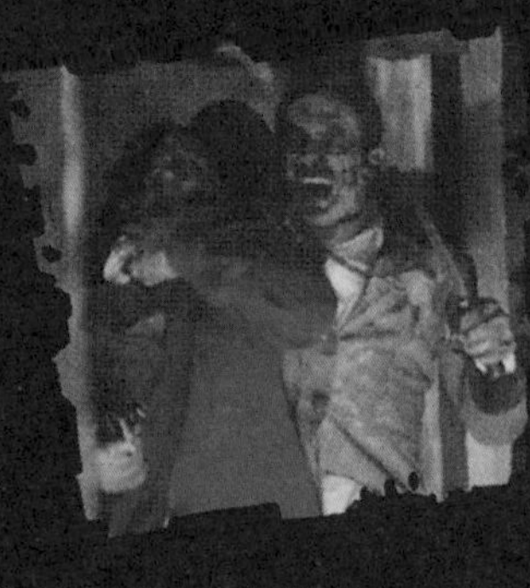

Yesterday, today, forever: *Blood Screams.* You will, too.

0 85393 50863 0

ISBN 0-7907-0085-9

NTSC

The linear audio tracks on this tape have been encoded with Dolby B-type noise reduction.

*Registered service mark of the National Captioning Institute Inc.

Concorde

R

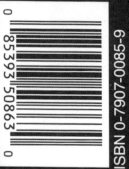

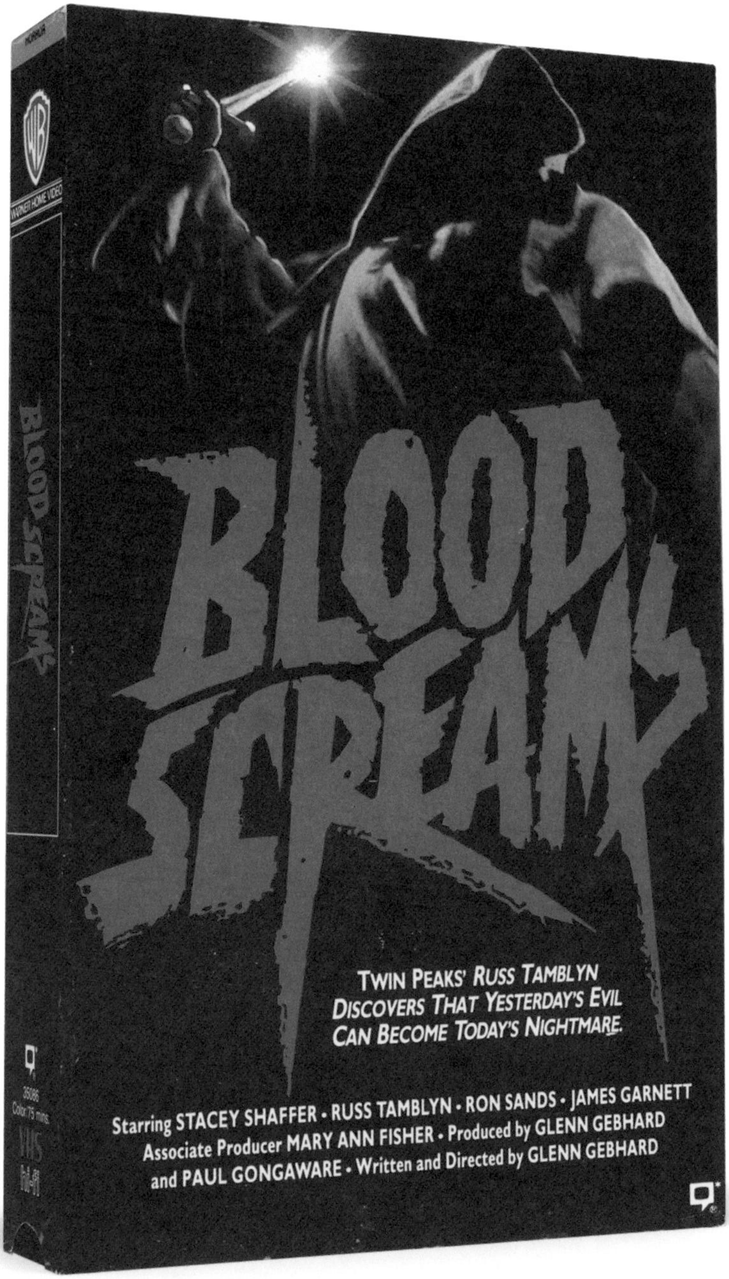
WARNER HOME VIDEO
BLOOD SCREAMS
BLOOD SCREAMS
TWIN PEAKS' RUSS TAMBLYN
DISCOVERS THAT YESTERDAY'S EVIL
CAN BECOME TODAY'S NIGHTMARE.
Starring STACEY SHAFFER • RUSS TAMBLYN • RON SANDS • JAMES GARNETT
Associate Producer MARY ANN FISHER • Produced by GLENN GEBHARD
and PAUL GONGAWARE • Written and Directed by GLENN GEBHARD
35086
Color/75 mins.

slithis

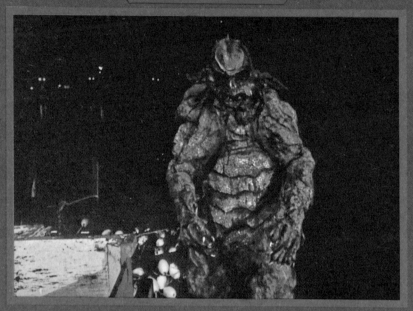

Color/86 Minutes

Finally nature unleashes it's revenge!

From the pollution of our nuclear waste came the killer we couldn't destroy. Our worst nightmares come to life with the terrifying, scaly monster — Slithis.

LOS ANGELES, CALIF.

MEDIA®

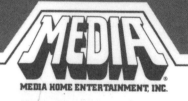

MEDIA HOME ENTERTAINMENT, INC.

VHS
M138
FINALLY, NATURE UNLEASHES IT'S REVENGE!
FROM THE POLLUTION OF OUR NUCLEAR WASTE,
CAME THE KILLER WE COULDN'T DESTROY!
HELL HATH
NO FURY... LIKE
slithis
WARNING!
YOU MUST BE PROTECTED
NOMINATED FOR 2 AWARDS BY SCI-FI HORROR ACADEMY!
MEDIA
MEDIA HOME ENTERTAINMENT, INC.
slithis
MEDIA

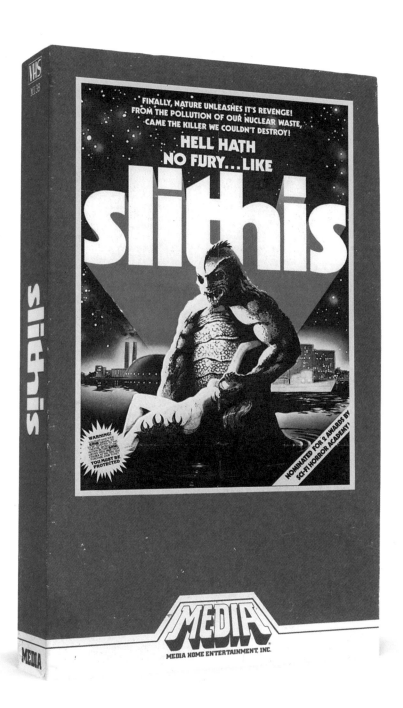

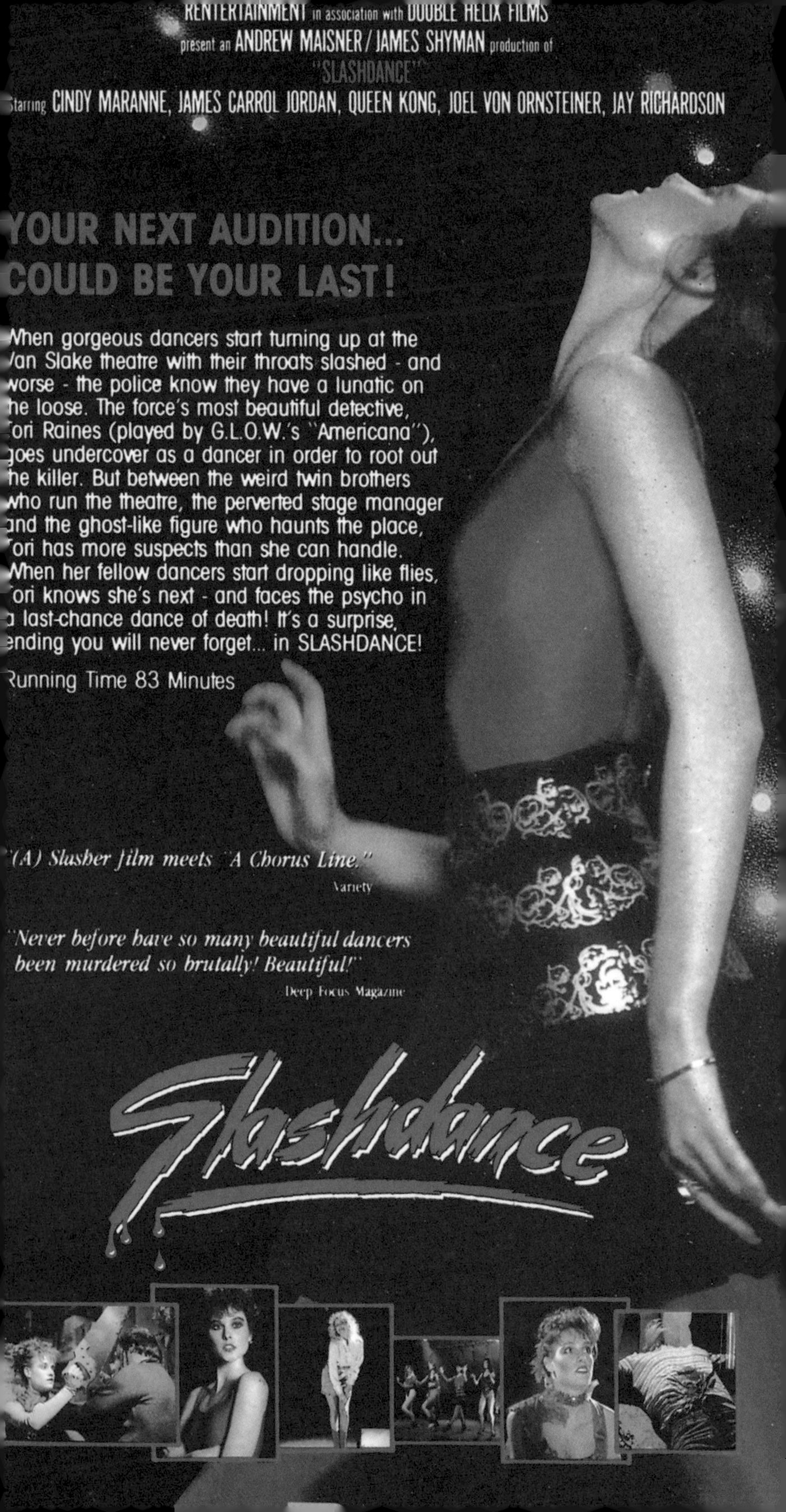
RENTERTAINMENT in association with DOUBLE HELIX FILMS
present an ANDREW MAISNER / JAMES SHYMAN production of
"SLASHDANCE"
Starring CINDY MARANNE, JAMES CARROL JORDAN, QUEEN KONG, JOEL VON ORNSTEINER, JAY RICHARDSON
YOUR NEXT AUDITION...
COULD BE YOUR LAST!
Vhen gorgeous dancers start turning up at the /an Slake theatre with their throats slashed - and vorse - the police know they have a lunatic on he loose. The force's most beautiful detective, Tori Raines (played by G.L.O.W.'s "Americana"), goes undercover as a dancer in order to root out he killer. But between the weird twin brothers who run the theatre, the perverted stage manager and the ghost-like figure who haunts the place, Tori has more suspects than she can handle. When her fellow dancers start dropping like flies, Tori knows she's next - and faces the psycho in a last-chance dance of death! It's a surprise, ending you will never forget... in SLASHDANCE!
Running Time 83 Minutes
"(A) Slasher film meets "A Chorus Line."
Variety
"Never before have so many beautiful dancers been murdered so brutally! Beautiful!"
Deep Focus Magazine
Slashdance

SAVE THE LAST DANCE... FOR HELL!

HORROR

Slashdance

RENTERTAINMENT in association with DOUBLE-HELIX FILMS
present an ANDREW MAISNER / JAMES SHYMAN production of
"SLASHDANCE"
Starring CINDY MARANNE, JAMES CARROL JORDAN, QUEEN KONG, JOEL VON ORNSTEINER, JAY RICHARDSON
Music by EMILIO KAUDERER Edited by LARRY ROSEN Written Directed by GEZA SINKOVICS

VHS
S L

BLOODSHED

A nightmare journey into the psychologically bizarre acts that occur when a young girl dies a horrible and bloody death. This hideous event is witnessed through a one-way mirror by a sadistic psychopath. In order to protect himself he stores the decaying body and brutally murders all who venture to discover his secret.

LASZLO PAPAS / BEVERLY ROSS
Written and Directed by
RICHARD CASSIDY

COLOR   88 MIN.   R1027
1983   RATED R

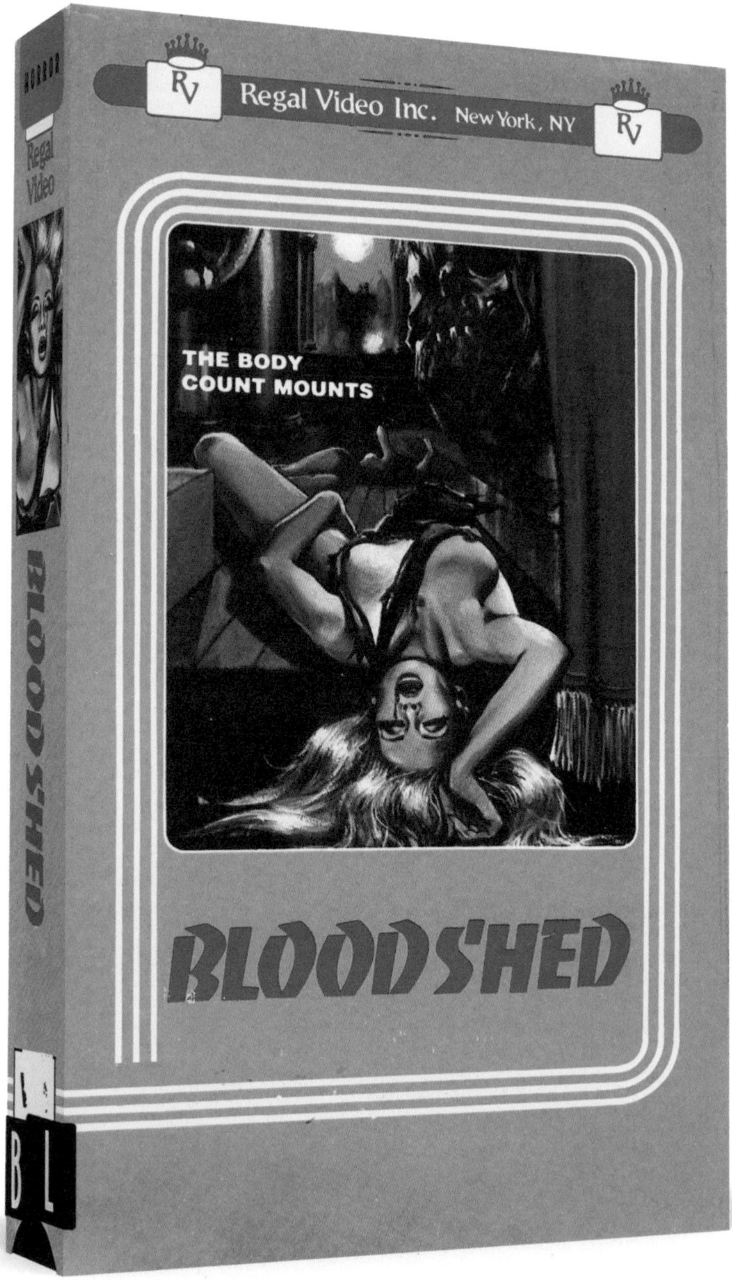
Regal Video Inc. New York, NY
THE BODY
COUNT MOUNTS
BLOODSHED
HORROR
Regal Video
BLOODSHED
BL

THE BLACK PANTHER
is a film of horrifying realism

which traces the bizarre and violent action of Donald Neilson—Britain's answer to Charles Manson! A film that has been hailed as "far more gripping than a fictional thriller," "guaranteed to hold you on the edge of your seat" and "a film not to miss," THE BLACK PANTHER is a suspenseful ride through Neilson's twisted mind.

Donald Neilson is now serving a life sentence for a series of brutal murders including the sadistic kidnapping and torture of a beautiful heiress in Britain during the 1970's. He earned his nickname of THE BLACK PANTHER from his dark, chilling, slitted hood—the only lead police had to go on. Re-trace the frightful steps that kept an entire country in panic—a calculating killer with no remorse for his actions. From family man to Death Row, find out what made him THE BLACK PANTHER!

PROGRAM TIME: APPROX. 90 MINUTES.
PROGRAM: COPYRIGHT © 1977 IMPICS LTD.
PACKAGE DESIGN AND SUMMARY: © 1986
VESTRON INCORPORATED. ALL RIGHTS
RESERVED. DISTRIBUTED BY VESTRON VIDEO,
P.O. BOX 4000, STAMFORD, CT 06907.
PRINTED IN U.S.A.

0 28485 14463

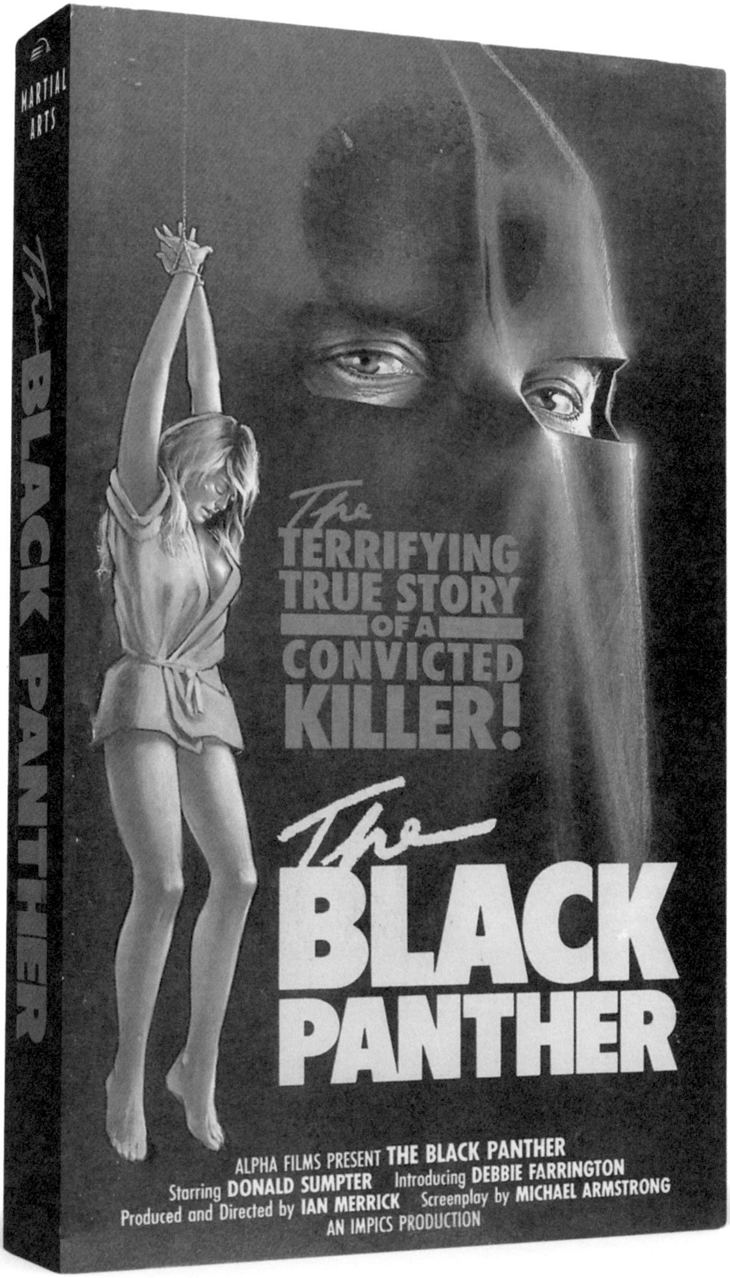
MARTIAL ARTS
The BLACK PANTHER
The TERRIFYING TRUE STORY OF A CONVICTED KILLER!
The BLACK PANTHER
ALPHA FILMS PRESENT THE BLACK PANTHER
Starring DONALD SUMPTER Introducing DEBBIE FARRINGTON
Produced and Directed by IAN MERRICK Screenplay by MICHAEL ARMSTRONG
AN IMPICS PRODUCTION

Johnny Bench

Collector Series

"Best syndicated sports series on television."
LA TIMES

Johnny Bench is regarded by many as the greatest catcher in baseball history. He is compared only to Bill Dickey, Mickey Cochrane, Roy Campanella and Yogi Berra.

Early in Bench's career Ted Williams autographed a ball to him as follows: "To Johnny Bench, a sure Hall of Famer."

In 1970, Bench was on his way to making a prophet of Williams. He hit 45 home runs, drove in 148 runs—leading the league in both departments—and was the National League's Most Valuable Player, an award he won again 2 years later when he hit 40 home runs and drove in 125 runs.

A superlative defensive catcher, Bench has won as much admiration for his defensive skills as for his hitting. His natural talents are so great that he has always made hard plays look easy and impossible plays look routine.

Host: Ken Howard
Time: 30 Minutes
In Color

No: 13110

Exclusive Distributors
Sports Legends Video, Inc.
154 Northfield Ave., Bldg. 410
Edison, New Jersey 08837

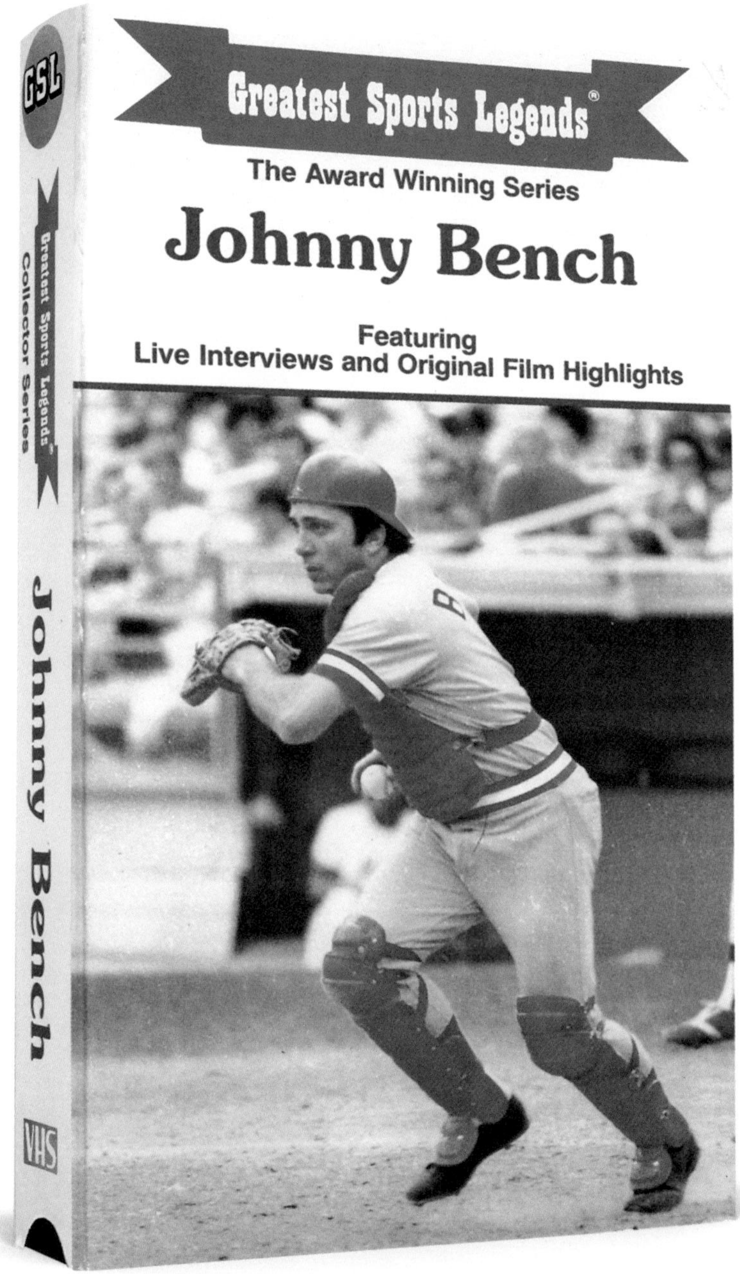
GSL
Greatest Sports Legends®
The Award Winning Series
Johnny Bench
Featuring
Live Interviews and Original Film Highlights
Greatest Sports Legends®
Collector Series
Johnny Bench
VHS

THE BLOOD SPATTERED BRIDE

Starring   **SIMON ANDREW**
MARIBEL MARTIN
DEAN SELMIER

TILL DEATH DO US PART . . .

That is the horrible lesson a pair of young newlyweds
learn when they honeymoon in an isolated mansion.
After the husband digs up a strange woman (literally
digs up) she stays the night, only to be possessed
by the spirit of a bloody murderess who died more
than 200 years go.

The deadly glint of razor-sharp knives slash through
the darkened corridors of the mansion, claiming
helpless victims in a nightmare of gore that will
leave you glued to your seat until the shattering climax!

Although not rated this film contains nudity and
scenes of graphic violence.

Color   Approx. 84 min.

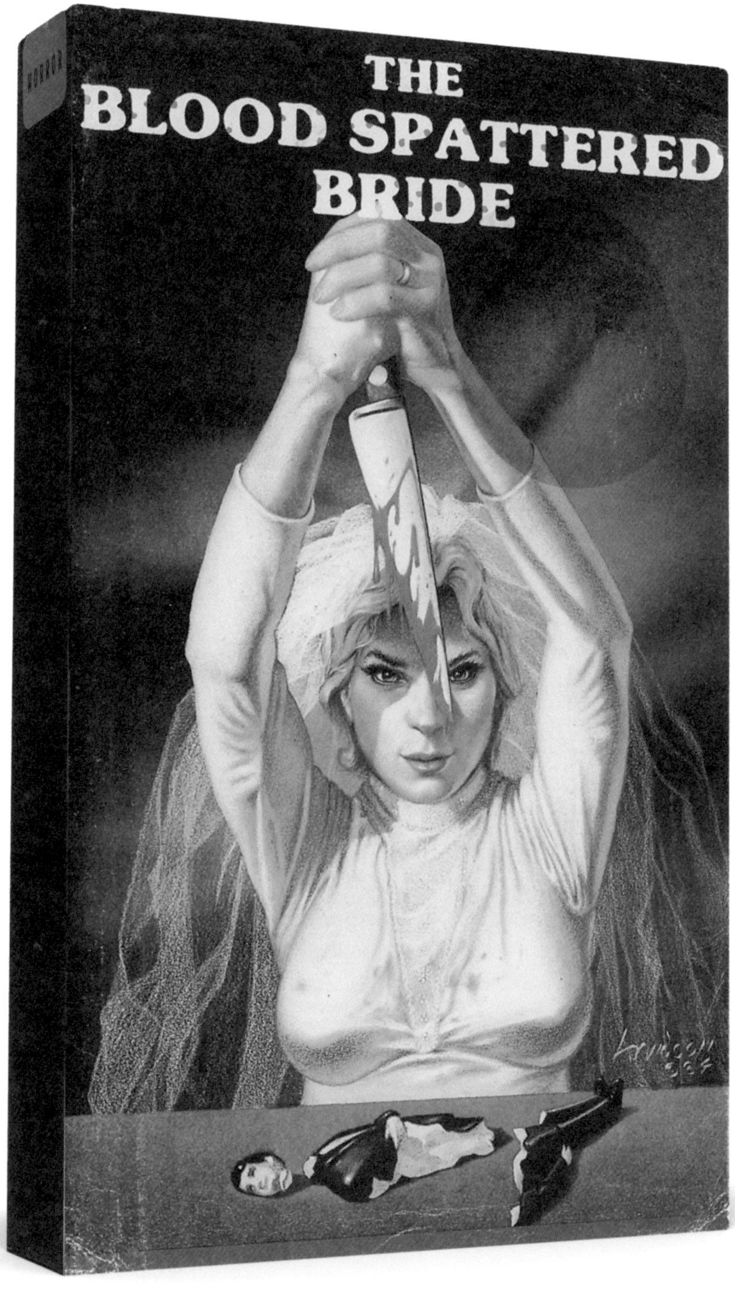
HORROR
THE
BLOOD SPATTERED
BRIDE

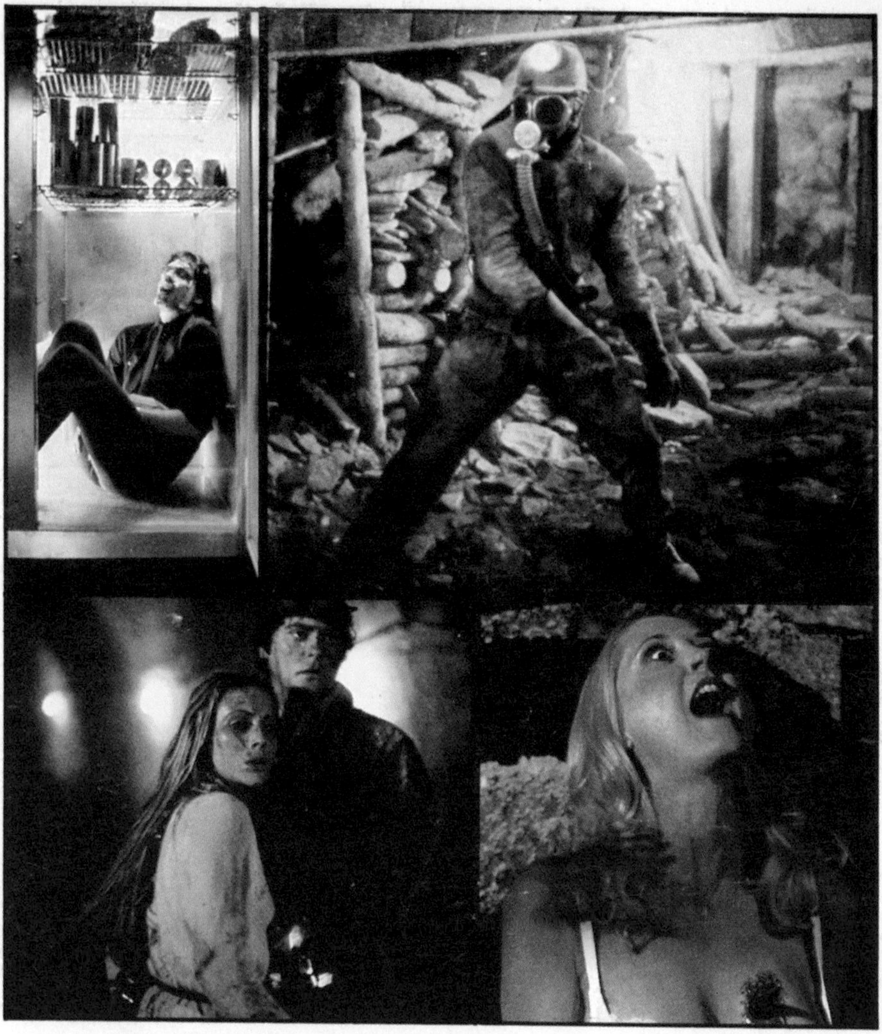

Twenty years ago, a tragic accident in a mine on St. Valentine's day took the lives of five miners. The disaster occurred while supervisors left their posts to attend the town's annual Valentine's Day dance. The only survivor, Harry Warden, was confined to a mental institution after the ordeal. On the disaster's first anniversary, he returned to the town for bloody revenge. That was nineteen years ago, and memories have dimmed. Young lovers T.J. (Paul Kelman) and Sarah (Lori Hallier) and friend Axel (Neil Affleck) are among the townspeople attending another Valentine's party. Then, a box of Valentine candy arrives, containing an ominous message and a blood-soaked heart. Before the night is over, terror will strike again and again and again . . .

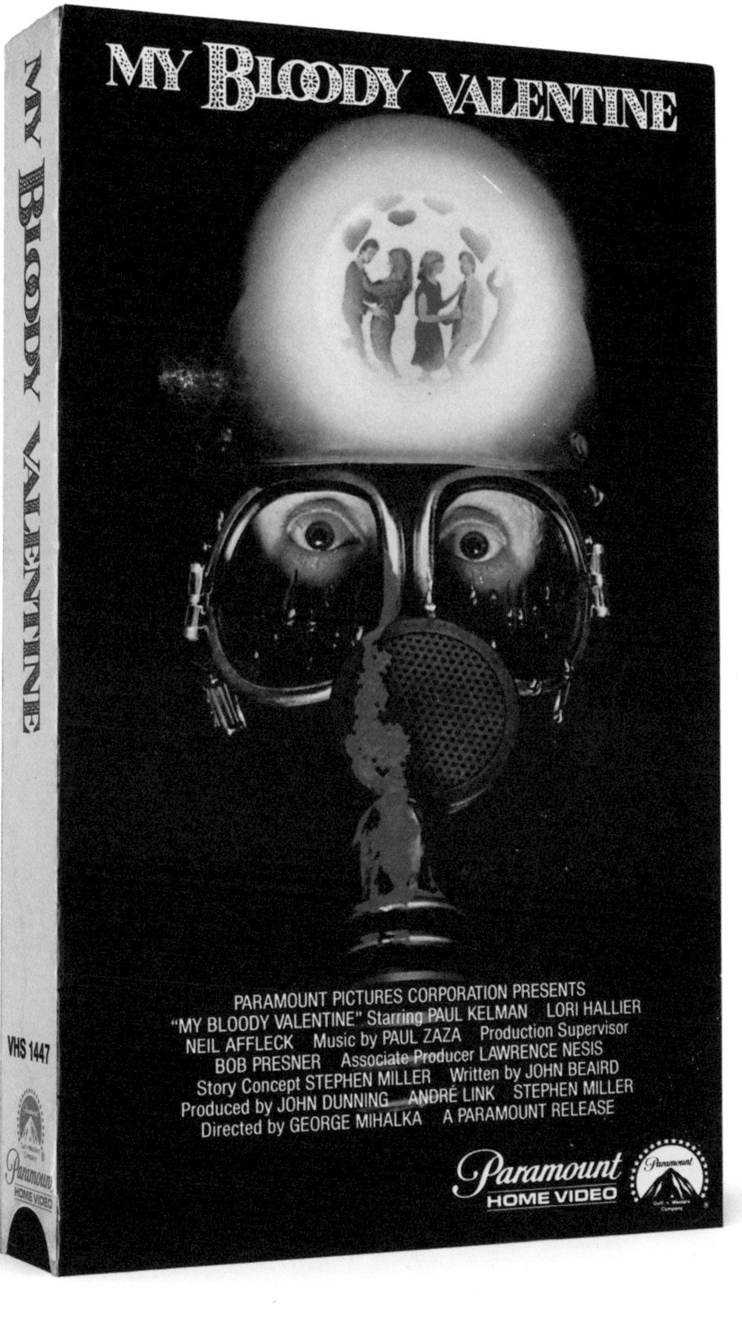
MY BLOODY VALENTINE
MY BLOODY VALENTINE
VHS 1447
Paramount
HOME VIDEO
PARAMOUNT PICTURES CORPORATION PRESENTS
"MY BLOODY VALENTINE" Starring PAUL KELMAN LORI HALLIER
NEIL AFFLECK Music by PAUL ZAZA Production Supervisor
BOB PRESNER Associate Producer LAWRENCE NESIS
Story Concept STEPHEN MILLER Written by JOHN BEAIRD
Produced by JOHN DUNNING ANDRÉ LINK STEPHEN MILLER
Directed by GEORGE MIHALKA A PARAMOUNT RELEASE
Paramount
HOME VIDEO

BOWHUNTING WHITETAILS: JUST FOR FUN!

With all the hoopla over record books and shooting trophy class bucks, sometimes it's easy to forget the real reason we ever started hunting in the first place – *"It's just plain fun"!*

BKS's ROGER RAGLIN has shot some tremendous whitetail bucks over the years, but he has never lost sight of the fact that personal satisfaction and enjoyment are the real reasons to spend time outdoors – not collecting heads for the wall.

In "Just for Fun", Roger will share some valuable tips with you on how to have, and keep 'fun' an intricate part of the bowhunting experience.

Oh, don't worry! There's plenty of hard core action too. With 5 vivid arrow impacts, one sequence includes a scene where Roger grunts and rattles in a charging one-horned buck to within 5 yards before he finally gets the buck's attention! You can only guess how he did that.

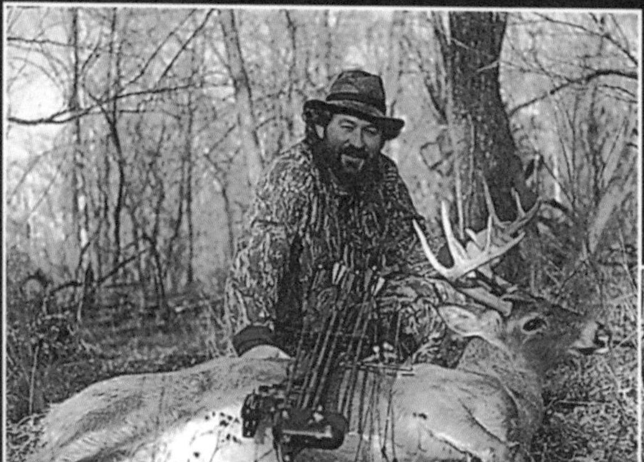

80 Minutes

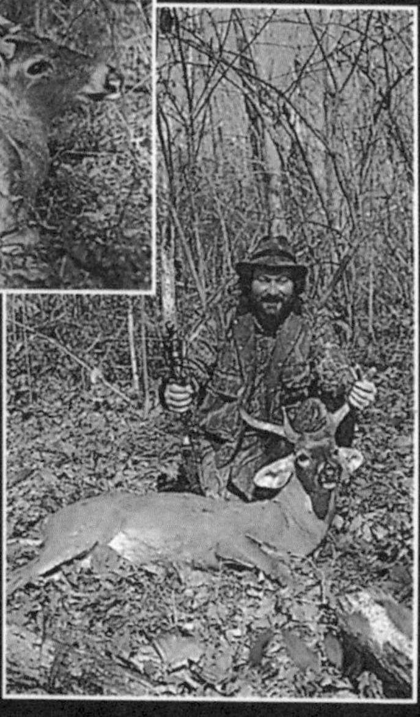

5 Vivid Arrow Impacts!

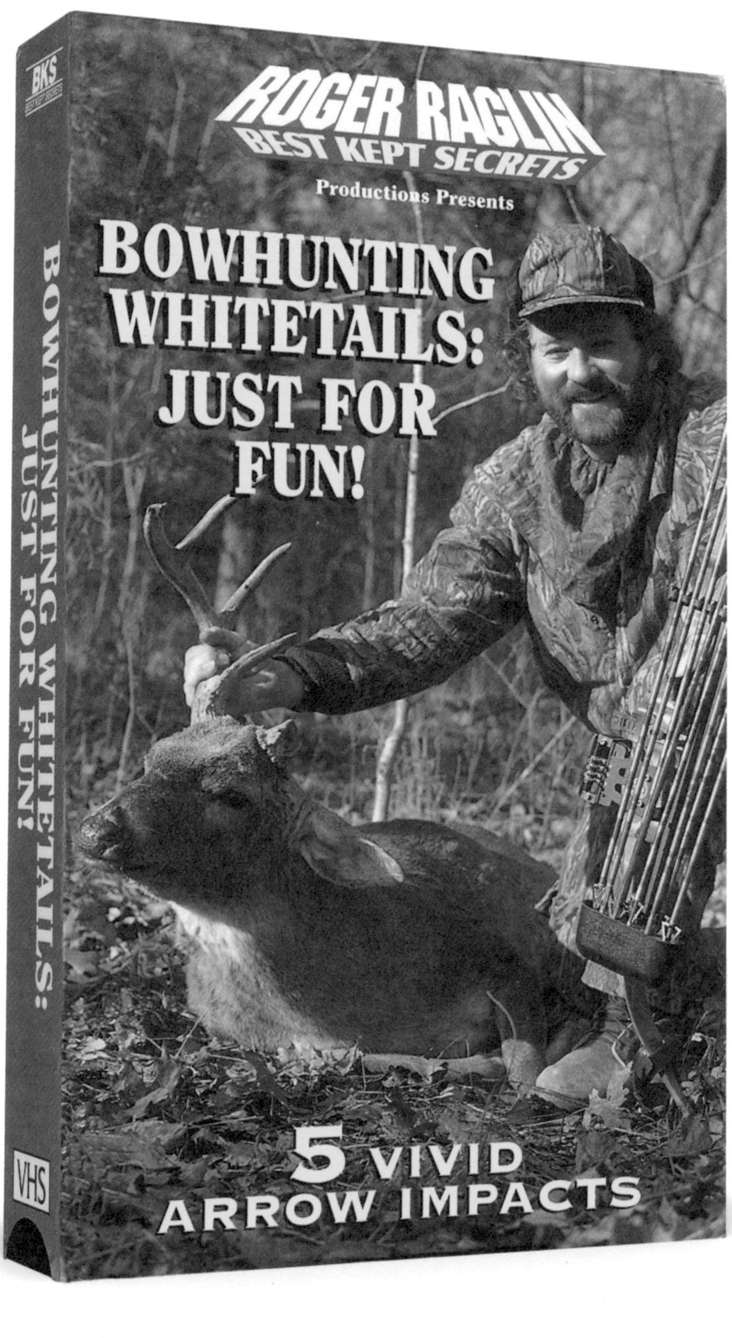
BKS
BEST KEPT SECRETS
ROGER RAGLIN
BEST KEPT SECRETS
Productions Presents
BOWHUNTING WHITETAILS: JUST FOR FUN!
BOWHUNTING WHITETAILS: JUST FOR FUN!
VHS
5 VIVID ARROW IMPACTS

the Seduction

Co starring COLLEEN CAMP, KEVIN BROPHY Music by LALO SCHIFRIN

Executive Producers JOSEPH WOLF, FRANK CAPRA, JR., CHUCK RUSSELL Executive in charge of production BLOSSOM KAHN

Associate Producer TOM CURTIS Produced by IRWIN YABLANS and BRUCE COHN CURTIS

Written and Directed by DAVID SCHMOELLER

Color/103 Minutes

Alone... Terrified... Trapped like an animal.

An erotic suspense-drama about a beautiful newscaster who is stalked and tormented by a photographer obsessed with her beauty. If he can't have her, no one will.

MEDIA HOME ENTERTAINMENT, INC.

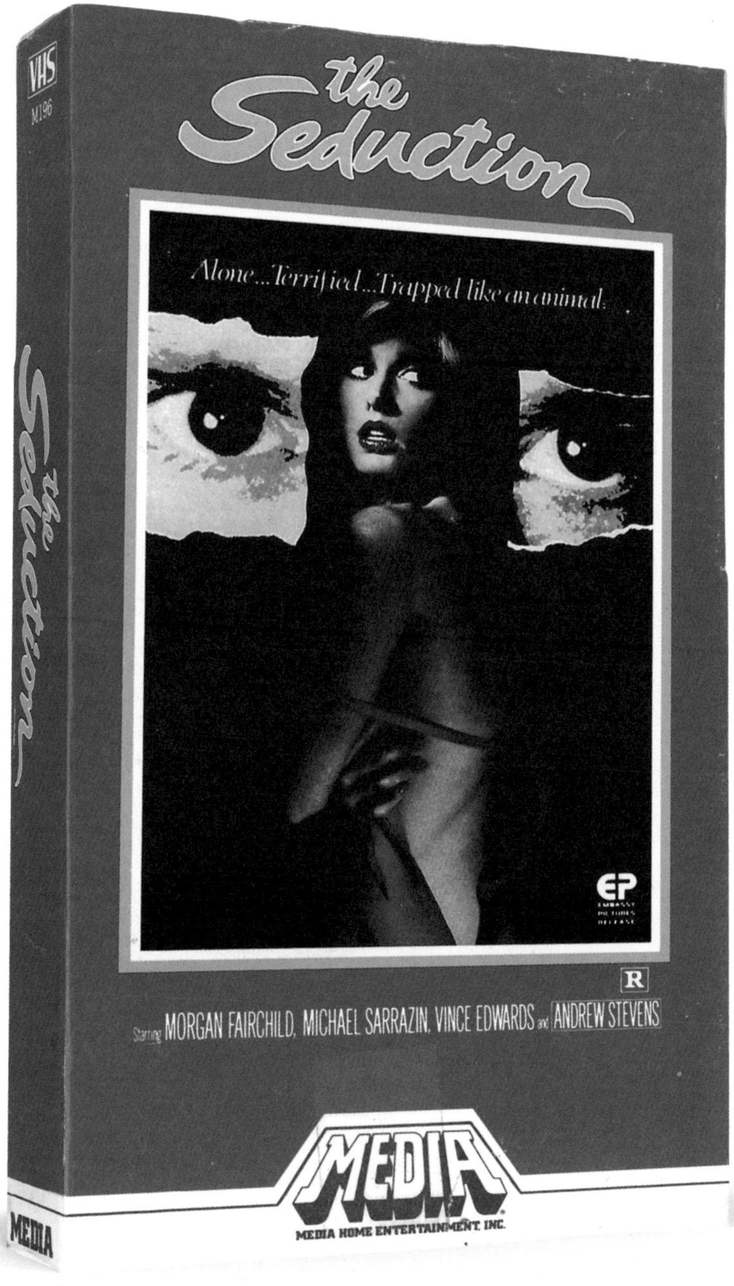
VHS
M196
the Seduction
Alone... Terrified... Trapped like an animal.
EP
R
Starring MORGAN FAIRCHILD, MICHAEL SARRAZIN, VINCE EDWARDS and ANDREW STEVENS
MEDIA
MEDIA HOME ENTERTAINMENT, INC.
the Seduction
MEDIA

SATAN'S BLACK WEDDING

• • • • • • • • •

A Blood Marriage
of Ghouls!

• • • • • • • • •

Starring:
GREG BRADDOCK
RAY MILES   LISA MILANO

• • • • • • • • • • • •

Chilling, supernatural events occur at
an old monastery located near the
scenic town of Monterey, California.
Vampires and ghouls prey on the
innocent, until the most diabolical
ritual imaginable takes place—
a Black Wedding!

1975—Color—61 minutes

• • • • • • • • • • • •

A HOME VIDEO RELEASE BY
WORLD VIDEO PICTURES, INC. LOS ANGELES, CA

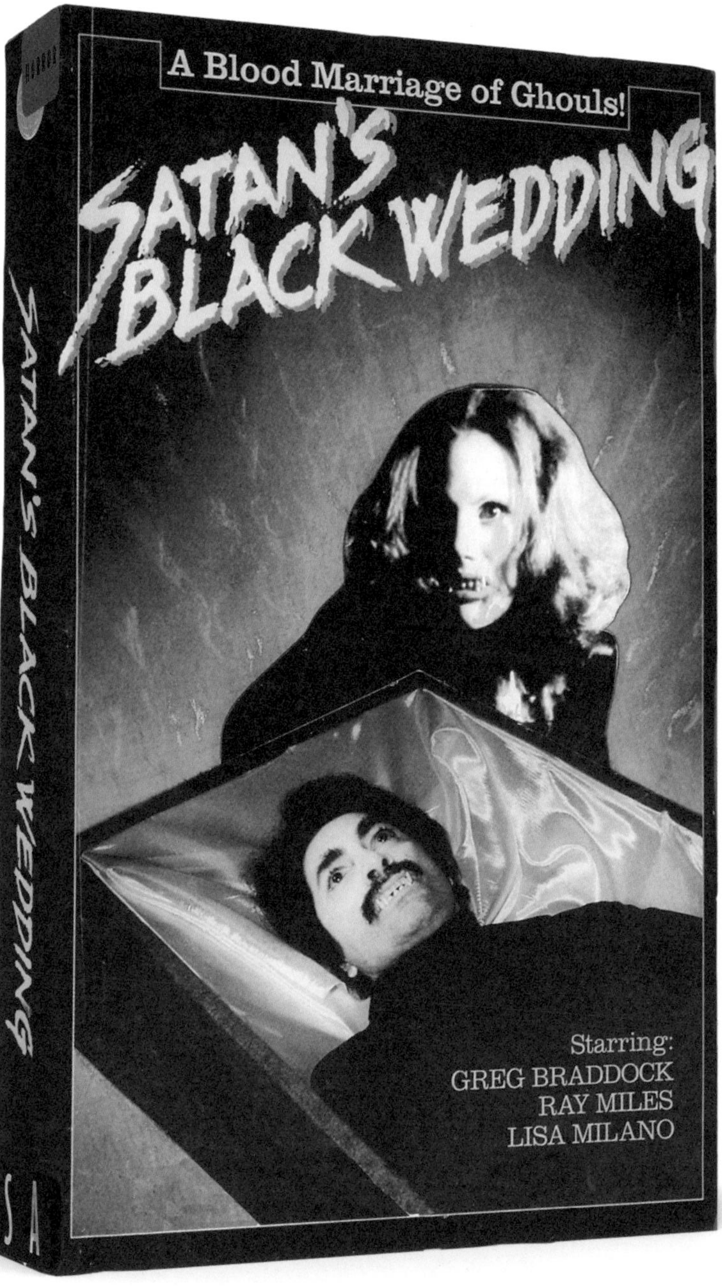
A Blood Marriage of Ghouls!
SATAN'S BLACK WEDDING
Starring:
GREG BRADDOCK
RAY MILES
LISA MILANO
SATAN'S BLACK WEDDING
S A

SCHWARZKOPF ON THE WAR
(The Briefing)

ISBN# 1-56278-104-9

0 30306-6445-3 0

"Stormin' Norman" Schwarzkopf predicted, back in 1983, that there would be a war in the Middle East. At that time, Schwarzkopf set out on his own to develop a plan in the event that a hostile nation would invade one of its neighbors. This plan became the groundwork for Operation Desert Shield.

This video contains the now famous military briefing, in its entirety, in which General Schwarzkopf explains the military tactics that led to the conclusion of the war. This very animated and informative account of the war by the General is presented by Peter Jennings and is further supplemented with an analytic view of the briefing by Jennings and resident military analysts Tony Cordesman and Lt. General Bernard E. Trainor.

Color   Approx. 70 min.   NR

ABC News 1991

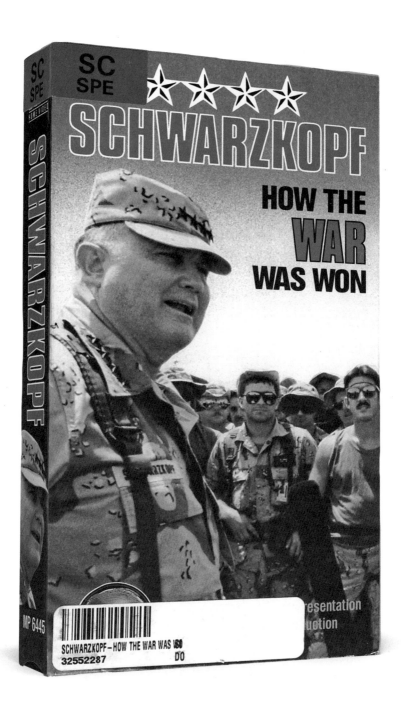

SC
SPE

SC
SPE

★ ★ ★ ★

SCHWARZKOPF

HOW THE
WAR
WAS WON

SCHWARZKOPF

resentation
uction

MP 6445

SCHWARZKOPF—HOW THE WAR WAS V60
32552287   D'O

AMERICAN ARTISTS INC. Presents "SLAUGHTERHOUSE" Starring JOE BARTON as "Buddy"
SHERRY BENDORF, DON BARRETT, WILLIAM HOUCK Director of Photography RICHARD BENDA
Original Soundtrack by VANTAGE POINT Original Score by JOE GARRISON
Executive Producer JERRY ENCOE Produced by RON MATONAK Written & Directed by RICK ROESSLER
AMERICAN ARTISTS AN AMERICAN ARTISTS RELEASE ©1987 American Artists, Inc.

He's young, he's big and he's always hungry. His name is Buddy, and please don't call him Bud.

This is the haunted story of Buddy Bacon, a brand new kind of American hero. A sweet guy, until you mess with one of his hogs...or cross his father. Then the other Buddy comes out, the one that will make you shiver in Slaughterhouse.

This Buddy has been given an urgent project: Revenge. Revenge against the so-called "Slaughterhouse conspirators" who caused his father's ruin. On their bone-crushing path, Buddy and his Daddy meet a few high school kids...whose luck just ran out.

One thing you'll learn about Buddy, he never misses a deadline. He's one of those conscientious dudes that just grinds it out, day in day out. He doesn't need pep talks, either. All he needs is an axe. A big axe. Get the picture?

"Dolby" and the double-D symbol are trademarks of Dolby Laboratories Licensing Corporation

1987, Color, 85 minutes, Horror.

hi-fi STEREO
DOLBY SURROUND ™
MONO COMPATIBLE

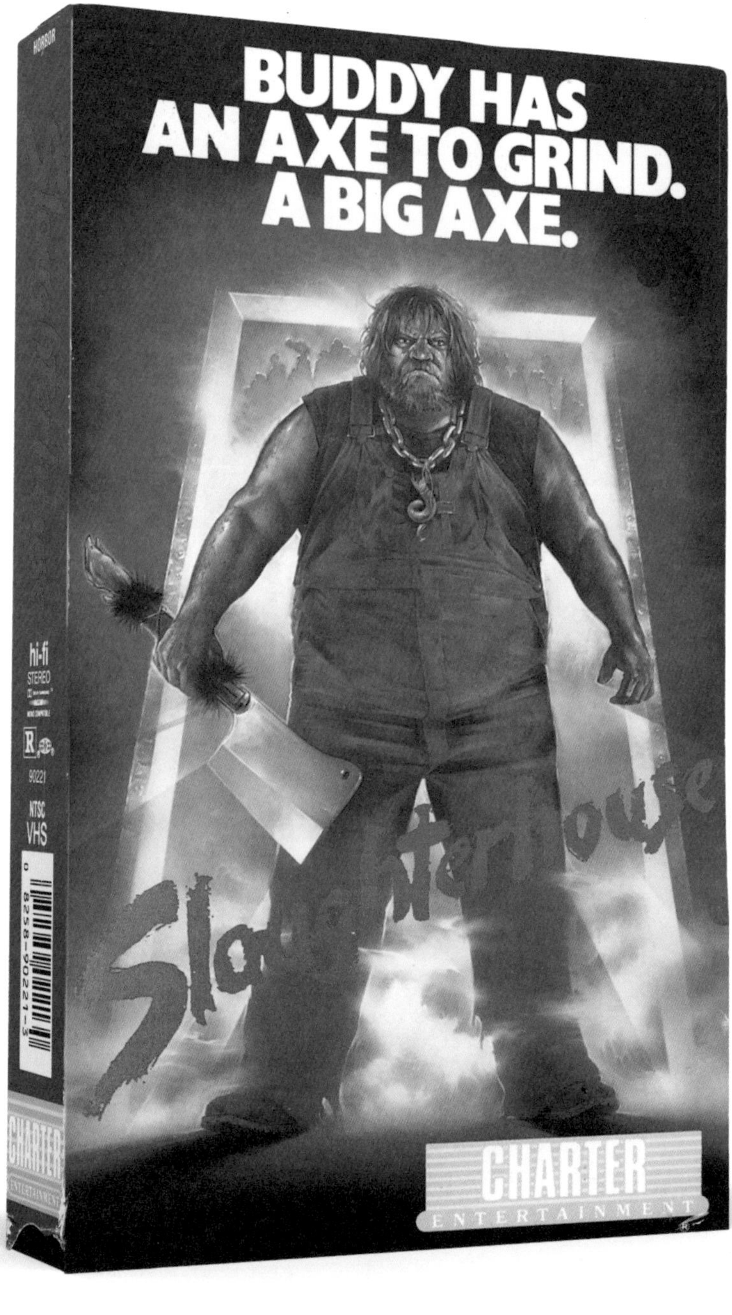
BUDDY HAS
AN AXE TO GRIND.
A BIG AXE.
Slaughterhouse
CHARTER
ENTERTAINMENT
hi-fi
STEREO
90221
NTSC
VHS
HORROR

CRAZED

Color/88 minutes

A Nightmare Journey Into The Dark Side Of Love.

A girl moves into a boarding house occupied by a reclusive voyeur who becomes obsessed by her. When she becomes the victim of an accidental drowning, he turns psychopathic by keeping her lifeless body—and murders intruders to keep his secret.

TWE TRANS WORLD ENTERTAINMENT 6430 Sunset Blvd., Suite 501 Hollywood, California 90028

Trans World Entertainment U.S.A.

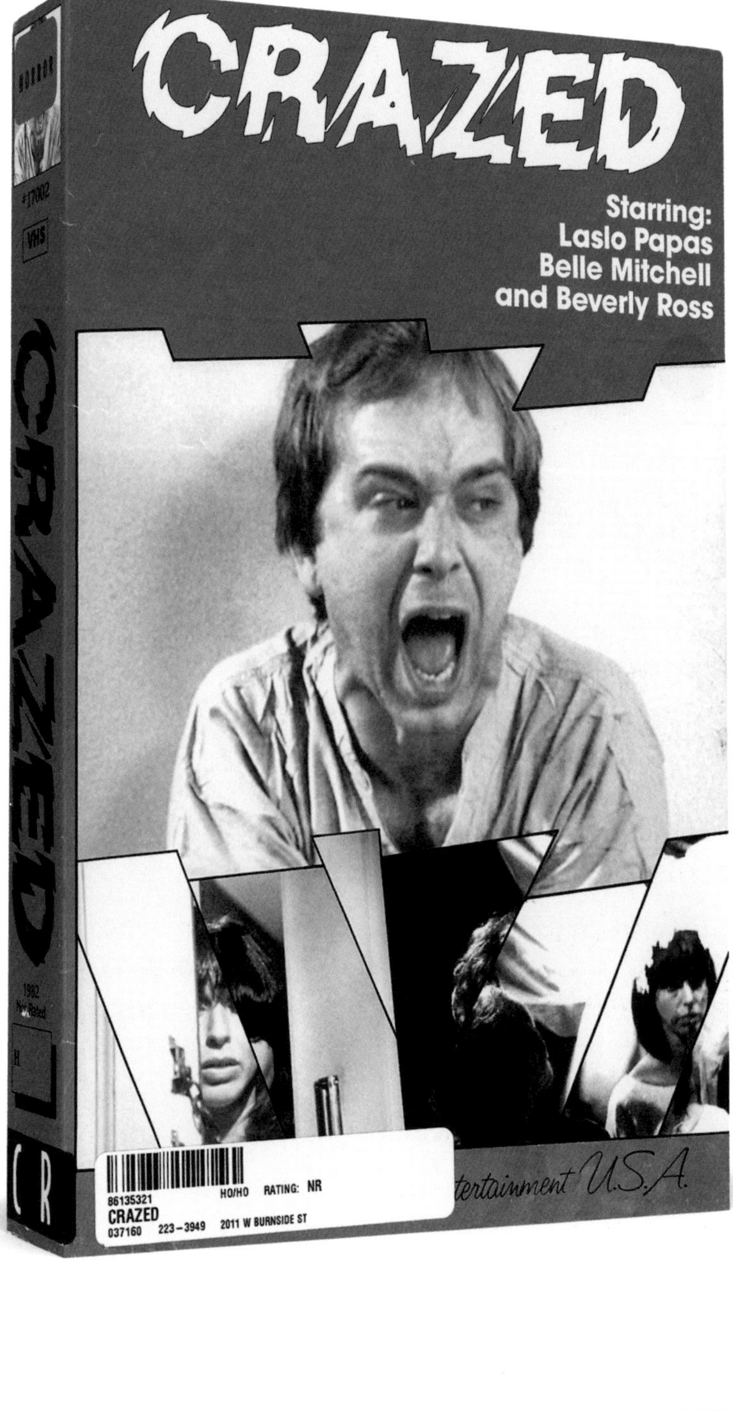
CRAZED
Starring:
Laslo Papas
Belle Mitchell
and Beverly Ross
HORROR
#17002
VHS
CRAZED
1982
Not Rated
CR
86135321
HO/HO RATING: NR
CRAZED
037160 223-3949 2011 W BURNSIDE ST
ntertainment U.S.A.

GARY COLEMAN
FOR SAFETY'S SAKE

Home Safety Can Be Fun! FOR SAFETY'S SAKE leads childre
and parents through a delightful series of live-action
segments designed to make the home the safe and sound
place that it was meant to be. Host Gary Coleman is joined b
his friends Jack and Jill Example, Nurse Helpquick, and the
colorful Fire-Captain Truck. Together they illustrate the
vital but often overlooked ABC's of self-care skills.

From accident prevention to common sense rules for being
home alone, from first-aid to kitchen safety, FOR SAFETY'S
SAKE provides entertaining and easily understood step-by-
step instruction. With its own "Be Prepared Guide" and tec
niques developed by the National Safety Council and the R
Cross, FOR SAFETY'S SAKE supplies the foundation for any
home safety program.

FOR SAFETY'S SAKE - it brings safety HOME!

COLOR 40 MINUTES

Starring **GARY COLEMAN**
With **AMY FOSTER· BOBBY JACOBY**
Executive Producer **PATTI JACKSON** Producer **PATRICIA STALLO**
Written by **DAVID MOOREHEAD** Director **LESLIE MARTINSO**

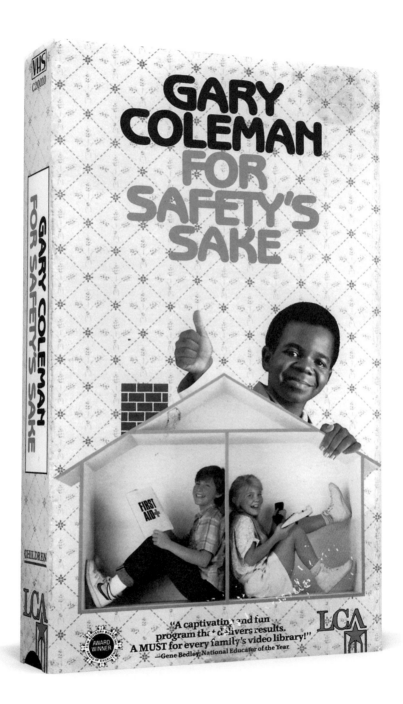

GARY COLEMAN FOR SAFETY'S SAKE

VHS
C20010

FIRST AID+

CHILDREN

LCA

AWARD WINNER

LCA

"A captivating and fun program that delivers results. A MUST for every family's video library!"
—Gene Bedley, National Educator of the Year

A Subterranean Horror Is Unleashed on New York City!

C.H.U.D.

John Heard, Daniel Stern and Christopher Curry

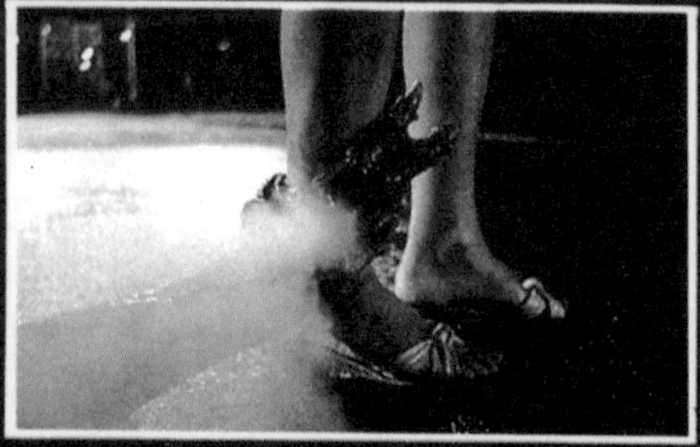

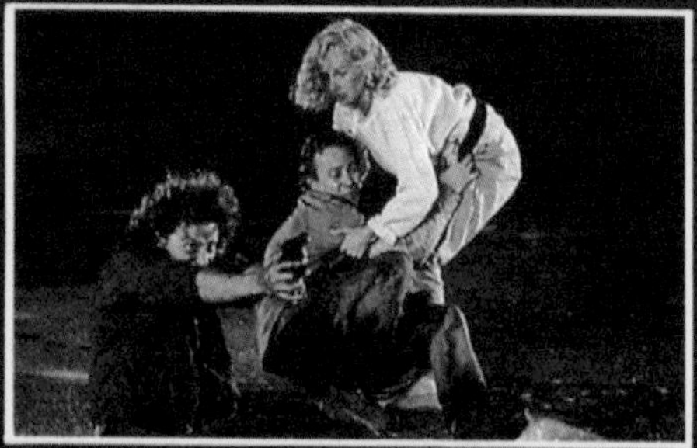

In the dank, putrid labyrinth of tunnels beneath the streets of New York City, a hideous transformation is taking place. An underground, ragtag colony of homeless derelicts is turning into a voracious tribe of grotesque mutants. They are turning into C.H.U.D.—*Cannibalistic Humanoid Underground Dwellers* who ooze up from their hellish depths after dark for the only food that satisfies their hunger—human flesh!!

JOHN HEARD *(CAT PEOPLE)* and DANIEL STERN *(BREAKING AWAY, DINER)* accidently learn of the government's covert subterranean dumping site of radioactive waste that is mutating the underground vagrants. Together with a Manhattan police captain, they attempt to unravel the government cover-up and to stop the carnivorous slaughter.

But they haven't got much time. Soon it will be dark on the streets of the city. Soon it will be feeding time.

Produced by ANDREW BONIME
Directed by DOUGLAS CHEEK
Screenplay by PARNELL HALL
Story by SHEPARD ABBOTT

Color/88 Minutes

R

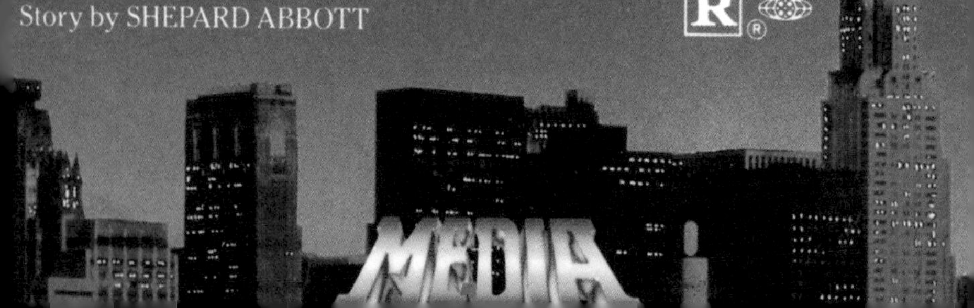

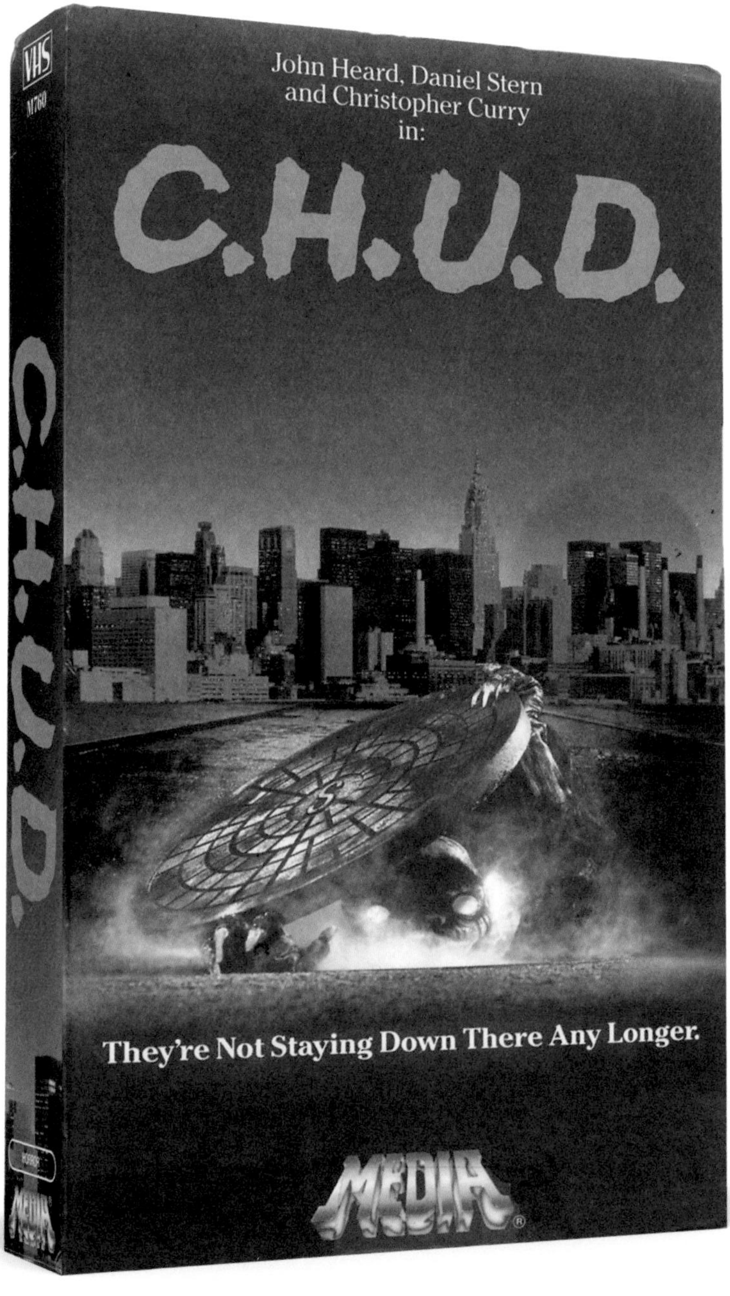
VHS
M760
John Heard, Daniel Stern
and Christopher Curry
in:
C.H.U.D.
They're Not Staying Down There Any Longer.
MEDIA
C.H.U.D.

The Prowler

The Human Exterminator . . . He has his own way of killing!

Starring
VICKY DAWSON • CHRISTOPHER GOUTMAN
CINDY WEINTRAUB
and **FARLEY GRANGER** as Sheriff George Fraser
Special Makeup and Effects by
TOM SAVINI
Music by
RICHARD EINHORN
Screenplay by
GLENN LEOPOLD and **NEAL F. BARBERA**
Produced by
JOSEPH ZITO and **DAVID STREIT**
Directed by
JOSEPH ZITO

A GRADUATION PRODUCTION

VHS

VC II™ LOS ANGELES, CA

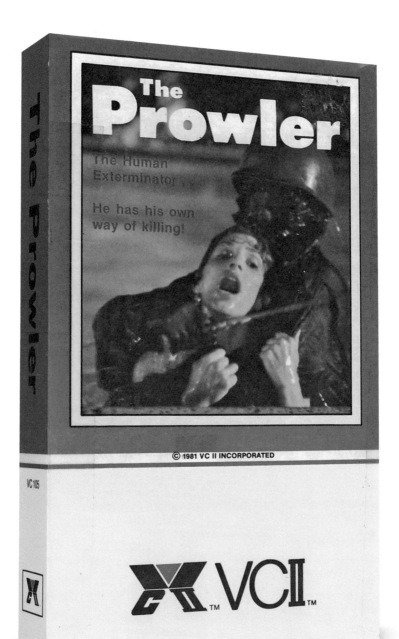

The Human
Exterminator

He has his own
way of killing!

The Prowler

VC 105

© 1981 VC II INCORPORATED

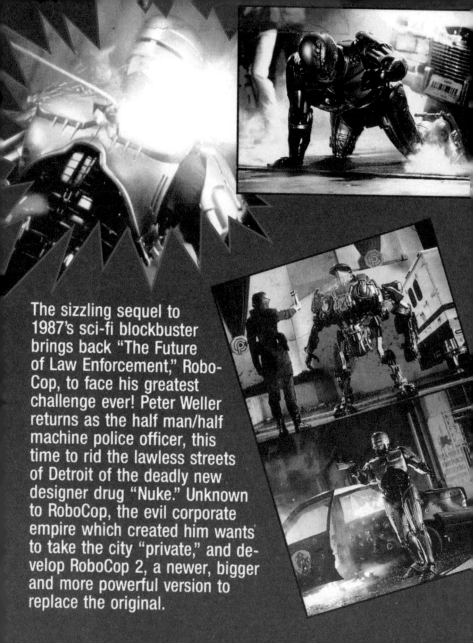

The sizzling sequel to 1987's sci-fi blockbuster brings back "The Future of Law Enforcement," Robo-Cop, to face his greatest challenge ever! Peter Weller returns as the half man/half machine police officer, this time to rid the lawless streets of Detroit of the deadly new designer drug "Nuke." Unknown to RoboCop, the evil corporate empire which created him wants to take the city "private," and develop RoboCop 2, a newer, bigger and more powerful version to replace the original.

1990, Color, 117 Minutes, 🔲® Closed Captioned, HI-FI Stereo, Rated R.

ROBOCOP 2 ™

A **Jon Davison** PRODUCTION ● AN **Irvin Kershner** FILM ● Peter Weller ● Nancy Allen ● "RoboCop_2" ● Daniel O'Herlihy
Tom Noonan ● Belinda Bauer ● Gabriel Damon ● DIRECTION OF PHOTOGRAPHY **Mark Irwin** ● VISUAL EFFECTS BY **Phil Tippett** ● ROBOCOP DESIGNED BY **Rob Bottin** ● MUSIC BY **Leonard Rosenman**
EXECUTIVE PRODUCER **Patrick Crowley** ● BASED ON CHARACTERS CREATED BY **Edward Neumeier** & **Michael Miner** ● STORY BY **Frank Miller** ● SCREENPLAY BY **Frank Miller** & **Walon Green**
ORION HOME VIDEO ● R ● 🔲 CLOSED CAPTIONED ● PRODUCED BY **Jon Davison** ● DIRECTED BY **Irvin Kershner** ● Prints By DeLuxe® ● An **ORION** PICTURES Release
1990 Orion Pictures Corporation. All Rights Reserved.
RoboCop is a Trademark of Orion Pictures Corporation.

ISBN 1-56255-076-4

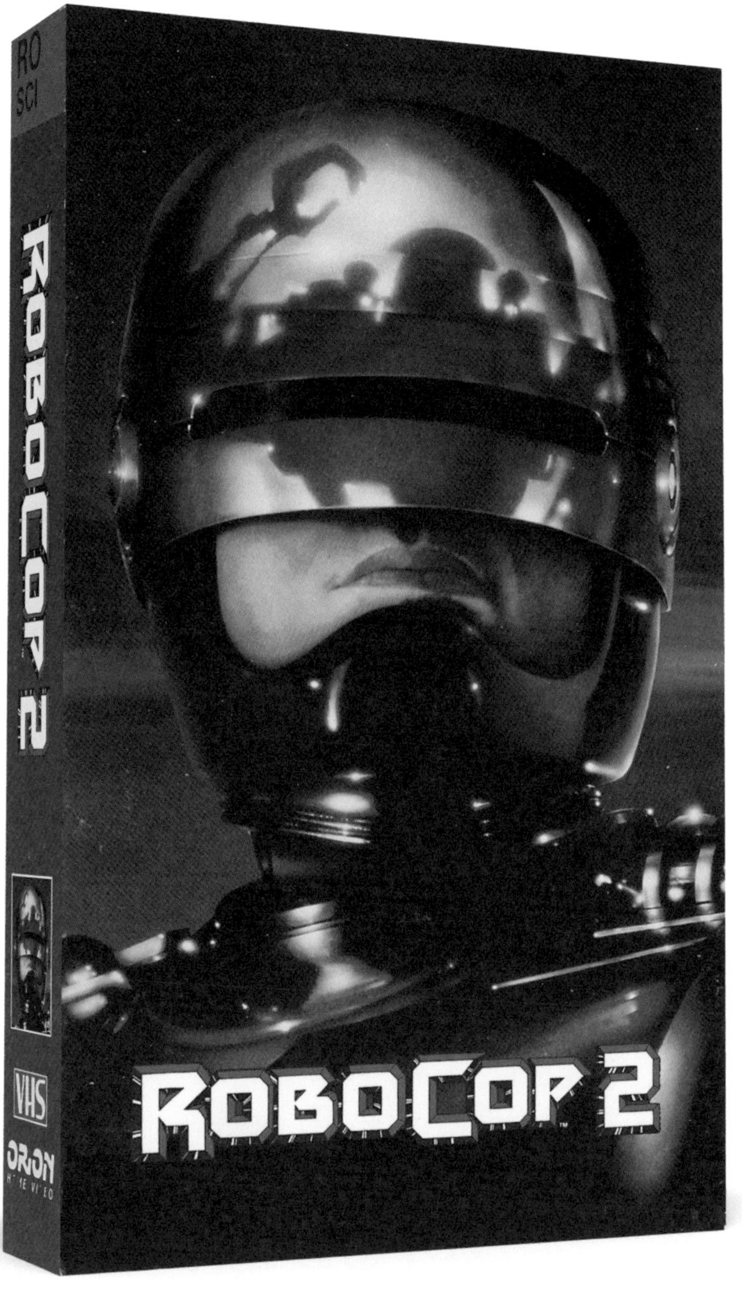
RO
SCI
ROBOCOP 2
ROBOCOP 2
VHS
ORION

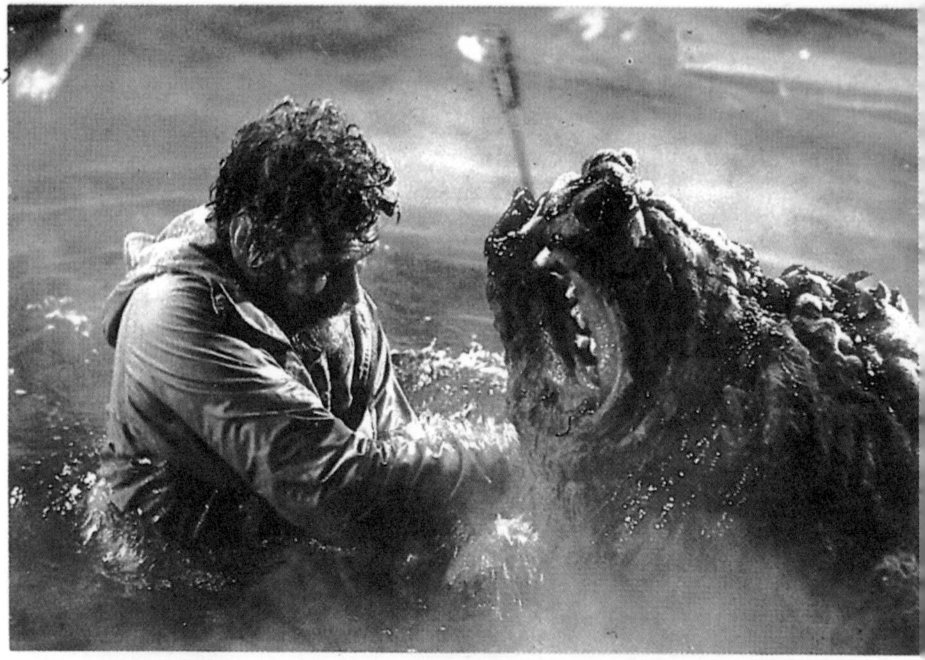

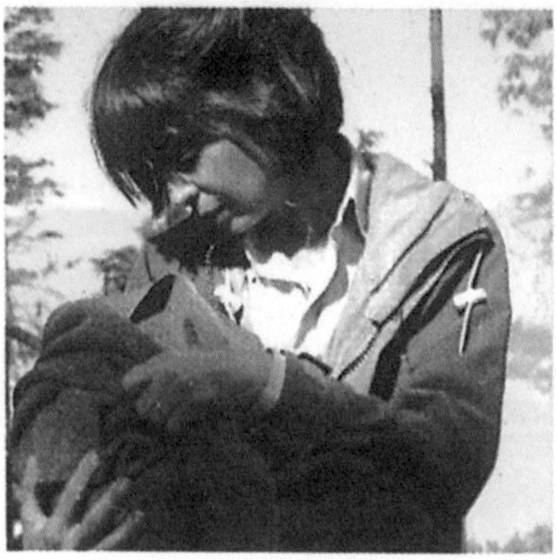

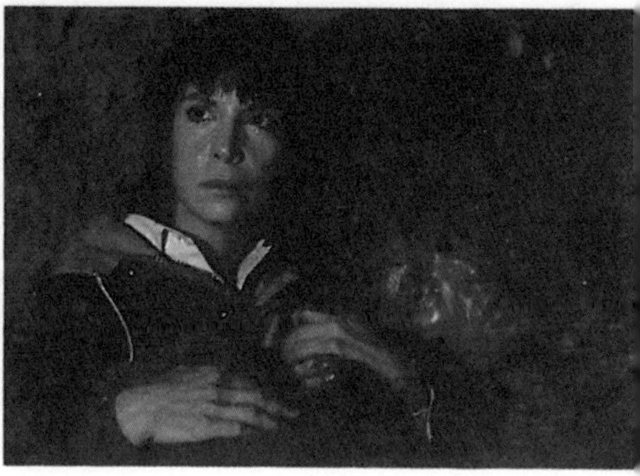

PROPHECY is a contemporary story of stark terror. Robert Foxworth and Talia Shire star as an idealistic doctor and his wife who, at the request of a concerned friend, travel to Maine to research the impact of the lumber industry on the local environment. They begin to investigate a succession of mysterious and terrifying events: ecological freaks of nature (including fish that grow many times their normal size), and a series of bizarre and grisly human deaths. Veteran suspense director John Frankenheimer manages to present PROPHECY as a "monster movie" as well as a suspenseful tale about the deadly forces which result from the pollution of our environment.

PG®

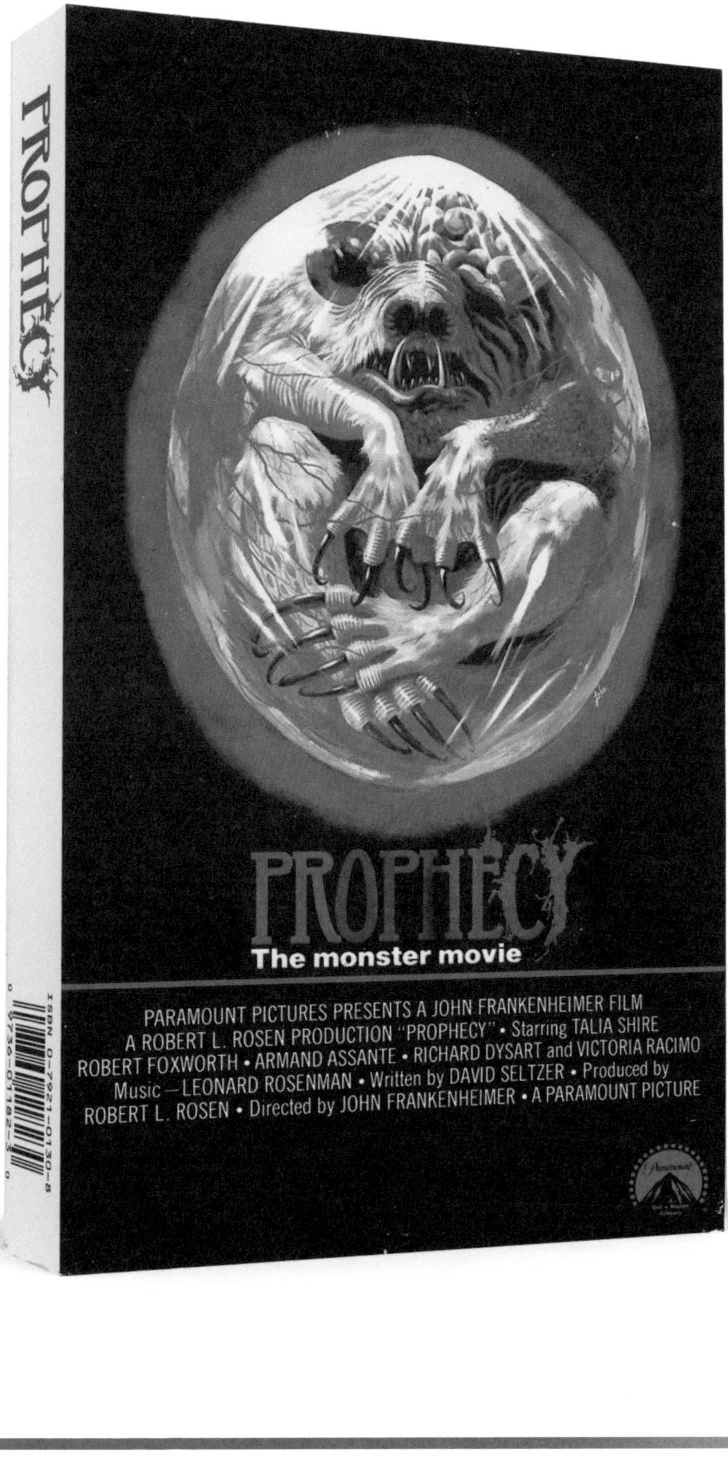
PROPHECY
ISBN 0-7921-0130-8
PROPHECY
The monster movie
PARAMOUNT PICTURES PRESENTS A JOHN FRANKENHEIMER FILM
A ROBERT L. ROSEN PRODUCTION "PROPHECY" • Starring TALIA SHIRE
ROBERT FOXWORTH • ARMAND ASSANTE • RICHARD DYSART and VICTORIA RACIMO
Music—LEONARD ROSENMAN • Written by DAVID SELTZER • Produced by
ROBERT L. ROSEN • Directed by JOHN FRANKENHEIMER • A PARAMOUNT PICTURE

SLAVE GIRLS FROM BEYOND INFINITY

BIG MOVIE.
BIG PRODUCTION.
BIG GIRLS.

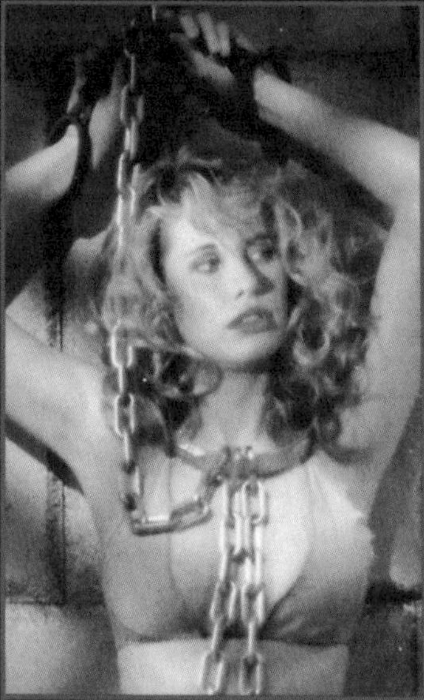

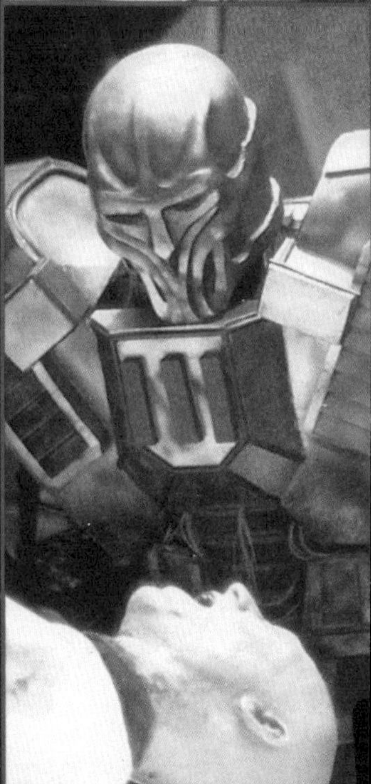

In the distant future, two beautiful young slaves are serving life on a prison galley. It's a no win situation. With high hopes and no map, they escape, convinced that any fate will be an improvement. But what do slave girls know? Crash-landed on a strange planet, they meet Zed, greatest hunter in the cosmos. His gracious hospitality fools them at first, but even these girls notice that Zed's other guests are disappearing one by one. What is the deadly secret locked behind the doors of Zed's trophy room? Is he a closet cosmetician? Sherlock Holmes never wore outfits like the SLAVE GIRLS FROM BEYOND INFINITY.

RUNNING TIME: 80 MINUTES

1987

Urban Classics VIDEO

A DIVISION OF EMPIRE ENTERTAINMENT, INC.
1551 N. LA BREA AVE.,
HOLLYWOOD, CALIFORNIA 90028

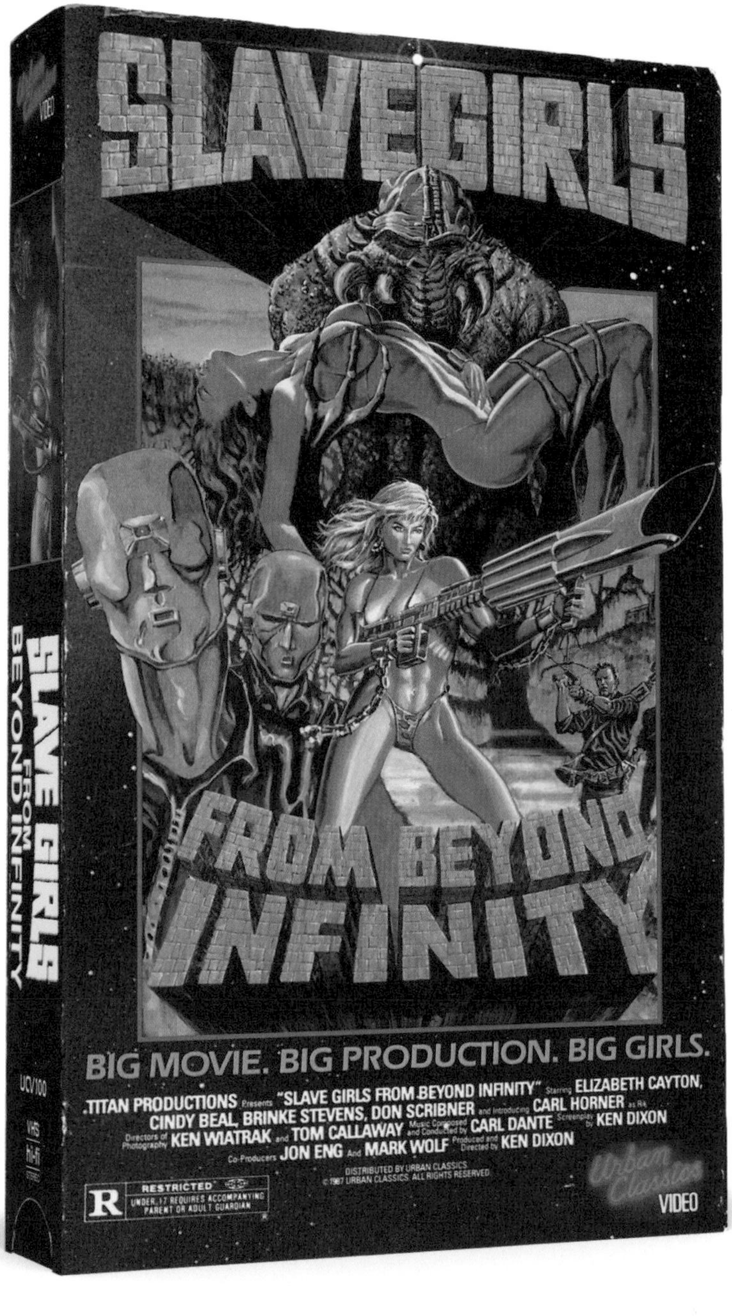
SLAVE GIRLS
FROM BEYOND INFINITY
BIG MOVIE. BIG PRODUCTION. BIG GIRLS.
TITAN PRODUCTIONS Presents "SLAVE GIRLS FROM BEYOND INFINITY" Starring ELIZABETH CAYTON,
CINDY BEAL, BRINKE STEVENS, DON SCRIBNER and introducing CARL HORNER as Rik
Directors of Photography KEN WIATRAK and TOM CALLAWAY Music Composed and Conducted by CARL DANTE Screenplay by KEN DIXON
Co-Producers JON ENG And MARK WOLF Produced and Directed by KEN DIXON
DISTRIBUTED BY URBAN CLASSICS
© 1987 URBAN CLASSICS. ALL RIGHTS RESERVED
R RESTRICTED
UNDER 17 REQUIRES ACCOMPANYING PARENT OR ADULT GUARDIAN
Urban Classics
VIDEO
SLAVE GIRLS FROM BEYOND INFINITY
UCV100
VHS
hi-fi

In a small town in Ireland, a young girl
becomes the victim of demonic possession.

After being informed by the priest of a
church robbery and disappearances of
newborn babies, police detective Barnes
arrests an old lady who is suspected of being
a witch. After rigid interrogation, the woman
kills herself by jumping out of a window.

In revenge, the old woman's spirit takes
possession of nine year old Susan, daughter
of Barnes, who in turn takes revenge on her
governess and on those who punished her in
her childhood.

Susan goes to the tomb of the old lady where
the forces of good and evil fight to the death
for...The Possessed.

The Possessed — a story of demonic terror
and witchcraft.

WARNING: Due to the graphic content of this
motion picture, viewer discretion is advised.

49008   Running Time: 87 minutes

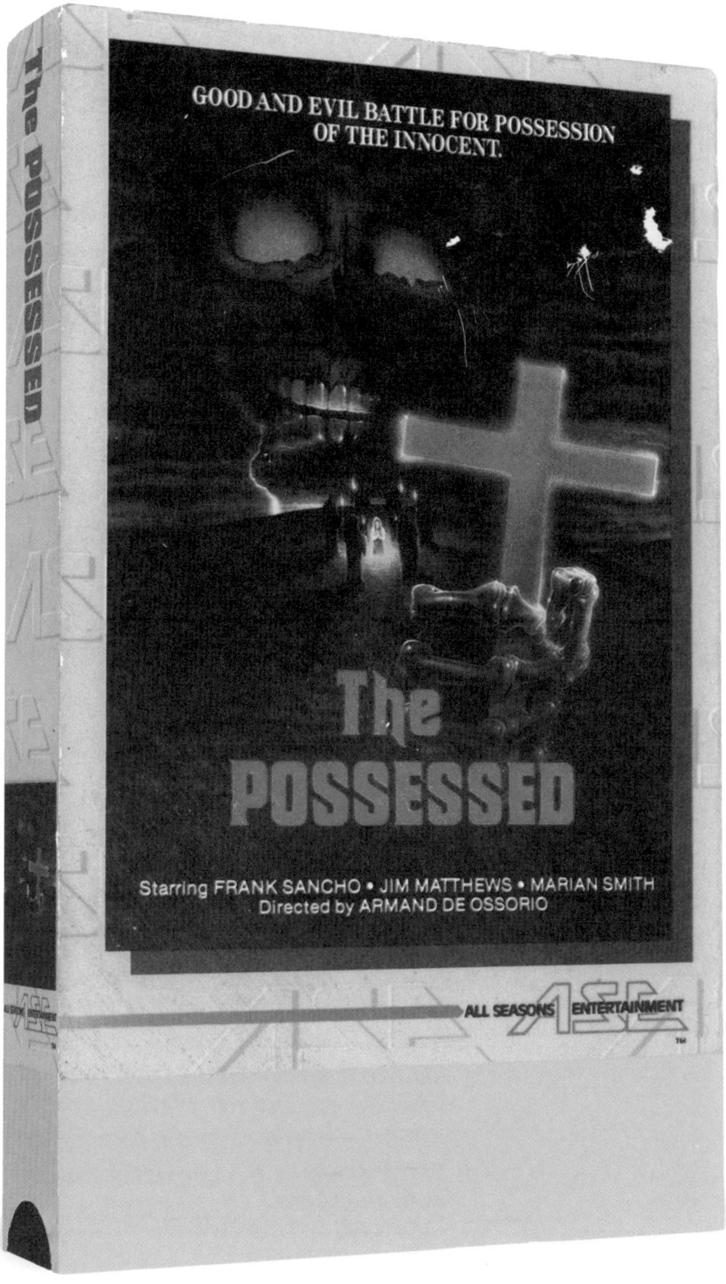
The POSSESSED
GOOD AND EVIL BATTLE FOR POSSESSION
OF THE INNOCENT.
The
POSSESSED
Starring FRANK SANCHO • JIM MATTHEWS • MARIAN SMITH
Directed by ARMAND DE OSSORIO
ALL SEASONS ENTERTAINMENT

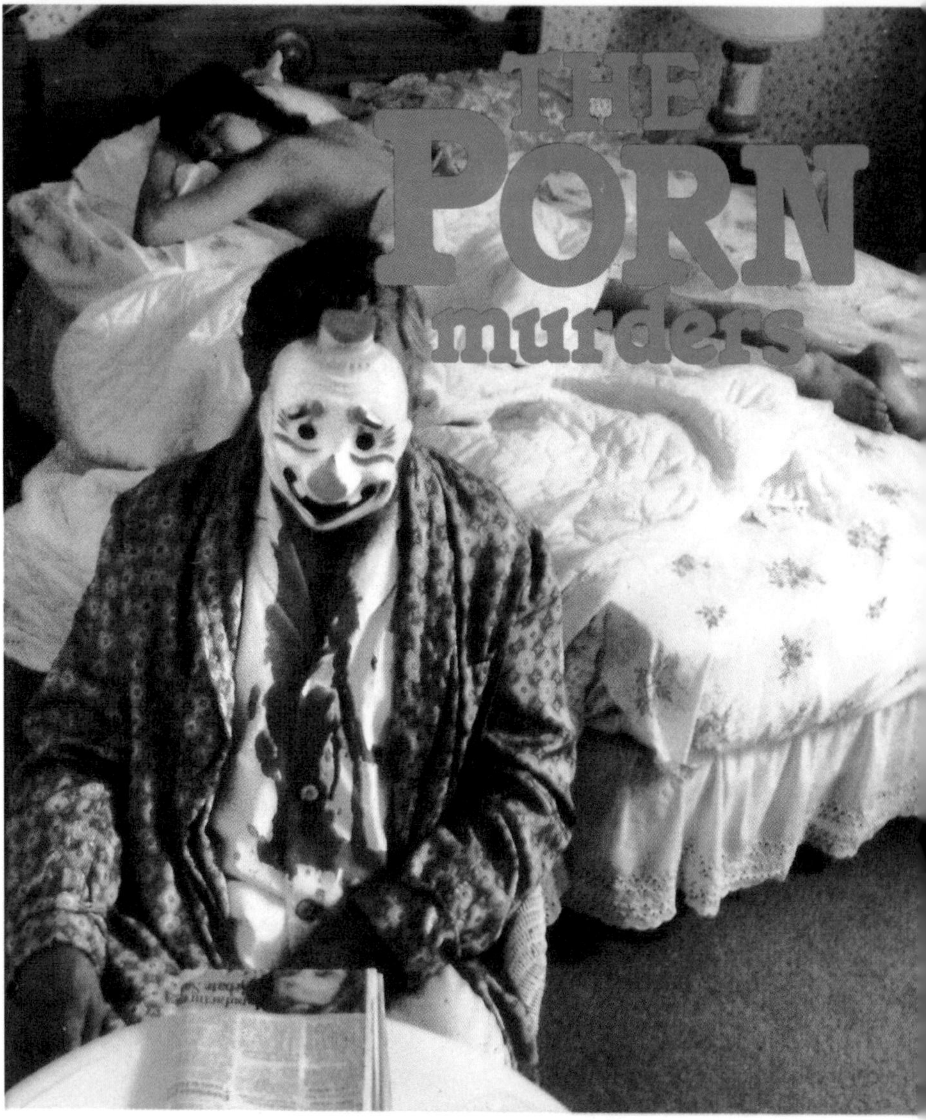
THE
PORN
murders

A hard-nosed homicide cop and a crime reporter team up to track down a killer crusading against pornography. At the scene of each grizzly murder the victim is wearing a bizzare clown's mask. While the duo and police follow one route the demented killer is closing in on more victims.

Starring: Jamie Spears, Terry Logan and Peter Brikmanis.
Written by: Jim Murray.
Produced and directed by: Charles Wiener.

AVEC

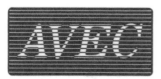

91 mins.

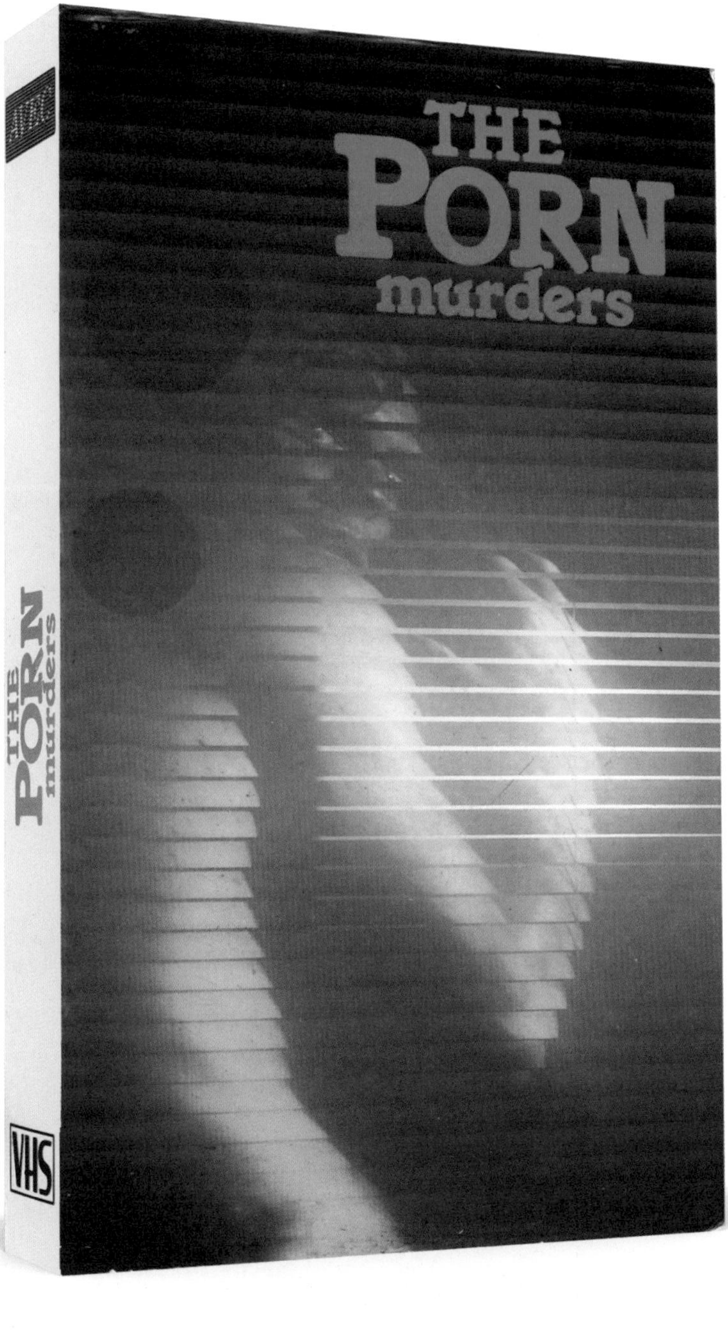
THE PORN murders
THE PORN murders
VHS

Because A Brain...

 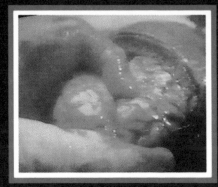

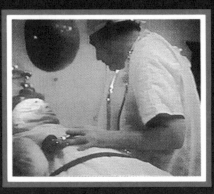 

Is A Terrible Thing
To Waste!

When a brilliant statesman & politician is diag-
nosed as having a terminal disease, he decides
the only viable solution is a brain transplant. He
discovers, only too late, that "innovative" doctor
that he has chosen to perform the surgery is quite
mad. The politician's brain is implanted into the body
of the deformed village idiot. Although he has a
great case for malpractice, he opts for revenge
because...a brain is a terrible thing to waste.

STARRING

GRANT WILLIAMS · KENT TAYLO

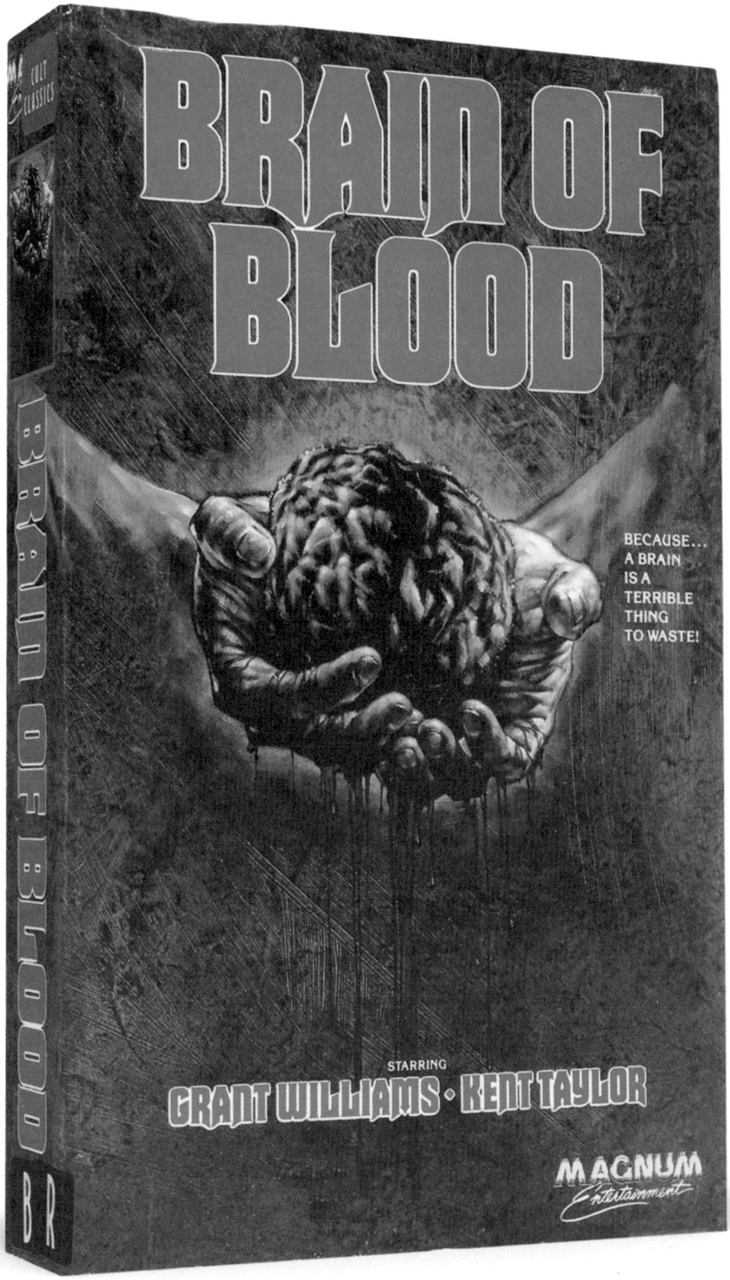
CULT CLASSICS
BRAIN OF BLOOD
BR
BRAIN OF BLOOD
BECAUSE... A BRAIN IS A TERRIBLE THING TO WASTE!
STARRING
GRANT WILLIAMS • KENT TAYLOR
MAGNUM
Entertainment

NIGHTMARE CIRCUS

Andrew Prine headlines as a psychotic ringmaster to his own bizarre circus, made up of captive women kept chained in his barn. In the center ring is the feature attraction of this psycho circus—a strange creature horribly mutated by a nuclear test blast in the nearby Nevada desert. It becomes difficult to tell who is more warped—the ringmaster or the mutant!

Starring

ANDREW PRINE   **MANUELLA THEIFF**

87 minutes   COLOR   R1020

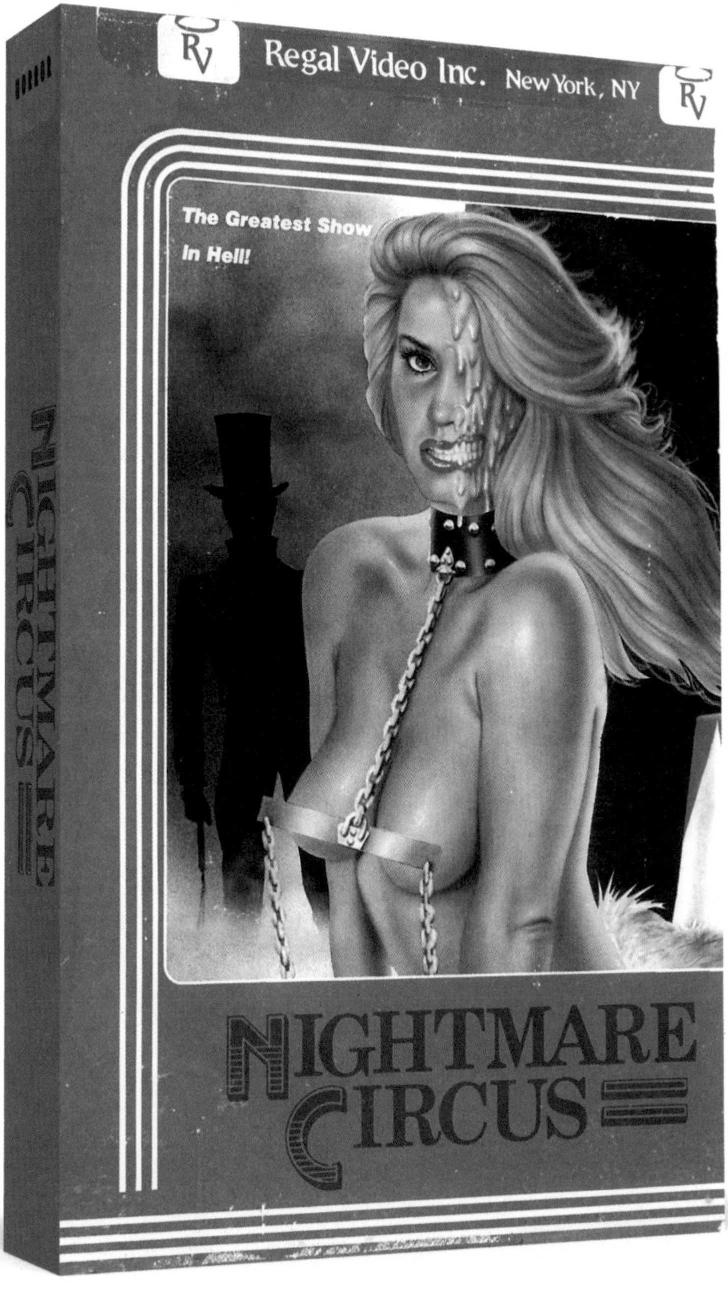
RV
Regal Video Inc. New York, NY
RV
The Greatest Show
In Hell!
NIGHTMARE
CIRCUS
NIGHTMARE
CIRCUS

BRIDES OF THE BEAST

Beautiful young virgins are sacrificed in orgiastic rights by the natives of a remote Pacific atoll. An arriving research scientist and his voluptuous blonde wife learn that the natives are appeasing a sex-mad mutant monster. The blood-craving creature is actually the master of the island, metamorphosized by the effects of earlier atomic radiation.

85 MINUTES / **COLOR**   R 1013

JOHN ASHLEY   **KENT TAYLOR**
                BEVERLY HILLS

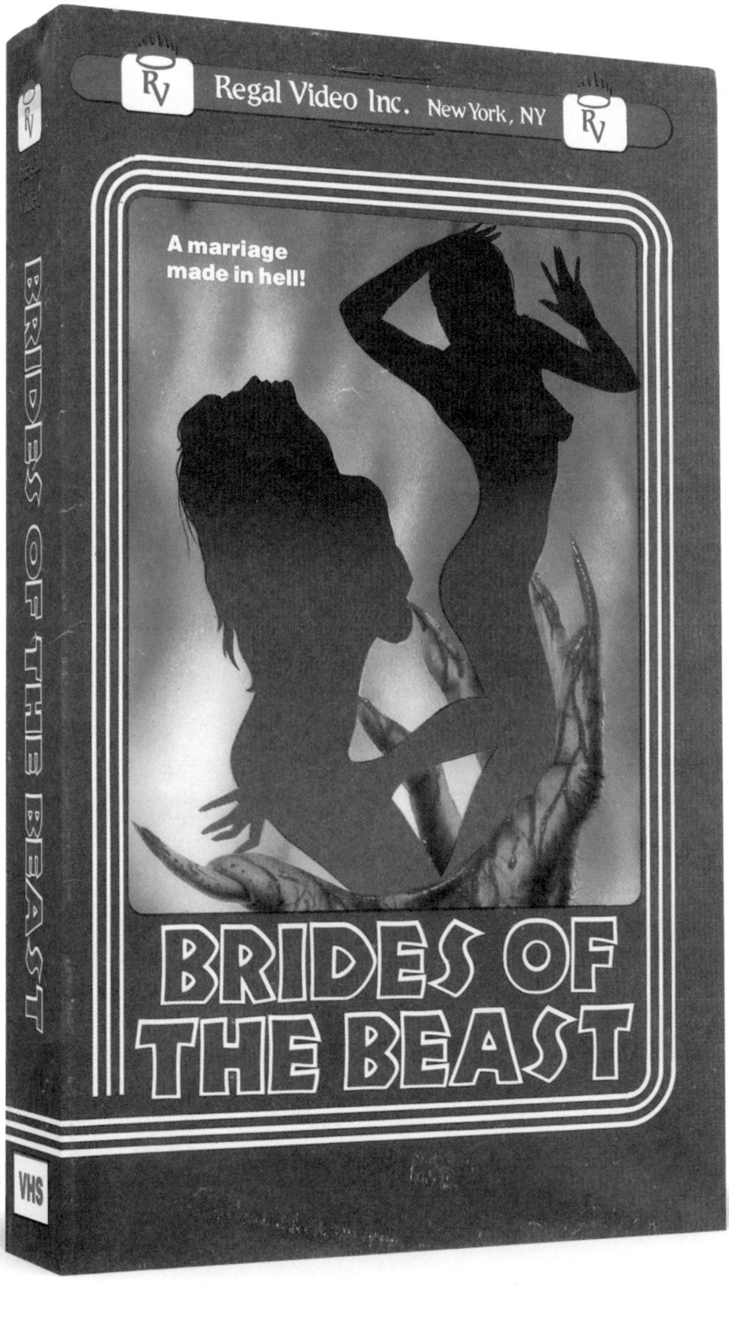
RV
Regal Video Inc. New York, NY
RV
A marriage made in hell!
BRIDES OF THE BEAST
Regal Video
BRIDES OF THE BEAST
VHS

Cat People

Some Music Rescored for Home Video.

Color/1 Hr. 59 Mins. R

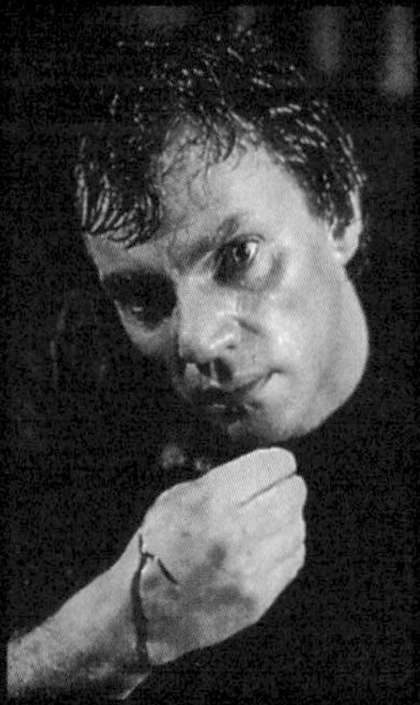

Nastassia Kinski stars in *Cat People* as Irena, a beautiful young woman on the bridge of sexuality; she discovers love for the first time only to find that the explosive experience brings with it tragic consequences. The tremendous passion of this girl's first romantic love is so strong, however, it by-passes the chaos around her—including her brother's (Malcolm McDowell) extraordinary demands—as it pushes her on to her own bizarre destiny. With a style as timeless as myth, *Cat People* is an erotic fantasy of the passion and terror that surround this girl's first love. Desire... passion...blood, her lust transforms her into one of the *Cat People*.

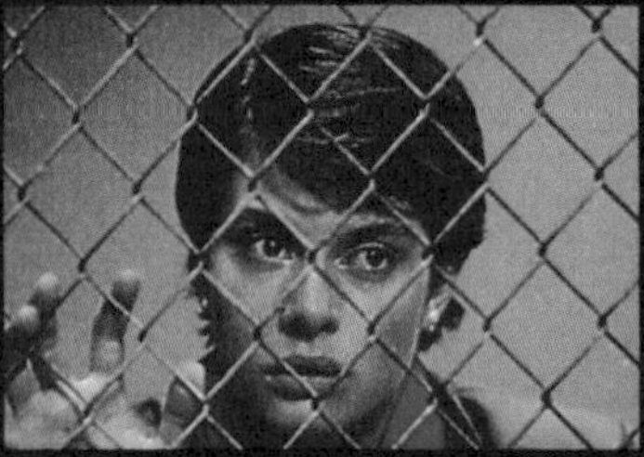

NASTASSIA KINSKI · MALCOLM McDOWELL · JOHN HEARD · ANNETTE O TOOLE

A CHARLES FRIES PRODUCTION A PAUL SCHRADER FILM

CAT PEOPLE

Screenplay by ALAN ORMSBY Based on the story by DEWITT BODEEN Special Visual Effects by ALBERT WHITLOCK Music by GIORGIO MORODER

Director of Photography JOHN BAILEY Executive Producer JERRY BRUCKHEIMER Produced by CHARLES FRIES Directed by PAUL SCHRADER

CAT PEOPLE theme sung by DAVID BOWIE • Lyrics by DAVID BOWIE Music by GIORGIO MORODER

An RKO Universal Picture

This videotape has been digitally mastered onto Hi Fi.

MCA HOME VIDEO

70 UNIVERSAL CITY PLAZA, UNIVERSAL CITY, CA 91608

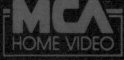

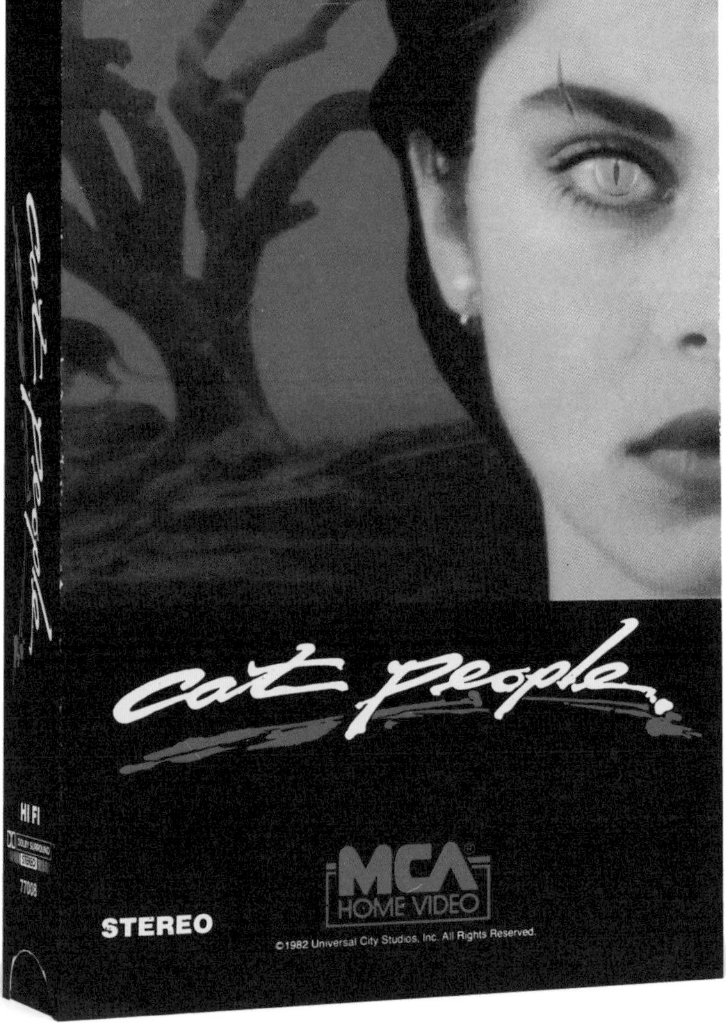

MCA HOME VIDEO
cat people
HI FI
STEREO
MCA HOME VIDEO
©1982 Universal City Studios, Inc. All Rights Reserved.

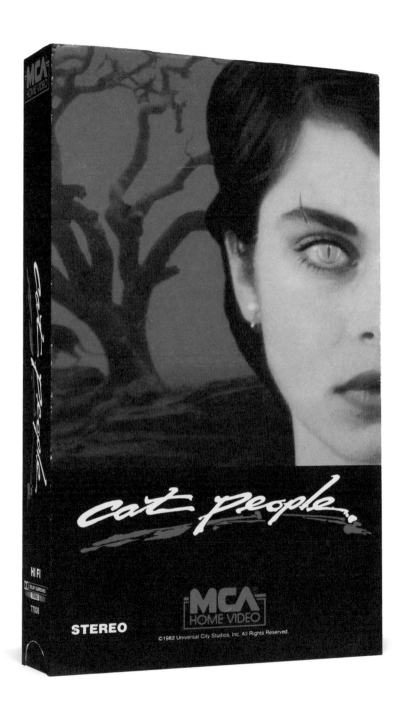

CAPTAIN FUTURE

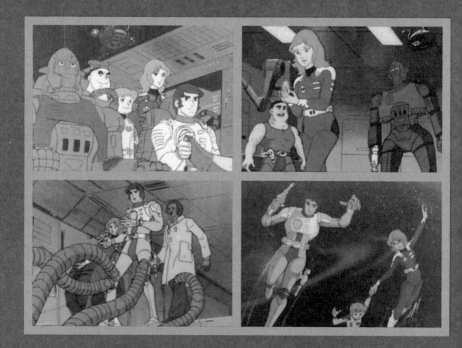

Color/54 Minutes

Captain Future's mission is to make the universe safe for mankind as he fights the evil emperor.

An animated adventure story set in outer-space, documenting the inter-galactic adventure of the legendary hero and his crew aboard the space ship Comet.

LOS ANGELES, CALIF.

MEDIA

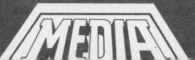

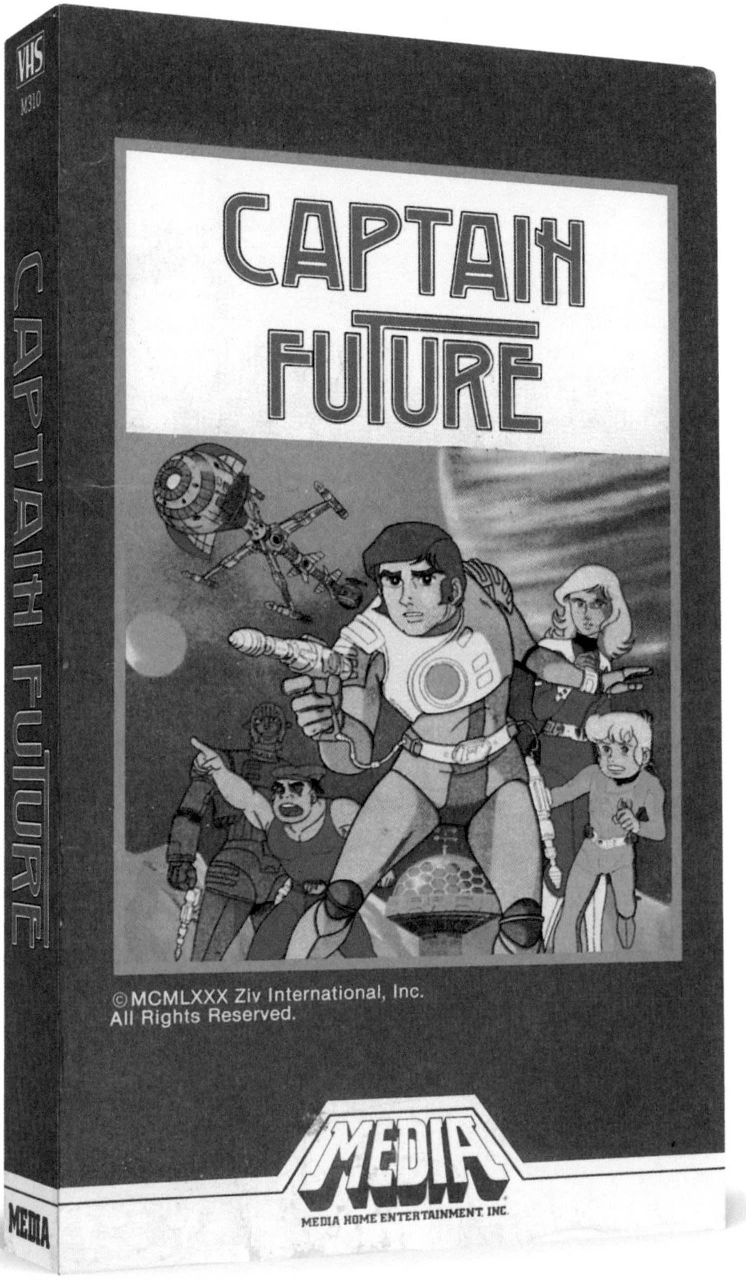

VHS
M310
CAPTAIN FUTURE
CAPTAIN FUTURE
©MCMLXXX Ziv International, Inc.
All Rights Reserved.
MEDIA
MEDIA HOME ENTERTAINMENT INC.
MEDIA

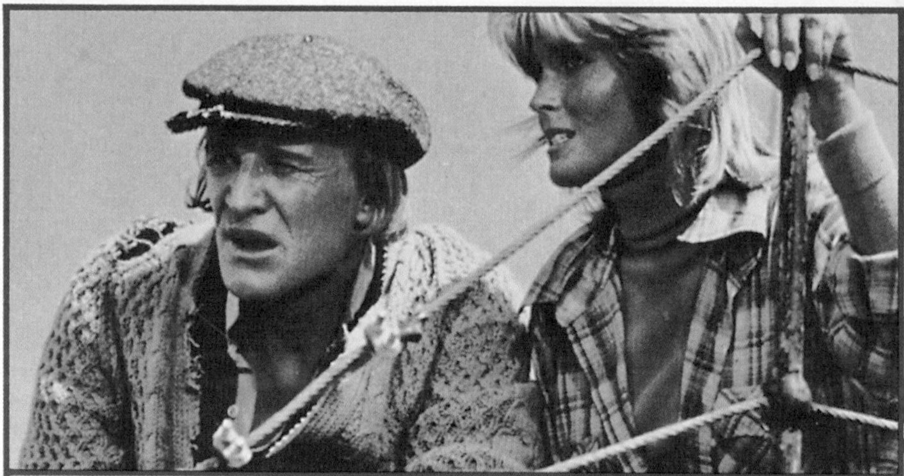

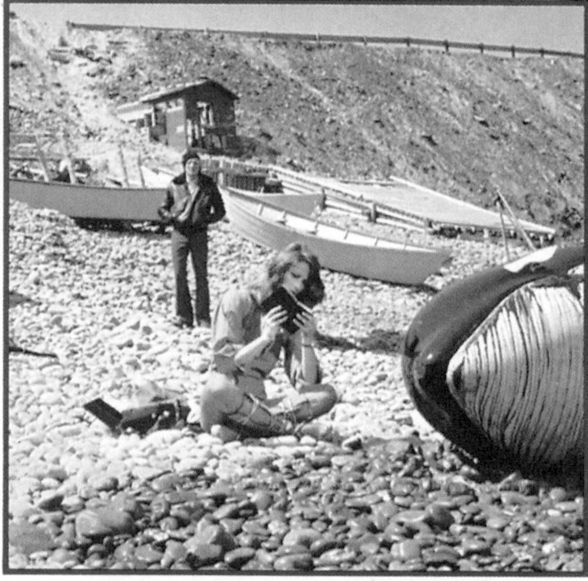

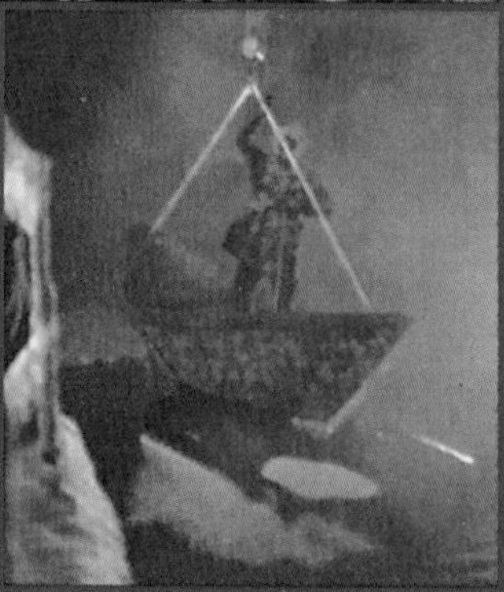

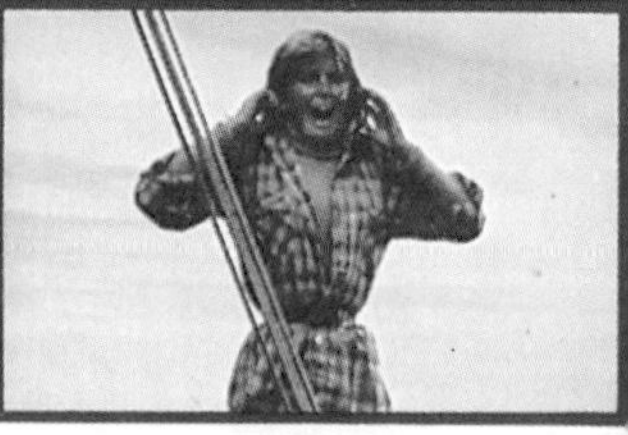

The natural beauty of Bo Derek in her screen debut and the supernatural spectacle of Dino De Laurentiis' *(King Kong)* masterful use of special effects on a gigantic scale highlights this rousing adventure story. It's the epic tale of one powerful being against another; a strong, determined fisherman (Richard Harris) versus an equally determined whale. When the giant whale's pregnant mate is maimed and killed by Harris, in a variation on *Moby Dick*, the whale seeks revenge on the man. Orca smashes boats, collapses buildings, and even manages to cause enormous destruction by fire. A suspenseful action drama.

PG®

VHS Hi-Fi playback requires VHS Hi-Fi VCR.
Beta Hi-Fi playback requires Beta Hi-Fi VCR.
5555 Melrose Ave., Hollywood, CA 90038.
Printed in U.S.A. Licensed for Sale Only in U.S. and Canada.

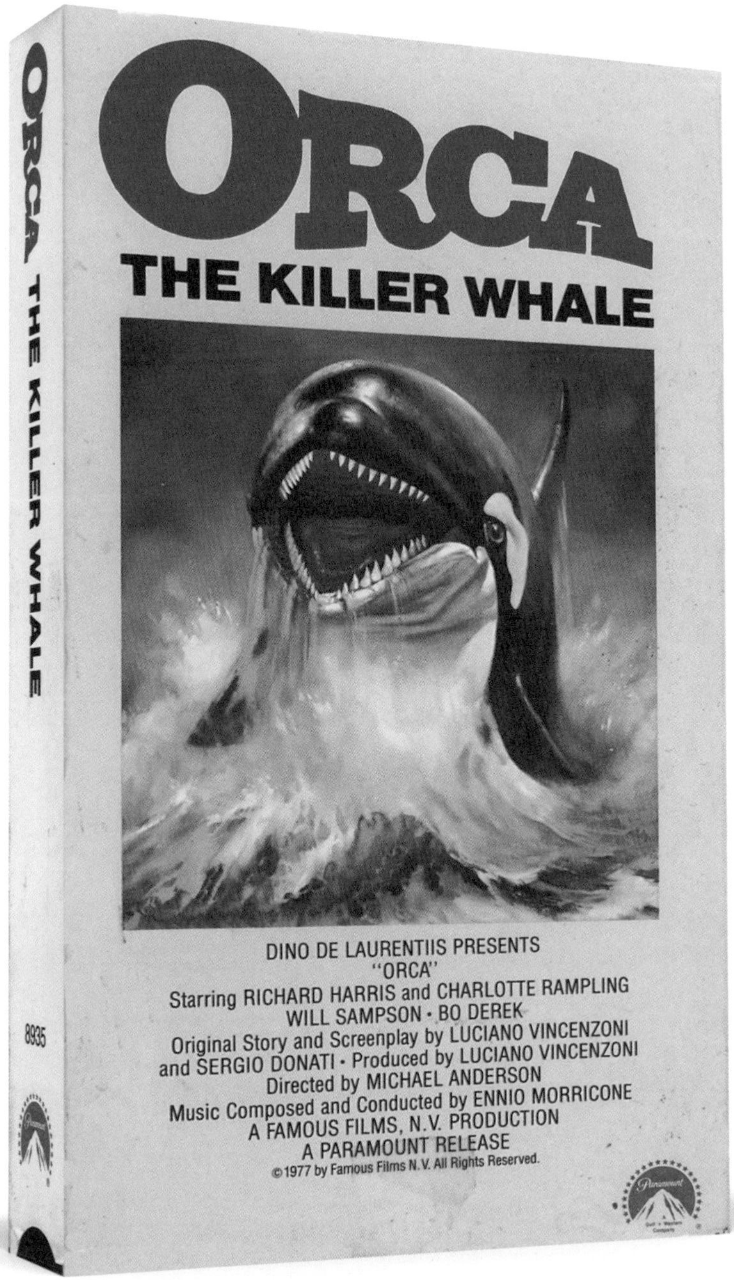

ORCA
THE KILLER WHALE
ORCA
THE KILLER WHALE
DINO DE LAURENTIIS PRESENTS
"ORCA"
Starring RICHARD HARRIS and CHARLOTTE RAMPLING
WILL SAMPSON • BO DEREK
Original Story and Screenplay by LUCIANO VINCENZONI
and SERGIO DONATI • Produced by LUCIANO VINCENZONI
Directed by MICHAEL ANDERSON
Music Composed and Conducted by ENNIO MORRICONE
A FAMOUS FILMS, N.V. PRODUCTION
A PARAMOUNT RELEASE
©1977 by Famous Films N.V. All Rights Reserved.
8935
Paramount

5555 Melrose Avenue, Hollywood, California 90038.
Printed in U.S.A. Licensed for Sale Only in U.S. and Canada.
TM & Copyright © 1990 by Paramount Pictures. All Rights Reserved.

Hi-Fi playback
requires Hi-Fi VCR.

VHS hi-fi

ISBN 0-7921-1028-5

0 9736-08774-3 4

DEATH WISH

An explosive story of revenge and urban violence. Charles Bronson plays Paul Kersey, a bleeding-heart liberal who has a change of opinion after his wife and daughter are violently attacked by a gang of thugs in their apartment. His daughter is raped, his wife raped and murdered. Bronson then turns vigilante as he stalks the mean streets of New York on the prowl for muggers, hoodlums and the like. A violent, controversial film which is frank and original in its treatment of urban crime and the average citizens' helplessness in dealing with it. Herbie Hancock wrote the musical score. And watch for a young Jeff Goldblum in his film debut as one of the thugs.

DINO DE LAURENTIIS PRESENTS CHARLES BRONSON in a MICHAEL WINNER FILM "DEATH WISH"
Co-Starring VINCENT GARDENIA WILLIAM REDFIELD and HOPE LANGE Music by HERBIE HANCOCK
From the Novel "DEATH WISH" by BRIAN GARFIELD Screenplay by WENDELL MAYES
Produced by HAL LANDERS and BOBBY ROBERTS Directed and Co-Produced by MICHAEL WINNER
A PARAMOUNT RELEASE

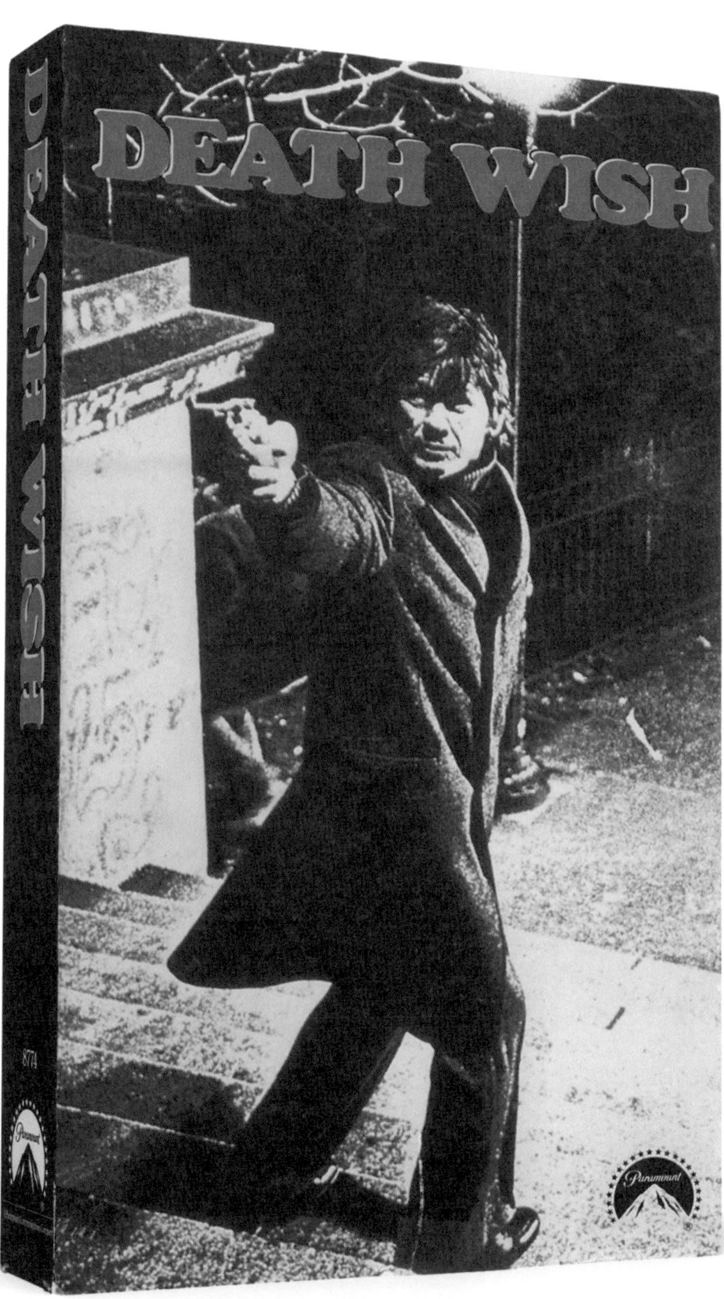
DEATH WISH
DEATH WISH
8774
Paramount
Paramount

NINJA: American Warrior

In his attempt to be the mos
powerful man in the world
Justin Taylor, leader of a sin
ister Ninja army, has becom
the largest narcotics smuggle
in the orient.

The U.S. Drug Enforcemen
Agency and the Hong Kong Polic
have joined forces with the CIA an
a brilliant policewoman, the awesom
Amazonia, to bring down Taylor b
any means, at any cost.

The CIA operative chosen for th
task ultimately realizes that the man h
must kill was his closest friend in the war. Torn betwee
justice and loyalty he's got to make the most crucia
decision of his life.

He has a choice that is no choice at all
—life or death...

90 Min./Color

IMPERIAL ENTERTAINMENT CORP
6430 Sunset Blvd., Suite 1500, Hollywood, CA 90028

0 2238-91201-3 1

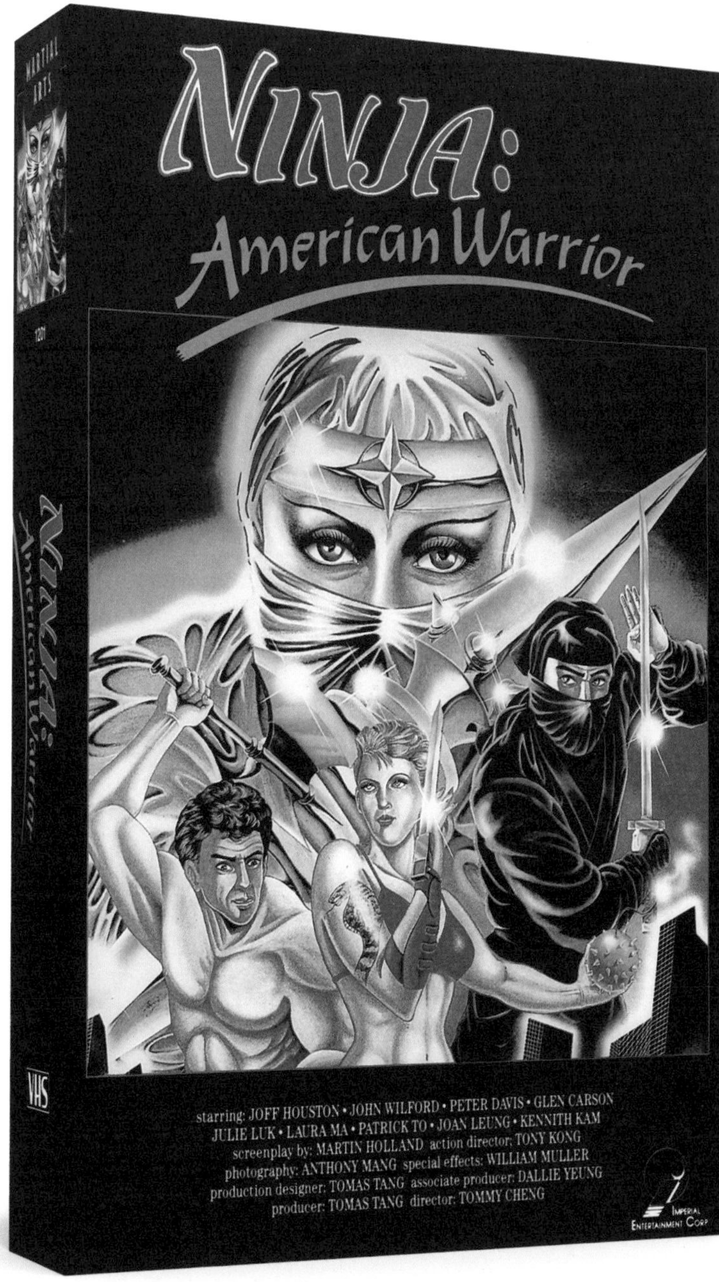
MARTIAL ARTS
1201
NINJA: American Warrior
VHS
NINJA: American Warrior
starring: JOFF HOUSTON • JOHN WILFORD • PETER DAVIS • GLEN CARSON
JULIE LUK • LAURA MA • PATRICK TO • JOAN LEUNG • KENNITH KAM
screenplay by: MARTIN HOLLAND action director: TONY KONG
photography: ANTHONY MANG special effects: WILLIAM MULLER
production designer: TOMAS TANG associate producer: DALLIE YEUNG
producer: TOMAS TANG director: TOMMY CHENG
IMPERIAL ENTERTAINMENT CORP

NINJA
BLACKLIST

Starring SHAN QUE, JUDI HI, CHAN WAI MAN
Produced By LI CHEN TSING   Directed By LO CHAUN

...g city crimelord spreads death and destruction. He mu...
...ped! His gang of thugs meet their match when they cross...
...two Ninja-trained comrades. Ninja blacklist features dy...
...ial art action in the first modern style action film from th...
...e rising sun.

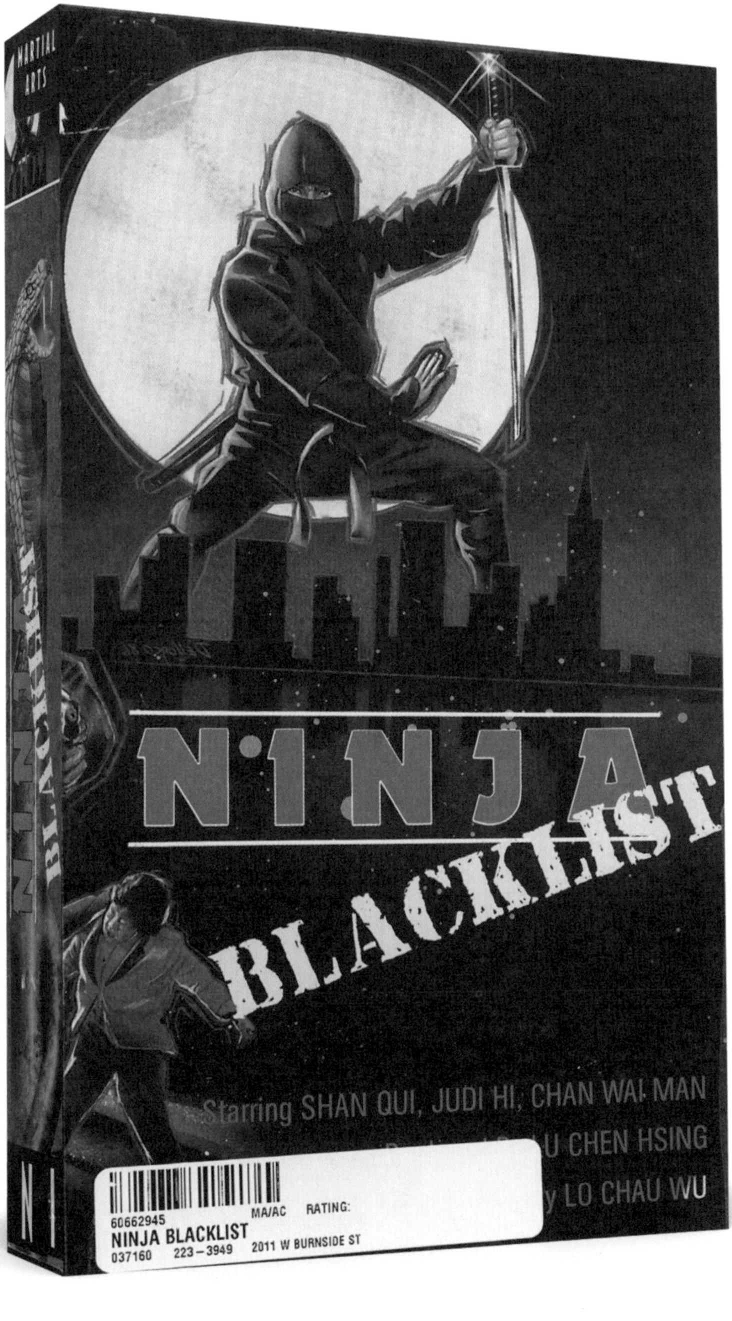
MARTIAL ARTS
NINJA
BLACKLIST
Starring SHAN QUI, JUDI HI, CHAN WAI MAN
U CHEN HSING
y LO CHAU WU
60662945 MA/AC RATING:
NINJA BLACKLIST
037160 223-3949 2011 W BURNSIDE ST

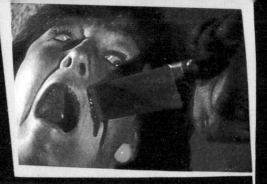

night-stalking killer
ose! The victims:
nsuspecting high
The method:
cally precise
ruesome, blood-
spree has the police
public terrified!
carved-up bodies
he mystery of the
identity—and
It's a gore-splattered
t will keep you
veting, nerve-

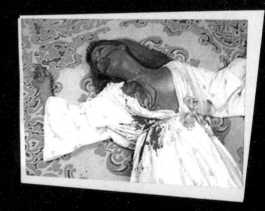

esent this exclusive WORLD PREMIERE RELEASE of NIGHT RIPPER—
luction, previously unseen anywhere.

RUNNING TIME 88 MINUTES—COLOR

VIDEO FEATURES PRESENTS
A JEFF HATHCOCK PRODUCTION

STARRING:
JAMES HANSEN, APRIL ANNE, LARRY THOMAS,
DANIELLE LOUIS, SIMON DE SOTO

PHOTOGRAPHED BY JOE DINH
MUSIC BY BILL PARSELY
PRODUCED BY JOHN TOMLINSON, JEFF HATHCOCK

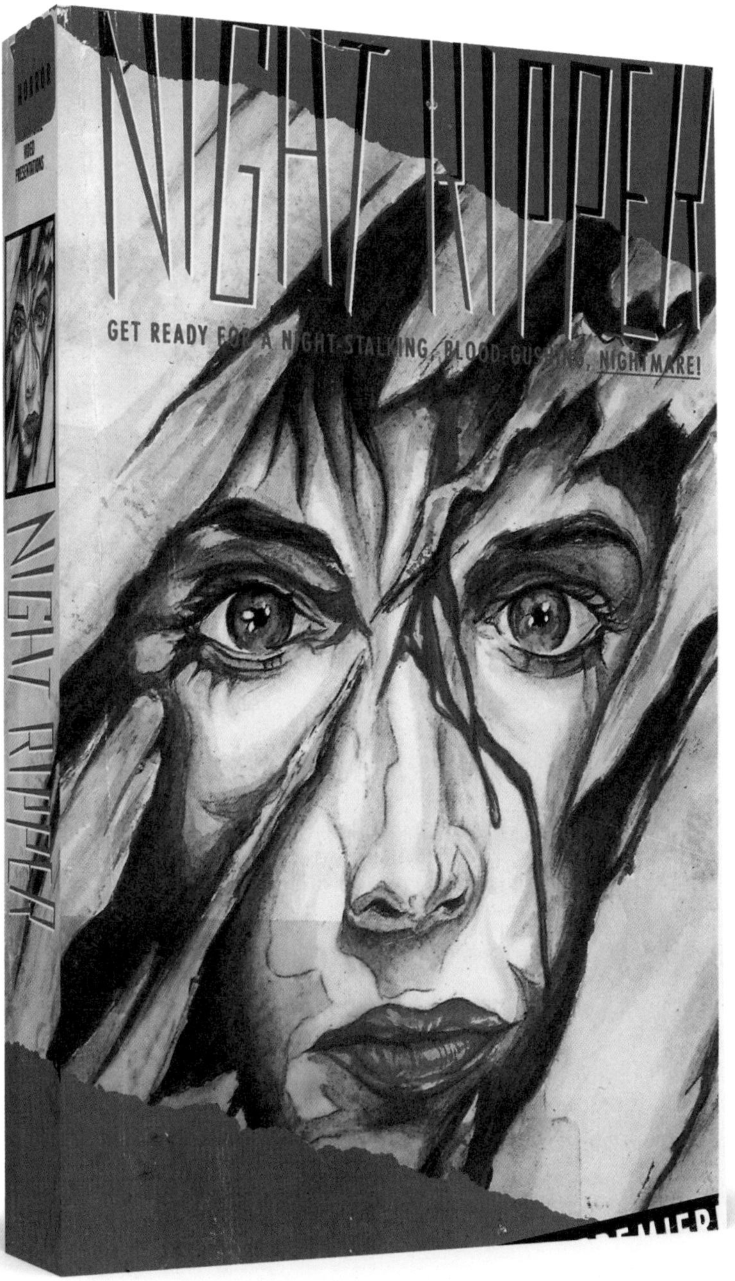
NIGHT RIPPER
GET READY FOR A NIGHT-STALKING, BLOOD-GUSHING, NIGHTMARE!
NIGHT RIPPER

COLOR ME BLOOD RED

Herschell Gordon Lewis continues his outrageous horror with "COLOR ME BLOOD RED," the final chapter in his classic trilogy of "gore" films.

A struggling artist, Adam Sorg, finds himself unable to sell any paintings until he accidentally discovers a shade of red…*blood red* … from his finger.

He murders one of his models and applies her bloodied face to his canvas. This painting technique gives him a "head-up" on other artists, and his newest creation becomes a big hit with the critics.

His first model begins to run dry, so he kills a couple of swimmers. He spears the man, and runs them both over with a boat. The fanatic artist then hangs the woman's body in the storeroom, to tap her vitals whenever the need for more blood occurs. With a fresh supply of blood hanging around, he buries the drained body of his first victim on the beach…which is discovered later in an advanced state of decomposition, depicted in full gory detail.

Horror fans will love the satiric approach H. G. Lewis takes with "COLOR ME BLOOD RED." The acts of violence, although graphic and shocking in nature, are treated so lightly by the artist, that the entire film takes on a slight feeling of comedy.

Running Time: 70 Minutes.
Not Rated. Directed by Herschell Gordon Lewis.

NEW STAR
VIDEO

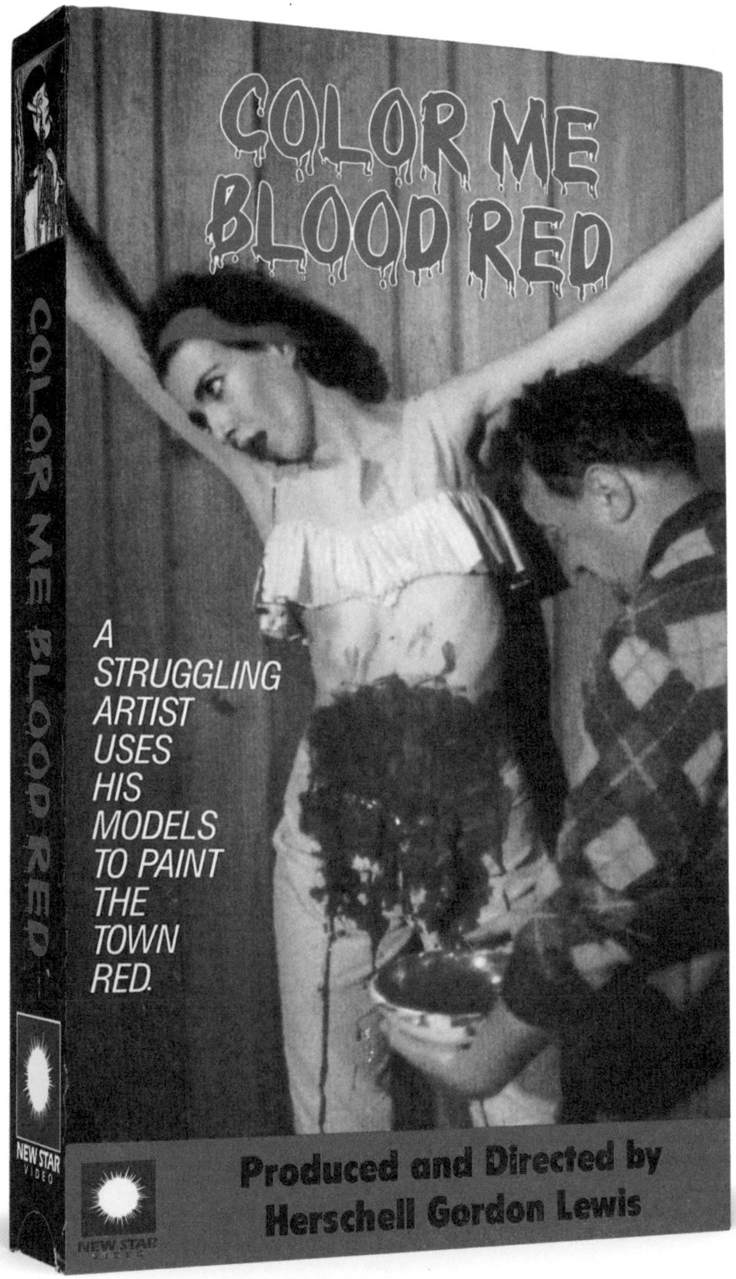
COLOR ME BLOOD RED
A STRUGGLING ARTIST USES HIS MODELS TO PAINT THE TOWN RED.
Produced and Directed by
Herschell Gordon Lewis
NEW STAR VIDEO
COLOR ME BLOOD RED
NEW STAR VIDEO

DON'T GO IN THE HOUSE

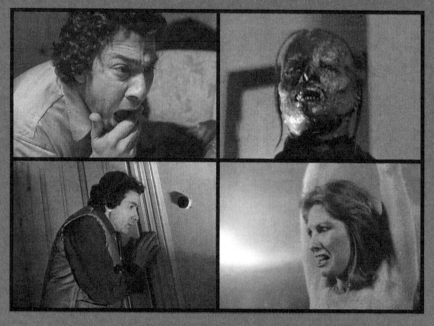

Color/90 Minutes

Tormented as a child, he takes vengeance....

A long, dormant psychosis is brought to life by the death of a young man's mother. He prepares his revenge by luring beautiful women, until the final act of vengeance comes from his victims!

LOS ANGELES, CALIF.

MEDIA

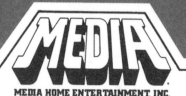

MEDIA HOME ENTERTAINMENT, INC.

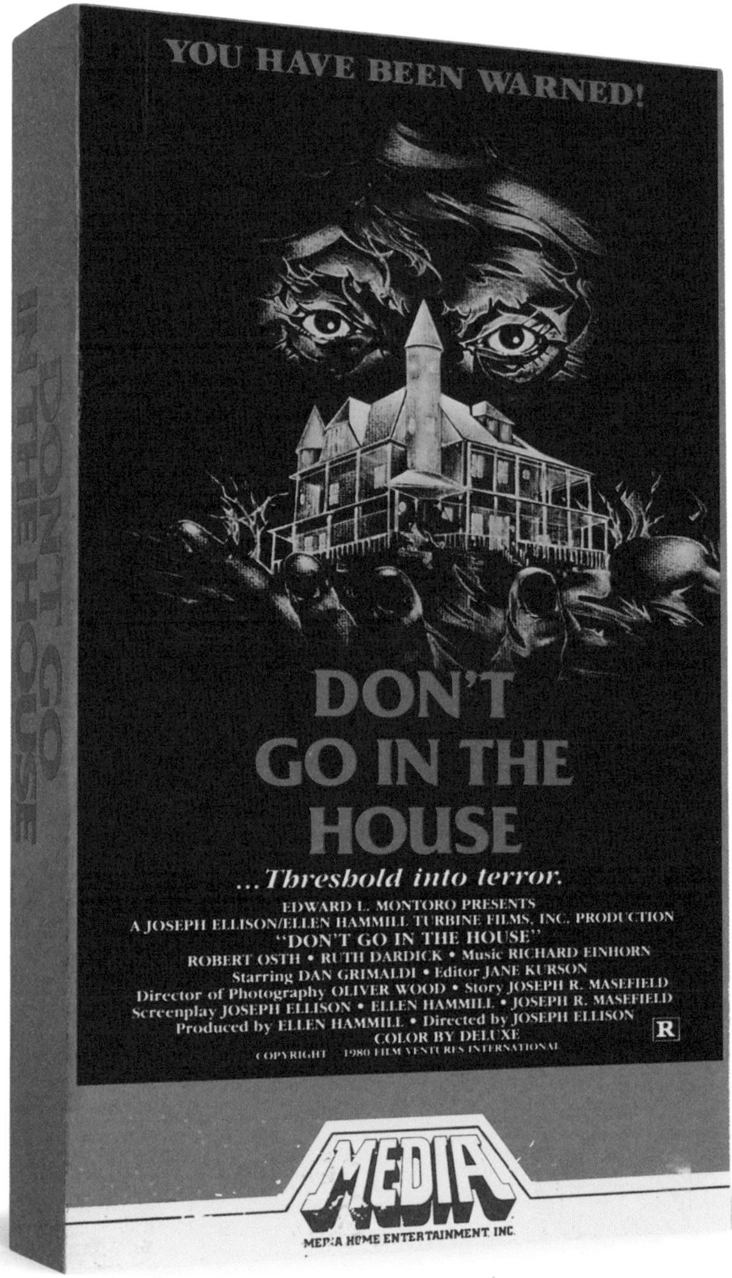
YOU HAVE BEEN WARNED!
DON'T GO IN THE HOUSE
...Threshold into terror.
EDWARD L. MONTORO PRESENTS
A JOSEPH ELLISON/ELLEN HAMMILL TURBINE FILMS, INC. PRODUCTION
"DON'T GO IN THE HOUSE"
ROBERT OSTH • RUTH DARDICK • Music RICHARD EINHORN
Starring DAN GRIMALDI • Editor JANE KURSON
Director of Photography OLIVER WOOD • Story JOSEPH R. MASEFIELD
Screenplay JOSEPH ELLISON • ELLEN HAMMILL • JOSEPH R. MASEFIELD
Produced by ELLEN HAMMILL • Directed by JOSEPH ELLISON
COLOR BY DELUXE
R
COPYRIGHT 1980 FILM VENTURES INTERNATIONAL
MEDIA
MEDIA HOME ENTERTAINMENT INC.
DON'T GO IN THE HOUSE

DELIRIUM

THEY SHALL HAVE MURDER
WHEREVER THEY GO...

Charlie kills women indiscriminately and grotesquely. And Charlie is going to go on killing! The police have no real clue to his identity, but the behaviour of one contact leads them to widen their investigations. The law closes in and violence explodes in a terrifying twist of stunning fury and suspense.

RUNNING TIME: Approx. 89 Min.

R	RESTRICTED ⬤
	UNDER 17 REQUIRES ACCOMPANYING PARENT OR ADULT GUARDIAN

©1982 PARAGON • LAS VEGAS, NEVADA

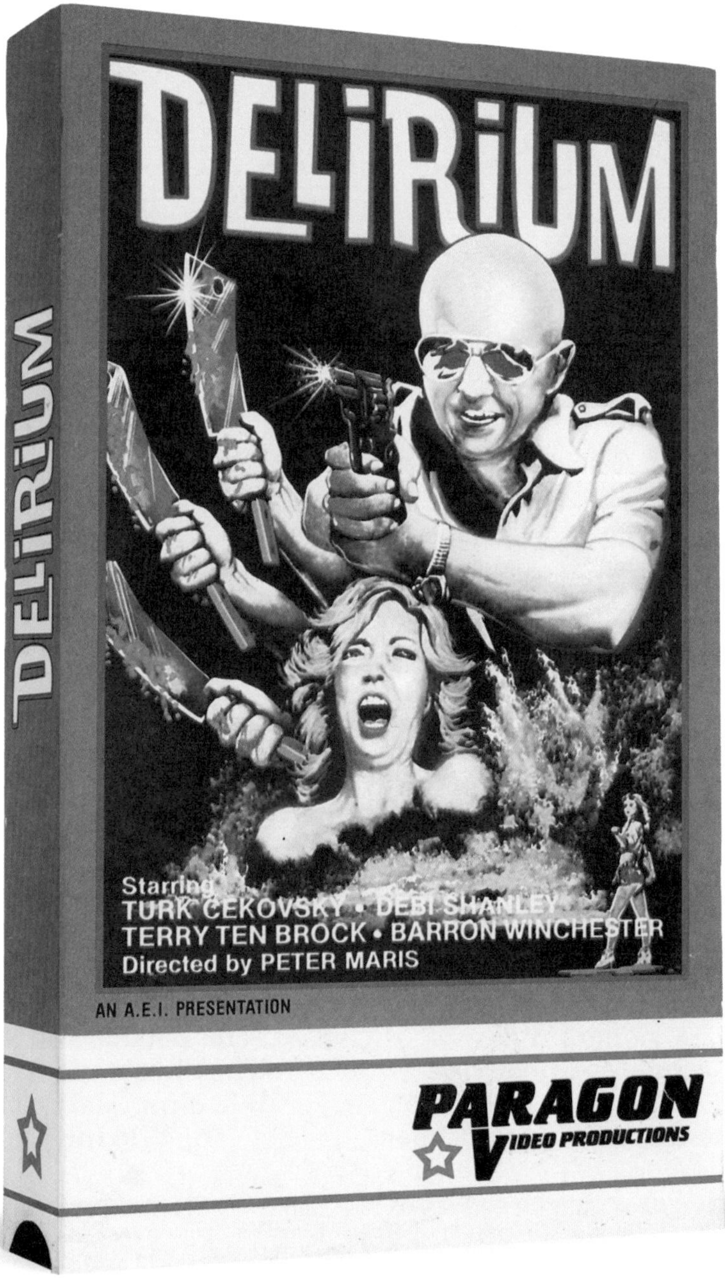
DELIRIUM
Starring
TURK CEKOVSKY • DEBI SHANLEY
TERRY TEN BROCK • BARRON WINCHESTER
Directed by PETER MARIS
AN A.E.I. PRESENTATION
PARAGON
VIDEO PRODUCTIONS
DELIRIUM

Hi-Fi playback requires Hi-Fi VCR.

VHS hi-fi

DOLBY B NR
ON LINEAR TRACKS

Dolby and the DD are trademarks of Dolby Laboratories Licensing Corporation.

ISBN 0-7921-1664-X

0 9736-12822-3 7

THE ANIMATED ADVENTURES OF

DICK TRACY

"Calling all Crimestoppers! This is Dick Tracy, inviting you to join me and my crime-busting pals, Joe Jitsu, GoGo Gomez, Hemlock Holmes and The Retouchables, and Heap O'Callory in our animated TV series based on the comic strip created by Chester Gould. Watch us battle notorious villains like Pruneface, BB Eyes, Flattop, The Mole, The Brow, Mumbles and more. And don't miss my very own Crimestopper Tips. They're the best things since the two-way wrist radio!"

Dick Tracy's adventures on this volume include:

Hot On The Trail	The Catnap Caper
Bomb's Away	The Boomerang Ring
Cheater Gunsmoke	The Skyscraper Caper
Grandma Jitsu	Wheeling And Stealing
The Copped Copper Caper	The Vile Inn Case

DICK TRACY A UPA/HENRY G. SAPERSTEIN PRESENTATION FROM UPA PRODUCTIONS OF AMERICA
Based on the comic strip created by CHESTER GOULD DICK TRACY'S voice by EVERETT SLOANE
other voices by MEL BLANC JUNE FORAY PAUL FREES JOAN GARDNER
Executive Producer HENRY G. SAPERSTEIN Directed by ABE LEVITOW
Copyright © 1989 UPA Productions of America
All Rights Reserved.

Paramount

Artwork on this box based upon "The Animated Adventures Of Dick Tracy."

5555 Melrose Avenue, Hollywood, California 90038.
Printed in U.S.A. Licensed for Sale Only in U.S. and Canada.
TM & Copyright © 1990 by Paramount Pictures. All Rights Reserv

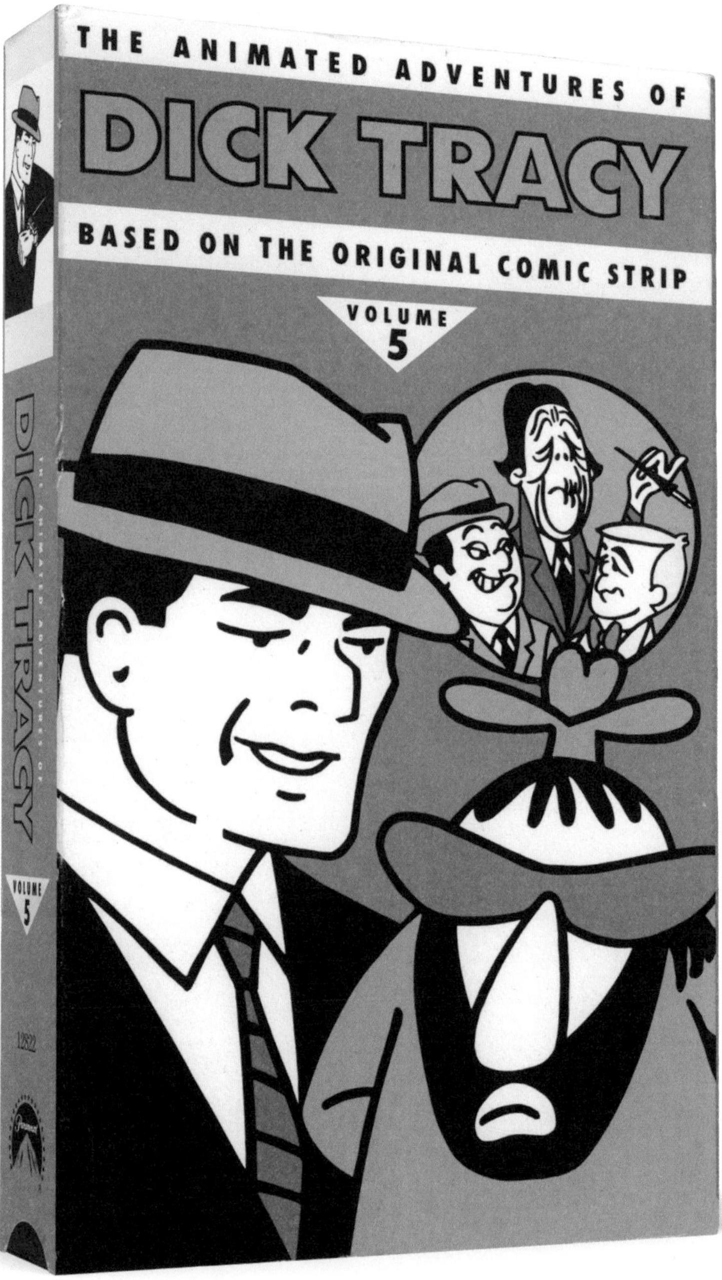
THE ANIMATED ADVENTURES OF
DICK TRACY
BASED ON THE ORIGINAL COMIC STRIP
VOLUME
5
DICK TRACY
VOLUME
5

NIGHT OF THE STRANGLER

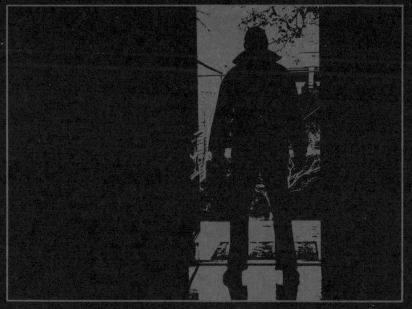

THE TIME: NOW - THE PLACE: NEW ORLEANS

A young, beautiful Southern society white girl falls in love with a young handsome black man...a tragic love affair that leads to seven brutal, bizarre murders.

RUNNING TIME: Approx. 88 Min.

R — RESTRICTED — UNDER 17 REQUIRES ACCOMPANYING PARENT OR ADULT GUARDIAN

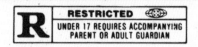

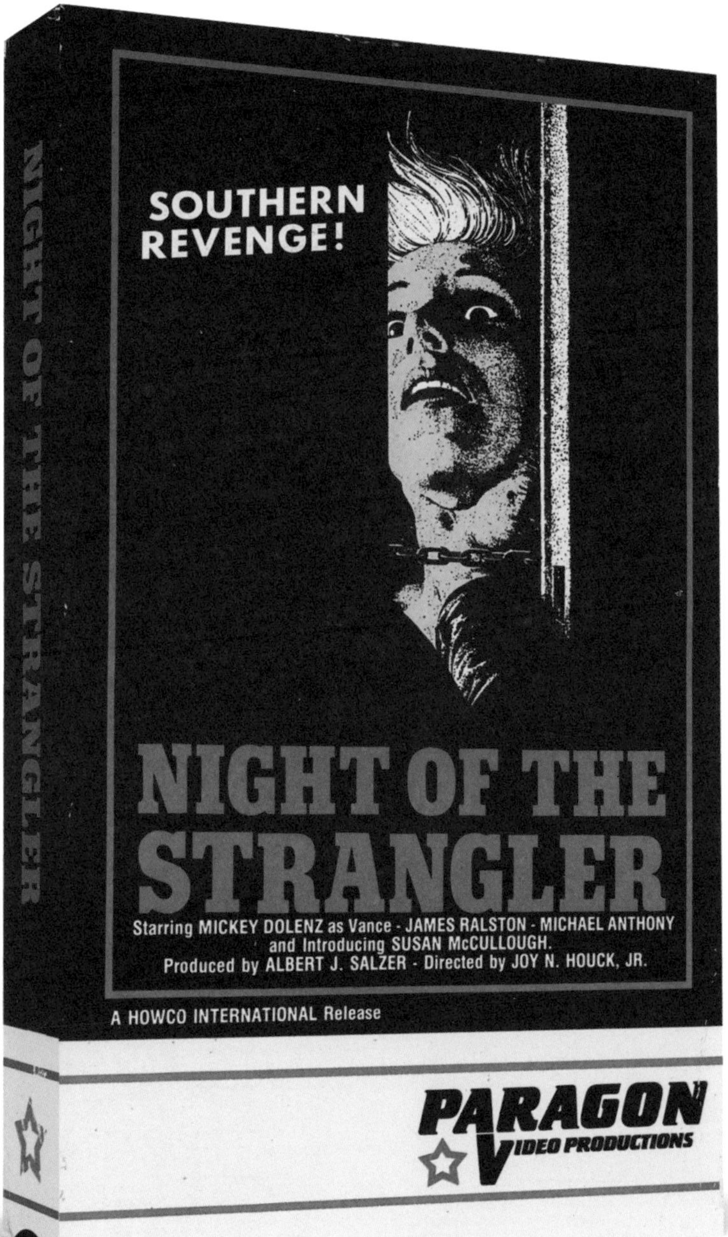
NIGHT OF THE STRANGLER
SOUTHERN REVENGE!
NIGHT OF THE STRANGLER
Starring MICKEY DOLENZ as Vance - JAMES RALSTON - MICHAEL ANTHONY
and Introducing SUSAN McCULLOUGH.
Produced by ALBERT J. SALZER - Directed by JOY N. HOUCK, JR.
A HOWCO INTERNATIONAL Release
PARAGON
VIDEO PRODUCTIONS

NIGHT OF BLOODY HORROR

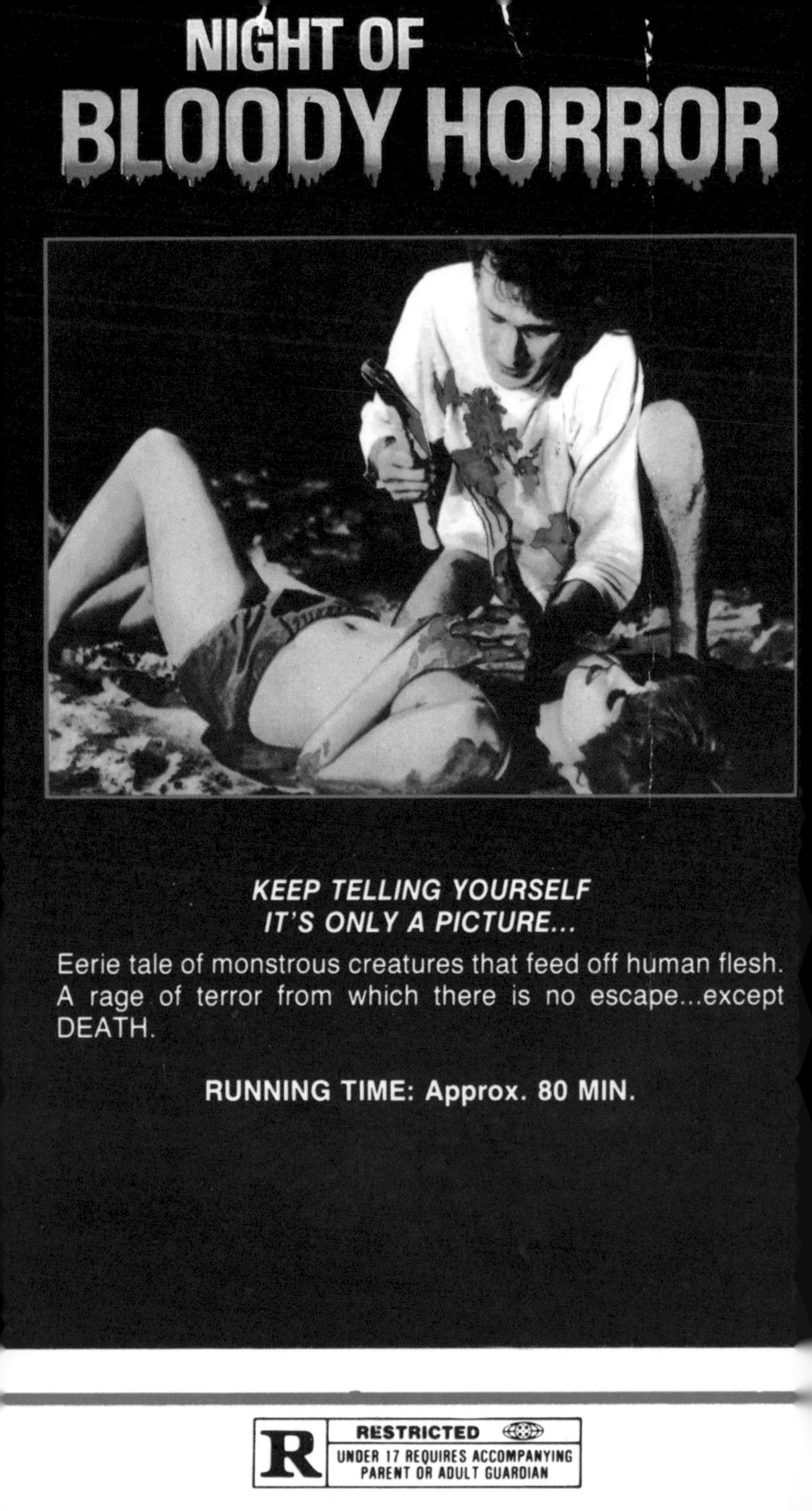

KEEP TELLING YOURSELF
IT'S ONLY A PICTURE...

Eerie tale of monstrous creatures that feed off human flesh. A rage of terror from which there is no escape...except DEATH.

RUNNING TIME: Approx. 80 MIN.

R RESTRICTED
UNDER 17 REQUIRES ACCOMPANYING PARENT OR ADULT GUARDIAN

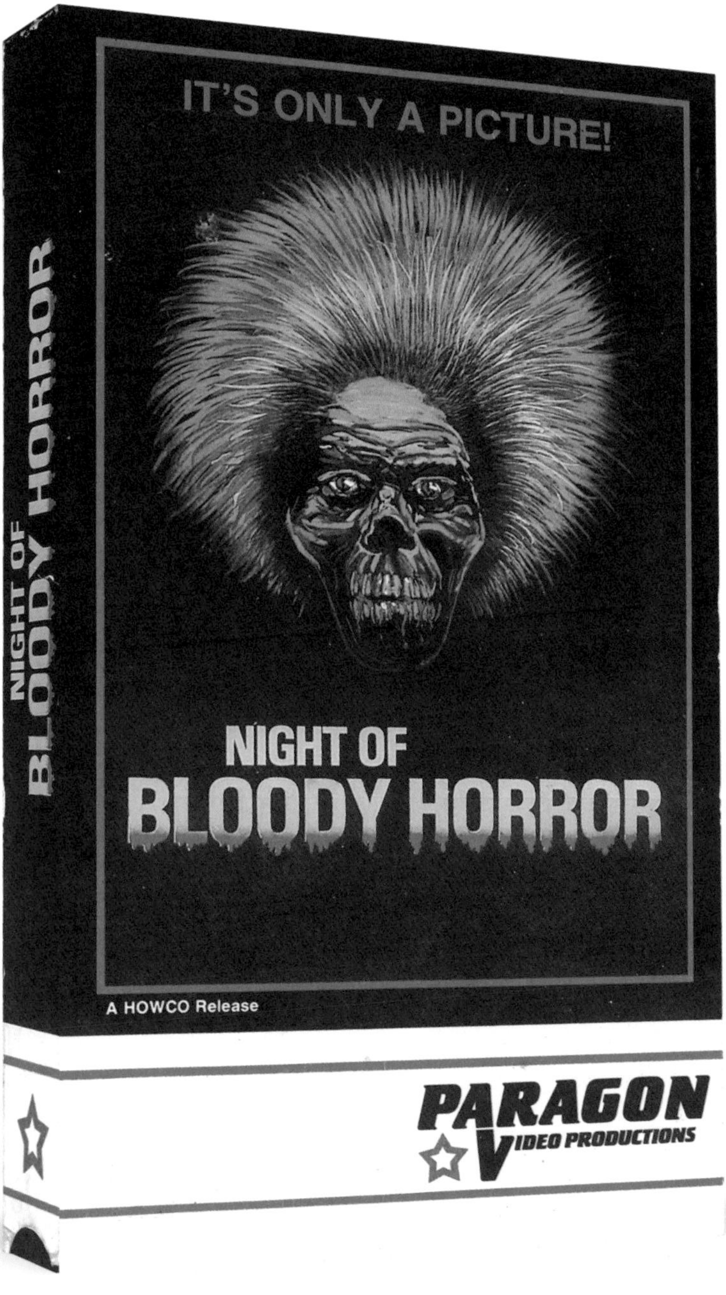
IT'S ONLY A PICTURE!
NIGHT OF
BLOODY HORROR
A HOWCO Release
PARAGON
VIDEO PRODUCTIONS
NIGHT OF
BLOODY HORROR

“‘Network’ is ou
brilliantly, savag

—Vi

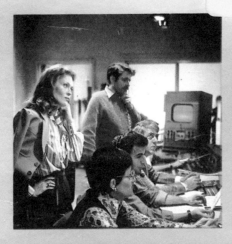

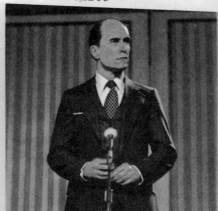

It’s a behind-the-screen look at the tyrants of television and what they’ve done to us—writer Paddy Chayefsky’s savage satire, Network.

Peter Finch gives an unforgettable, Oscar-winning performance as Howard Beale, the man who goes from dispassionate newscaster to national folk hero with his famous battle cry, “I’m mad as hell, and I’m not going to take it anymore!”

Network is also the story of the fierce fights for power among the network officials.

Finch plays a top TV anchorman who announces one day that he’ll blow his brains out in prime time, for the sake of the ratings…

Faye Dunaway as the vicious Vice President of Programming, William Holden as the News Division President and Robert Duvall as the cold hatchet man for the corporation all participate in glorifying its star—and in his ultimate destruction.

In addition to the Oscars for Best Actor and Screenplay, Network has achieved top honors for Faye Dunaway as Best Actress and Beatrice Straight as Best Supporting Actress.

R RESTRICTED
UNDER 17 REQUIRES ACCOMPANYING PARENT OR ADULT GUARDIAN

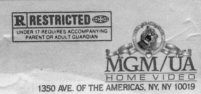

MGM/UA
HOME VIDEO
1350 AVE. OF THE AMERICAS, NY, NY 10019

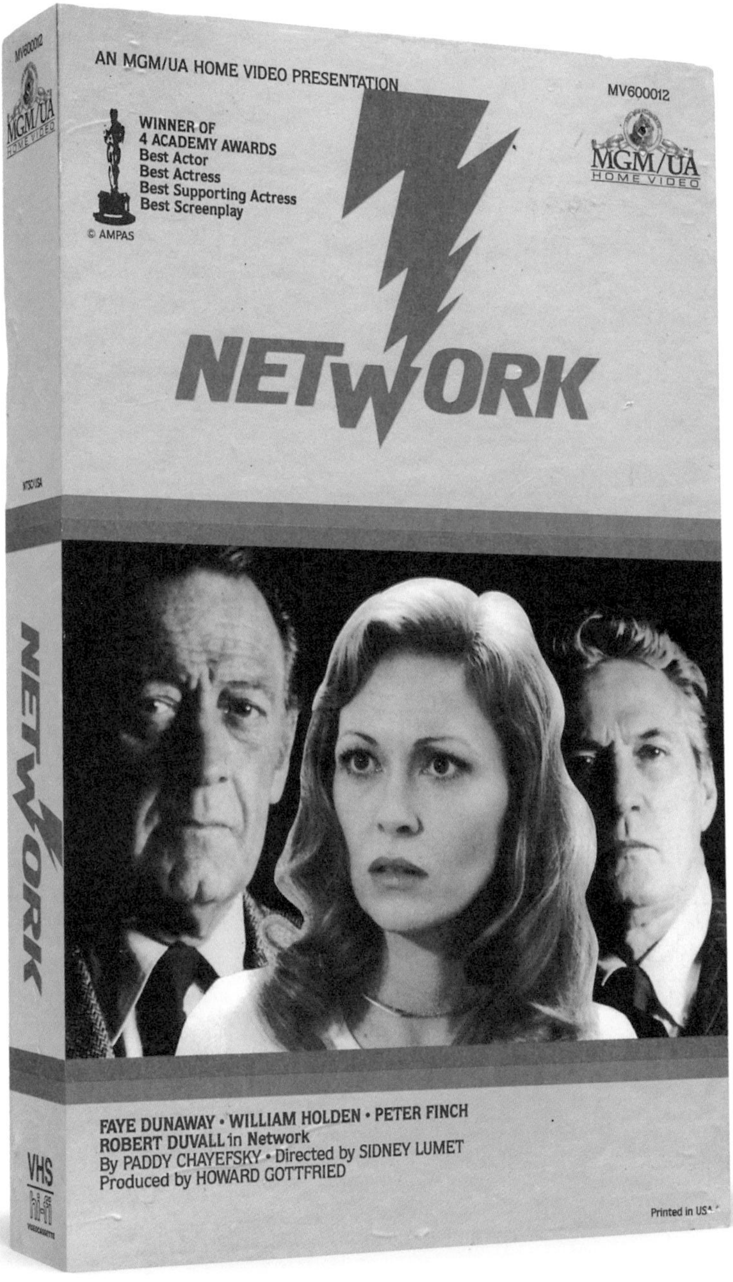
AN MGM/UA HOME VIDEO PRESENTATION
MV600012
MGM/UA
HOME VIDEO
WINNER OF
4 ACADEMY AWARDS
Best Actor
Best Actress
Best Supporting Actress
Best Screenplay
© AMPAS
NETWORK
FAYE DUNAWAY • WILLIAM HOLDEN • PETER FINCH
ROBERT DUVALL in Network
By PADDY CHAYEFSKY • Directed by SIDNEY LUMET
Produced by HOWARD GOTTFRIED
VHS
NETWORK

A Tale of Blinding Horror

A blood curdling film starring *JOHN RICHARDSON, MARTINE BROCHARD, IVES PELLIGRINI, GEORGE RIGAUD* and *SILVA SOLAR.*

A group of tourists from New York board a sightseeing bus. Their trip is a pleasant one until a bizarre crime sets the passengers on edge and threatens them all.

As the tension mounts, a murder is committed. One of the group is stabbed to death and hideously mutilated—the left eye is cut completely out of the corpse.

Suddenly the murders become epidemic and the butchering killer, clad in a blood-stained slicker and gloves, strikes again and again. Beautiful young women are stabbed and one by one their eyes are plucked out.

At last a young model tracks the killer to a remote museum and is forced to witness the last victim's death throes and disfigurement. In a bloody finale, the secret of the eyeball-killer is revealed.

ILLUSTRATION BY DICK BOUCHARD

© 84 D. BOUCHARD

A JOSEPH BRENNER ASSOCIATES, INC. RELEASE

PRINTED IN U.S.A. 1977 RELEASE NTSC

Prism Entertainment, 1875 Century Park East, Suite 1010, L.A., CA 90067

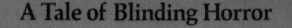

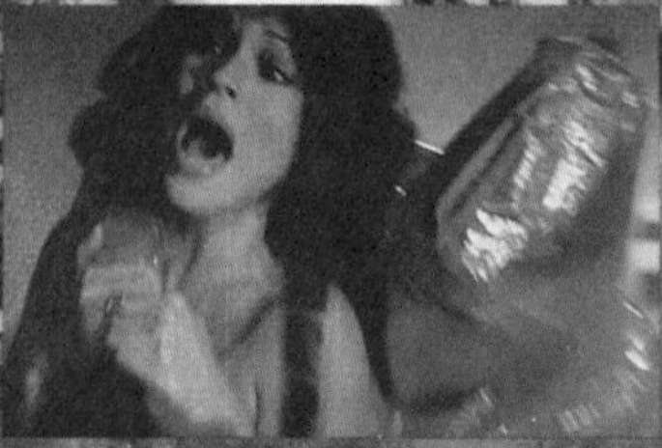

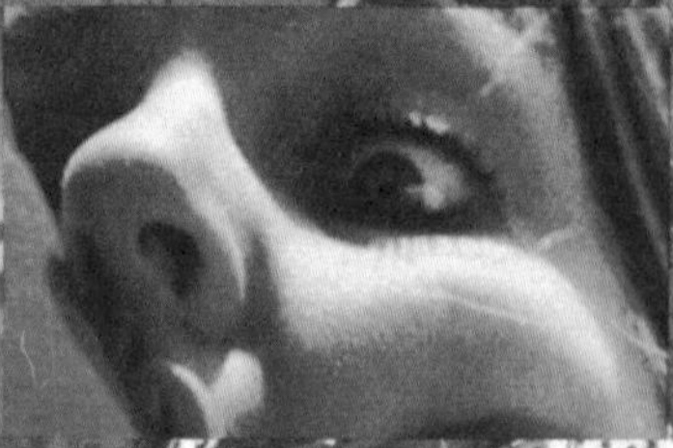

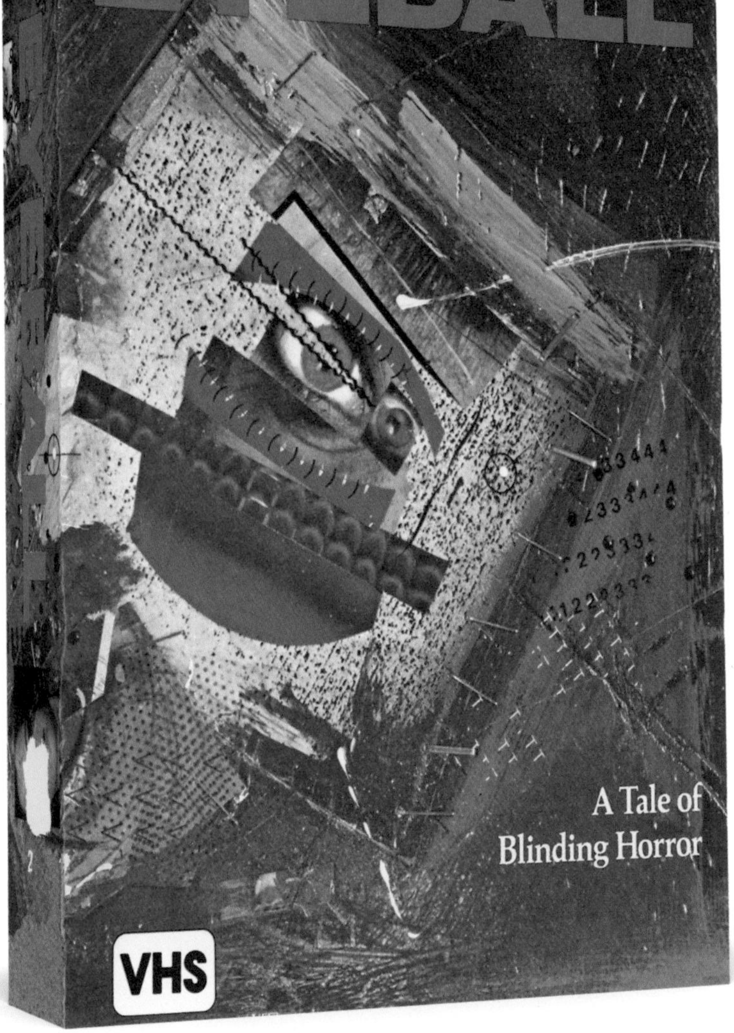
PRISM
ENTERTAINMENT
EYEBALL
A Tale of
Blinding Horror
VHS

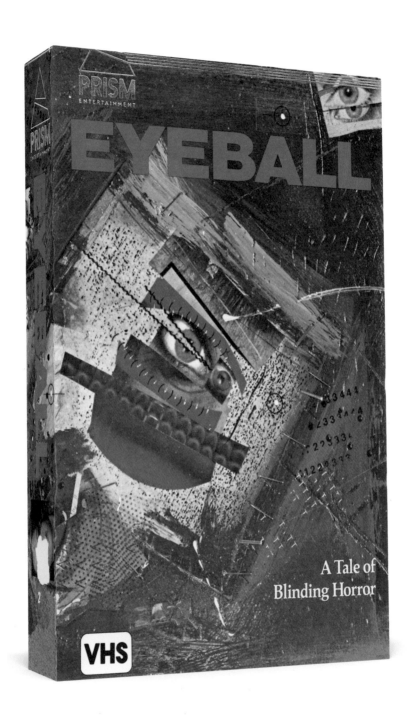

5555 Melrose Avenue, Hollywood, California 90038.
Printed in U.S.A. Licensed for Sale Only in U.S. and Canada.
™ & Copyright © 1990 by Paramount Pictures. All Rights Reserved.

Hi-Fi playback
requires Hi-Fi VCR.

VHS hi-fi

ISBN 0-7921-1774-1

0 9736-06525-3

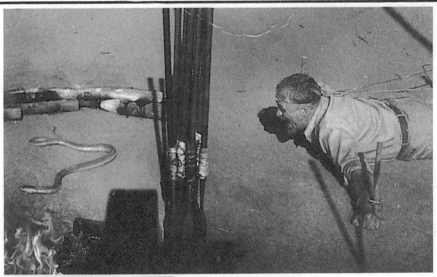

Locations in Maputi, Botswana and Zimbabwe provide magnificent backdrops for this dramatic action-adventure. Cornel Wilde is Man, the great white hunter whose safari is wiped out by angry tribesmen. Impressed with his bravery, they give him a "lion's chance" to save his life. He is stripped of clothes, weapons and given a head start. Then for four days and nights he struggles to survive with the village's best lion killers in close pursuit. But can he keep a few seconds distance between himself and pursuers' spears?

PARAMOUNT PICTURES PRESENTS A THEODORA PRODUCTION, INC.
CORNEL WILDE as Man in "THE NAKED PREY"
Co-starring KEN GAMPU • Written by CLINT JOHNSTON and DON PETERS
Produced and Directed by CORNEL WILDE

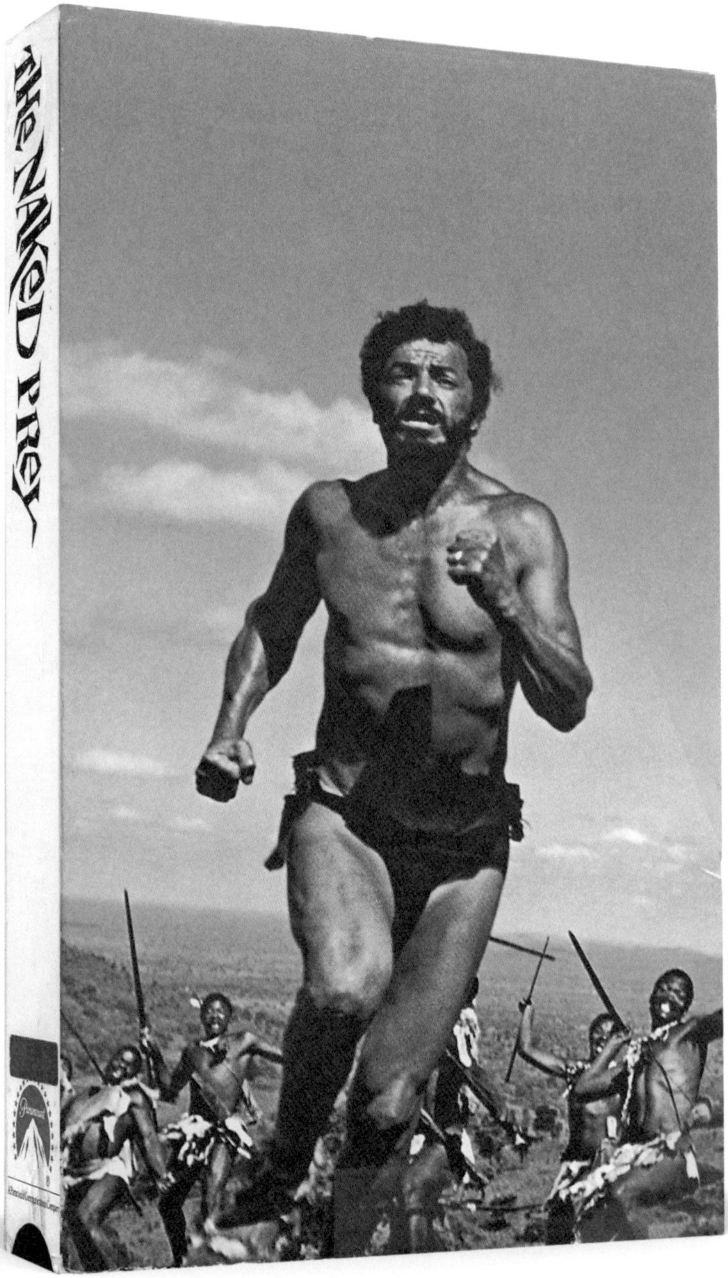
The NAKED PREY

MONGREL

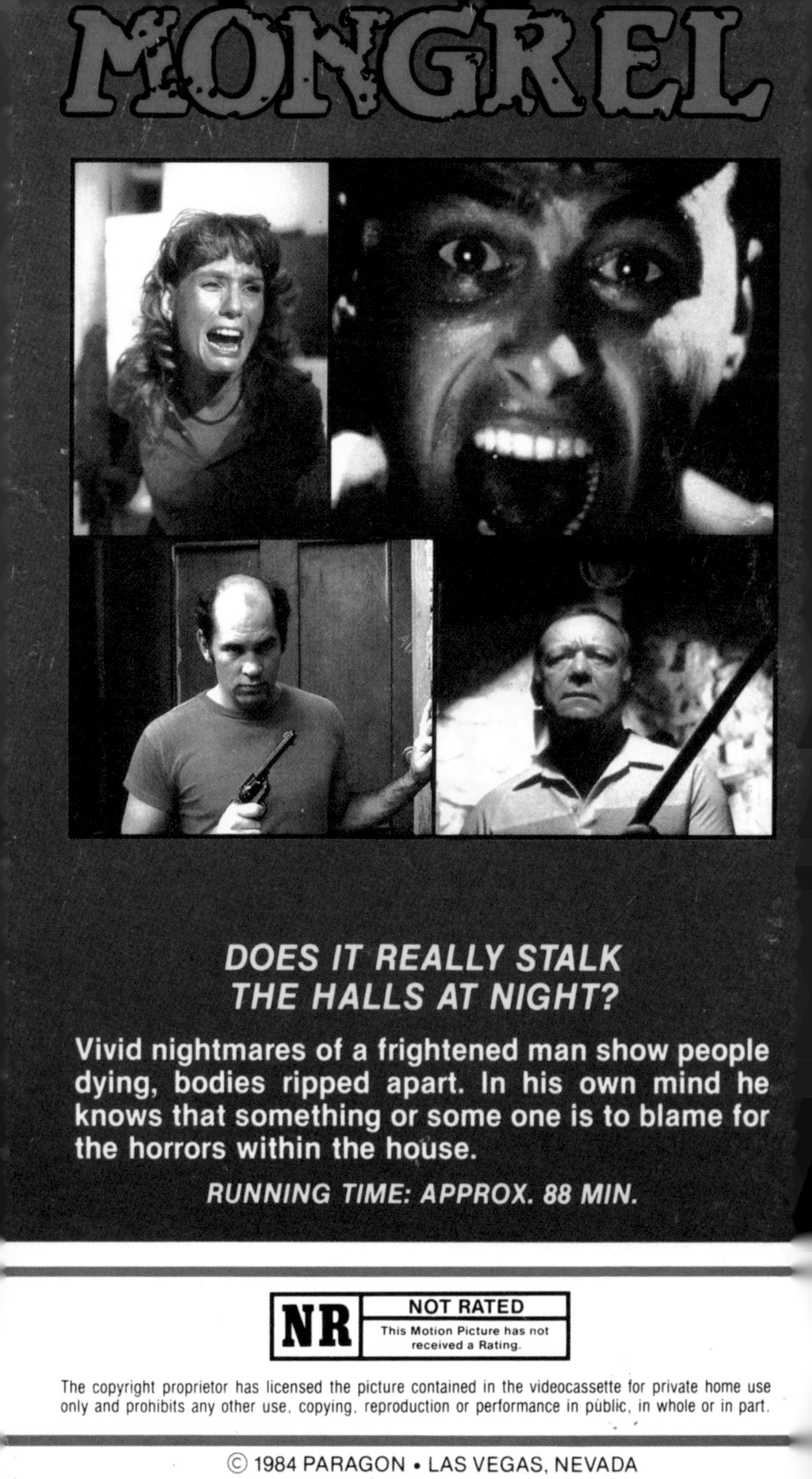

DOES IT REALLY STALK THE HALLS AT NIGHT?

Vivid nightmares of a frightened man show people dying, bodies ripped apart. In his own mind he knows that something or some one is to blame for the horrors within the house.

RUNNING TIME: APPROX. 88 MIN.

NR NOT RATED
This Motion Picture has not received a Rating.

MONGREL

Tormented visions
of a beast...

Starring ALDO RAY TERRY EVANS written & directed by Robert A. Burns produced by John Jenkins Sutherland

A JENKINS, RONDO, SUTHERLAND RELEASE

PARAGON
VIDEO PRODUCTIONS

ONE ARMED
EXECUTIONER

REVENGE IS SWEET...

His wife brutally murdered before his eyes - His arm
chopped off as a warning - His job, his pride, his con-
fidence gone...a young Interpol agent's rage for life
has but one meaning: REVENGE, REVENGE AND
REVENGE.

RUNNING TIME: Approx. 90 Min.

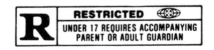

R | **RESTRICTED**
UNDER 17 REQUIRES ACCOMPANYING
PARENT OR ADULT GUARDIAN

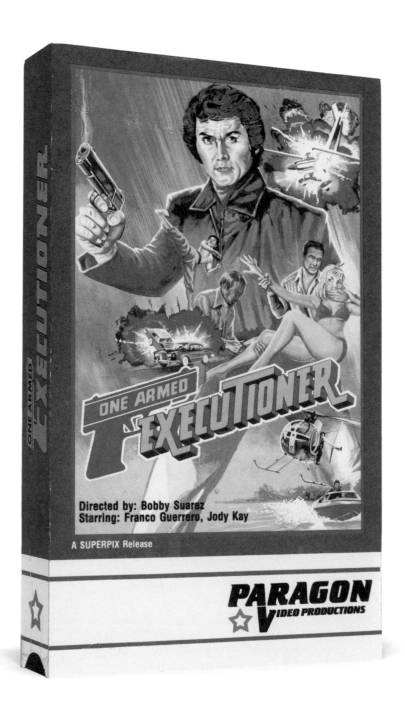

ONE ARMED EXECUTIONER

ONE ARMED
EXECUTIONER

Directed by: Bobby Suarez
Starring: Franco Guerrero, Jody Kay

A SUPERPIX Release

PARAGON
VIDEO PRODUCTIONS

DRIVE-IN MASSACRE

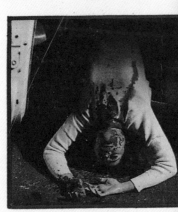

film you will love,

if it doesn't kill you!!

...ve-In Massacre is the story of a psychopathic killer who lurk... ...shadows to brutally murder unsuspecting patrons of the driv...

The police are totally baffled by this wanton mayhem, ...lthough the suspects are many: The arrogant theater manag... ...who hates the owner; The milk-toastish handyman who is ...rboring a burning hatred; The theater owner himself, who ... ...penchant for collecting exotic knives. Or perhaps the killer ...omeone even more dangerous — someone who kills for th... pure, sick pleasure of it.

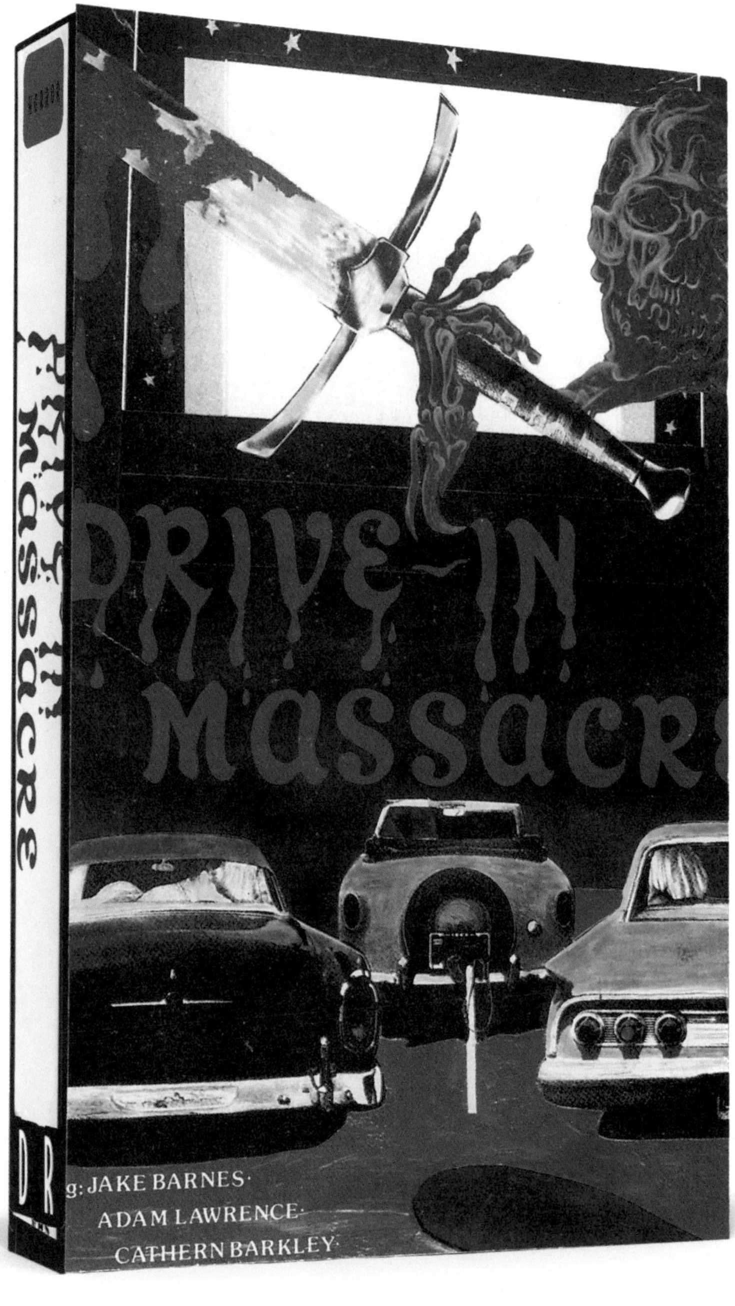
DRIVE-IN
MASSACRE
g: JAKE BARNES·
ADAM LAWRENCE·
CATHERN BARKLEY·
DRIVE-IN MASSACRE

EVEN STEVEN
PRODUCTIONS

IN 35MM COLOR

YOU
COULD
BE
NEXT!!

MIDNIGHT INTRUDERS

starring

Francoise Darc • Alain Mayniel
• Alexander Chapuies •
• Lyllah Michael Torrena •

Suggested Rating "R"

In a house, not unlike your own, on an average street in a neighborhood you might even know, Alice waits for her lover. When he arrives, the two are unprepared for the terror that comes when night creeps in and the lights are turned off. The upstairs window is unlocked and the curtains are drawn. That one night turns into a grisly adventure into a macabre. Alice's nightmare has just begun. No one is safe from the MIDNIGHT INTRUDER.

With
Tom Hart • Adrian Anderson
Barbara Keene • Jon Savage
• B.R. Connors •

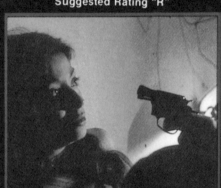

Producer—Dave Arthur • Written and Directed by Gary Graver • Director of Photography—Michael Stringer • Music—Ronald Burton • Costume and Set Design—Prudence Masseth

GRAPHICS BY FERGUSSON III

some scenes contain nudity

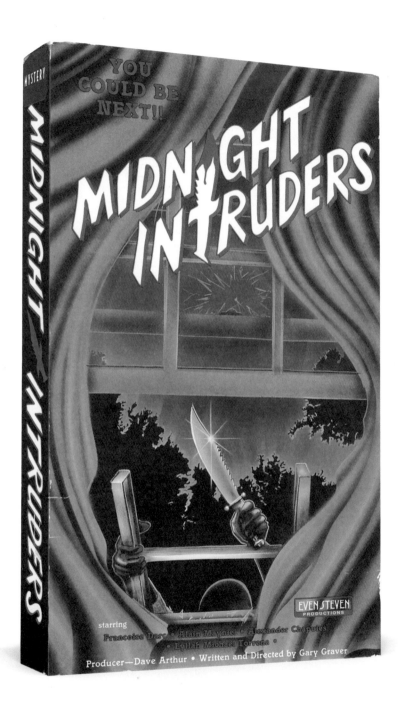

MYSTERY

MIDNIGHT INTRUDERS

YOU COULD BE NEXT!!

MIDNIGHT INTRUDERS

EVEN STEVEN
PRODUCTIONS

starring
Francoise Dav • Alain Maymlei • Alexander Charvies
• Lylah Michael Torrena •

Producer—Dave Arthur • Written and Directed by Gary Graver

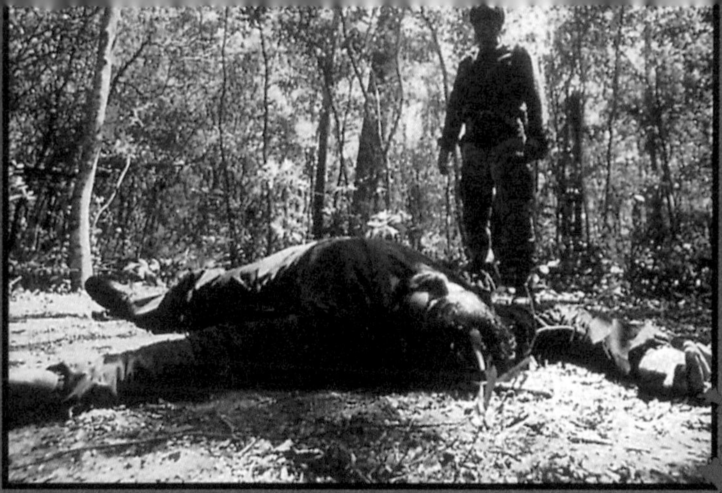

IMAGINE: *An overnight game of simulated military conflict and survival played in the rugged outdoors.*

YOUR GOAL: *To avoid booby traps and your "trigger-happy" opponents, and to gather packets of vital information that will lead you to your main objective—$50,000 in cash.*

YOUR WEAPONS: *Standard army gear, your keenest survival instincts and a special gun that shoots "blood pellets" to identify your "kills."*

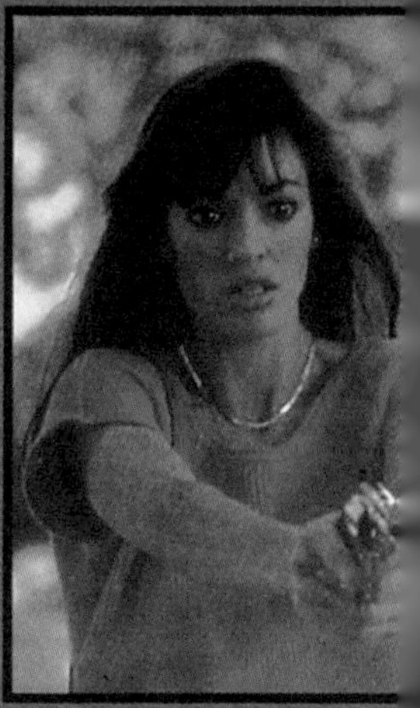

The MASTERBLASTER GRAND NATIONAL CHAMPIONSHIPS *begin deep within the Southern backwoods, where a cross-section of offbeat characters gather to compete for the big money. It's a good, clean competitive, all-American game.*

That is, until the killing becomes real...

Now the question is not who will win, but who will survive this ultimate game of ***DEATH?*** *And who is the* ***KILLER?***

CREDITS

Color, 94 min., Rated R.

Starring JEFF MOLDOVAN, DONNA ROSAE, JOE HESS and PETER LUNDBLAD
Original Story by RANDY GRINTER and RICHARD PITT
Screenplay by RANDY GRINTER
Executive Producer WILLIAM GREFE
Directed by GLENN R. WILDER

1888 Century Park East, Suite 1000
Los Angeles, California 90067

Printed in the U.S.A.

RADIANCE
FILMS INTERNATIONAL

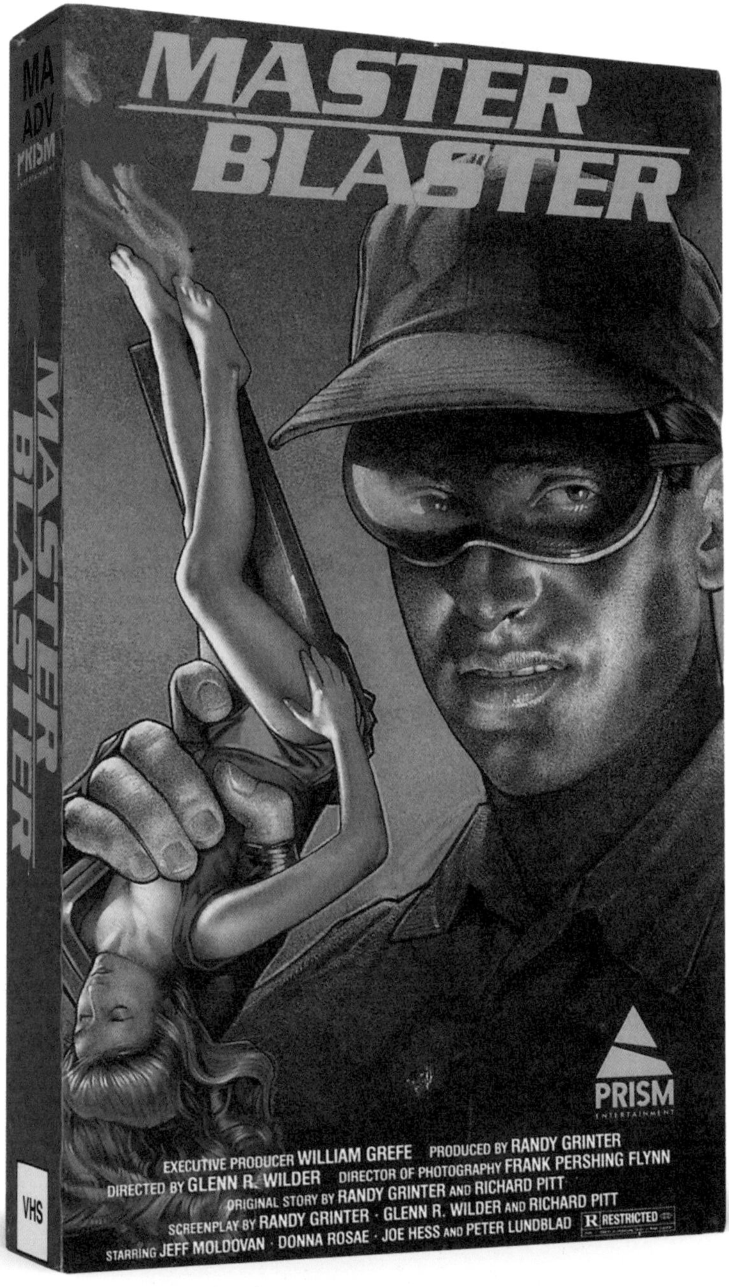
MASTER BLASTER
PRISM
EXECUTIVE PRODUCER WILLIAM GREFE PRODUCED BY RANDY GRINTER
DIRECTED BY GLENN R. WILDER DIRECTOR OF PHOTOGRAPHY FRANK PERSHING FLYNN
ORIGINAL STORY BY RANDY GRINTER AND RICHARD PITT
SCREENPLAY BY RANDY GRINTER · GLENN R. WILDER AND RICHARD PITT
STARRING JEFF MOLDOVAN · DONNA ROSAE · JOE HESS AND PETER LUNDBLAD
R RESTRICTED
MA
ADV
MASTER BLASTER
VHS

Bradley *(IVAN RASSIMOV)*, a daredevil photographer, travels upriver in Northern Thailand into a still-uncharted region, where time has stood still and the savage jungle tribes remain untouched by civilization. The ferocious natives net him from the river; they treat him as a "water creature," because of his blonde hair and strange diving gear.

Bradley is forced to endure bizarre torments at the hands of the natives in their remote village–he is staked in the sun, speared, and forced to drive piles into the river bed. Only the intervention of Marya *(ME ME LAY)*, the chief's daughter, spares the photographer from almost certain death. Accepted into the tribe after a traditional ritual of torture, he is allowed to marry Marya.

Just as Marya is giving birth to her first child, a bloodthirsty tribe of headhunters attack–and the "Man From Deep River" springs into action to defend his new, primitive home.

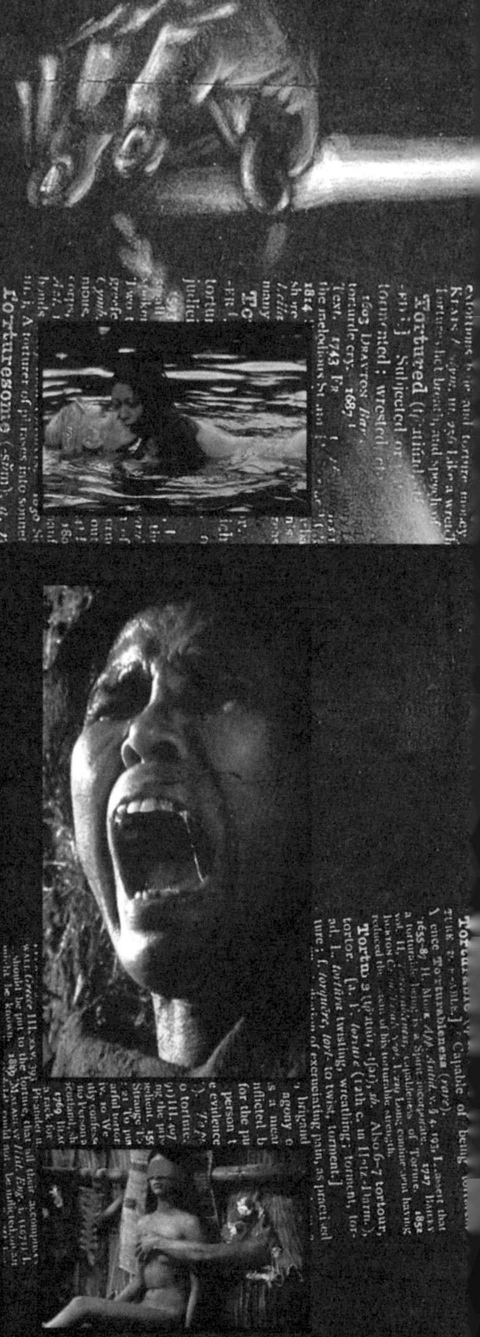

ILLUSTRATION BY CHRIS POLENTZ

PRINTED IN U.S.A. 1977 RELEASE TRC

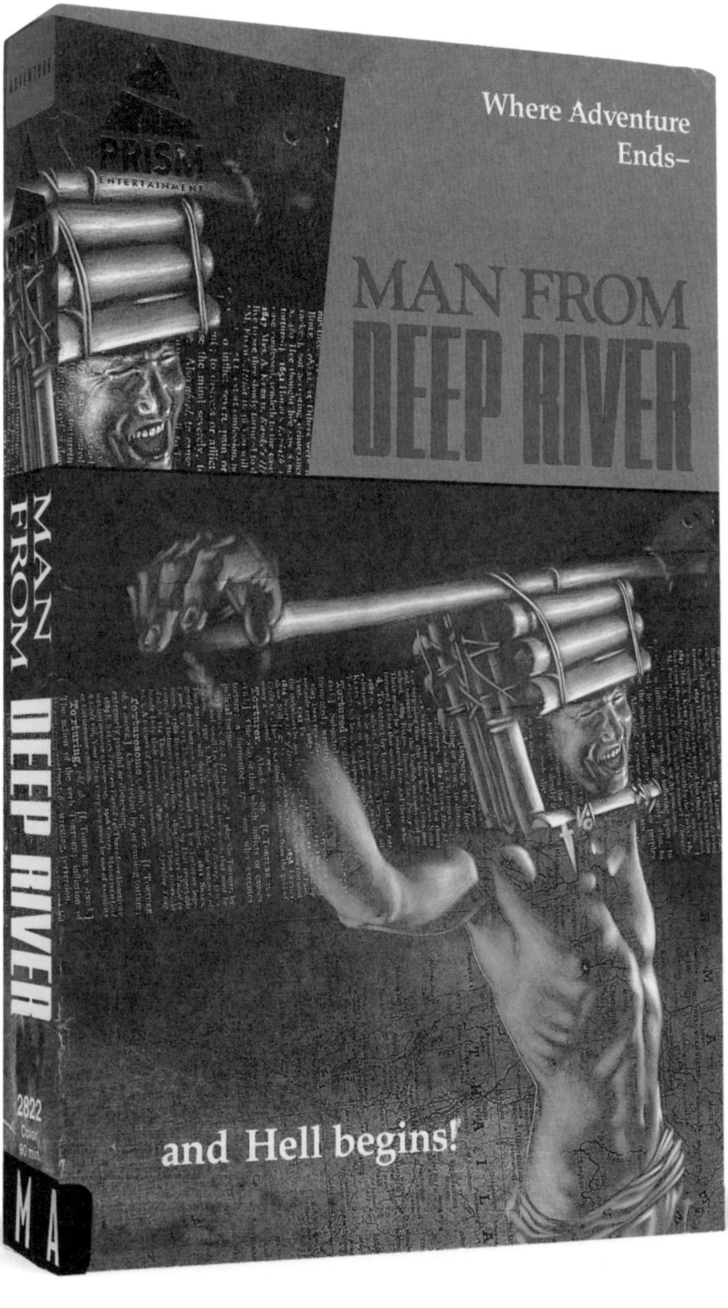
PRISM
ENTERTAINMENT
Where Adventure
Ends–
MAN FROM
DEEP RIVER
MAN
FROM
DEEP RIVER
2822
Color
90 min.
M A
and Hell begins!

A terrifying love story of two people caught in a bizarre web of circumstances, MAGIC creates an atmosphere of pulse-stopping horror from the first frame of the film. Ann-Margret stars as a beautiful woman seeking to recapture her lost illusions; with Anthony Hopkins as the ventriloquist who uses the brash, abrasive voice of his dummy to express his hidden fears and desires. Screenplay by William Goldman, based on his best-selling novel.

1978 Color, Running time: 106 minutes

Starring ANTHONY HOPKINS • ANN MARGRET
• BURGESS MEREDITH • ED LAUTER
Produced by JOSEPH E. LEVINE and
RICHARD P. LEVINE
• Directed by RICHARD ATTENBOROUGH
• Screenplay by WILLIAM GOLDMAN

© 1978 JOSEPH E. LEVINE
© 1983 Embassy Home Entertainment
1901 Avenue of the Stars
Los Angeles, CA 90067

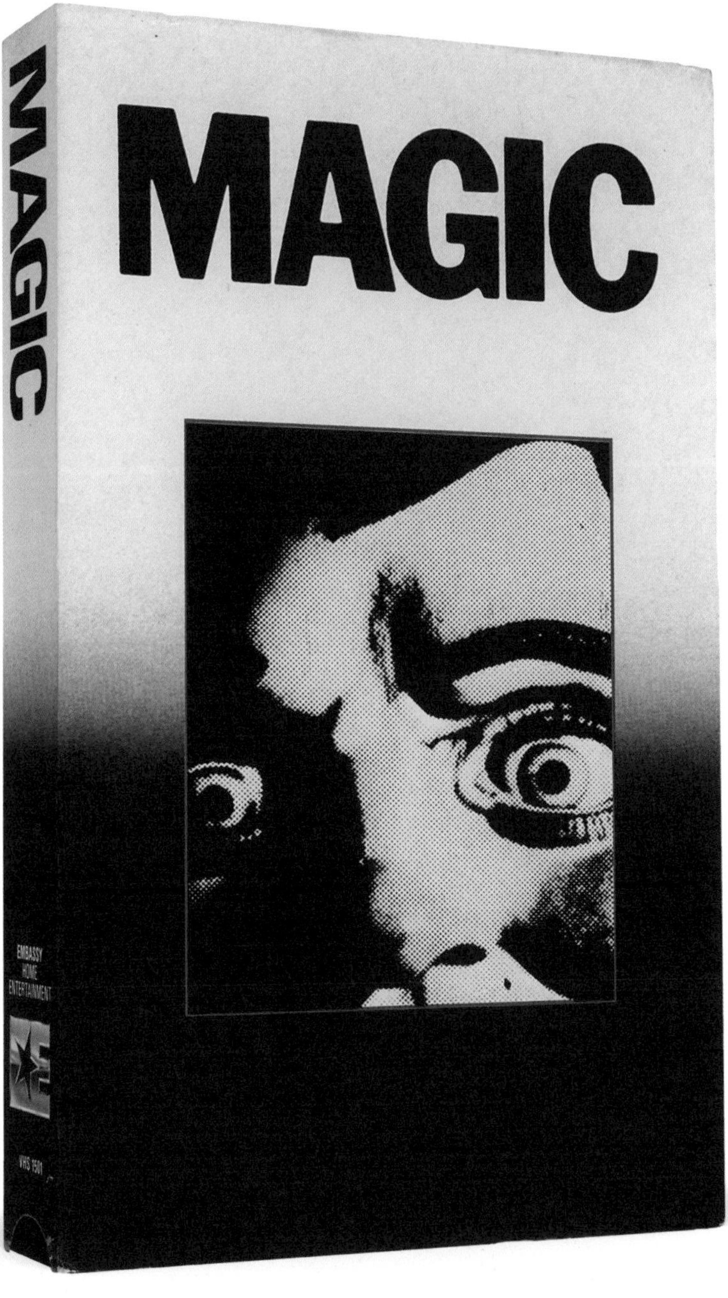
MAGIC
MAGIC
EMBASSY
HOME
ENTERTAINMENT
VHS 1501

A FORCE OF ONE

CHUCK NORRIS, JENNIFER O'NEILL, RON O'NEAL and CLU GULAGER

He hears the silence. He sees the darkness. He's the only one who can stop the killing.

A FORCE OF ONE is about a team of undercover narcotics agents whose investigation mysteriously begins to go haywire. One by one the squad is being eliminated by assassination. Those felled are left virtually unmarked...except for one cruel death mark—the work of a deadly martial artist.

To help discover the identity of the karate killer, the police enlist the aid of karate champion Matt Logan, played by Chuck Norris (six time undefeated world karate champion). Logan is in training to defend his title against Jerry Sparks (played by Bill Wallace).

Amanda Rust (Jennifer O'Neill), a key member of the undercover team is the first to put the pieces together. Can she warn Logan before he steps into the ring? Find out as non-stop action and suspense fill this high voltage martial arts drama.

Color   91 Min.

Video Treasures, Inc.
270 Oser Avenue
Hauppauge, New York 11788

Video Treasures™ are from the collection of
Video Treasures, Inc., distributed by
Video Cassette Sales, Inc.

0 13132 90530 3

RATED PG

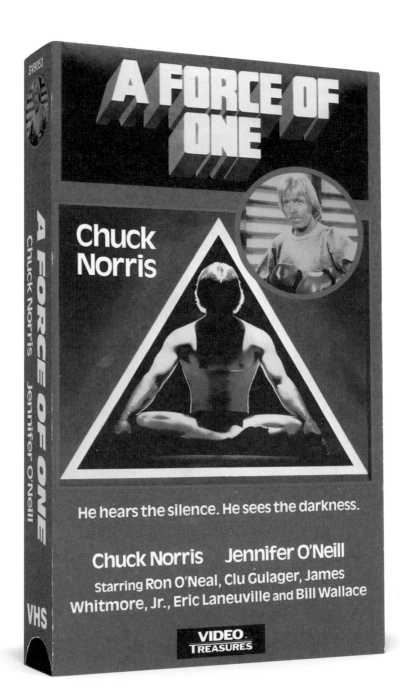

A FORCE OF ONE

Chuck
Norris

He hears the silence. He sees the darkness.

Chuck Norris   Jennifer O'Neill

Starring Ron O'Neal, Clu Gulager, James
Whitmore, Jr., Eric Laneuville and Bill Wallace

VIDEO.
TREASURES

VHS

SV9053

A FORCE OF ONE
Chuck Norris
Jennifer O'Neill

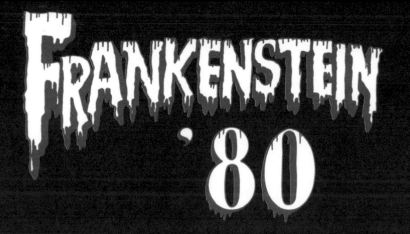

FRANKENSTEIN '80

Starring **JOHN RICHARDSON**
MARISA TRAVERS
GORDON MITCHEL

Once again we feel the maniacal terror of resurrected, restructured flesh.
But this time our monster wants more than life — he wants women and he wants them bad.
Driven by the pressure in his head and his loins ***Frankenstein '80*** leaves a trail of bloody women and baffled authorities.

Although not rated this film contains nudity and scenes of graphic violence.

Color — Approx. 90 min.

GORGON VIDEO

PRINTED IN U.S.A.

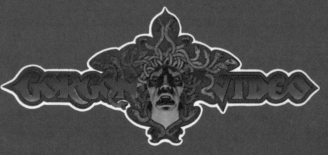

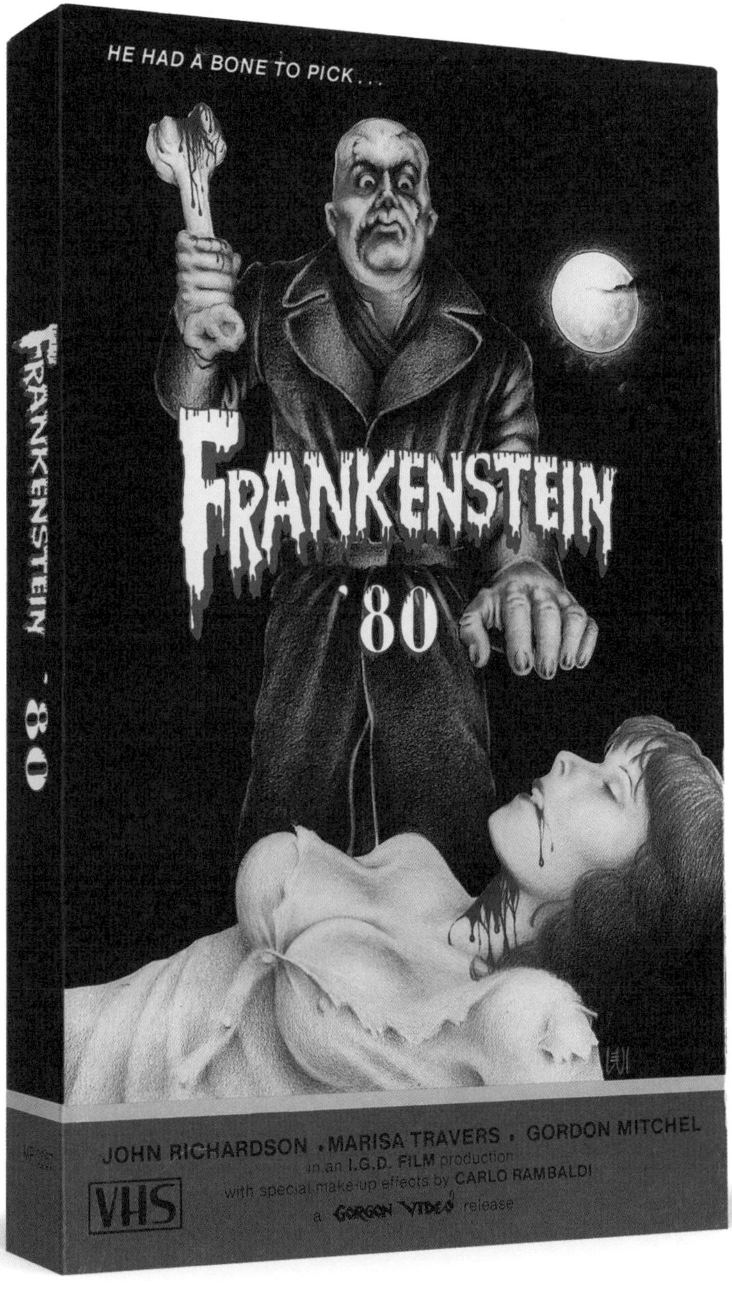
HE HAD A BONE TO PICK . . .
FRANKENSTEIN
80
FRANKENSTEIN '80
JOHN RICHARDSON • MARISA TRAVERS • GORDON MITCHEL
in an I.G.D. FILM production
with special make-up effects by CARLO RAMBALDI
a GORGON VIDEO release
VHS

Mardi Gras MASSACRE

Starring

Curt Dawson and Gwen Arment

MARDI GRAS MASSACRE is a contemporary story set in New Orleans around and during the Mardi Gras.

An Aztec Priest arrives on the scene to revive the blood ritual of human sacrifice to the Aztec god "Quetzalcoatl." The Priest sacrifices three victims considered evil by slicing the hand and the bottom of the foot, and cutting out the heart while the victim is still alive.

A New Orleans police detective relentlessly pursues the Priest throughout the events of the Mardi Gras. Ultimately, he catches up with the Priest while conducting a climactic nine-person sacrifice.

Replicas of the barbaric sacrificial instruments used by the Aztecs are seen in this thriller—**MARDI GRAS MASSACRE.**

VHS

VC II™• LOS ANGELES, CA

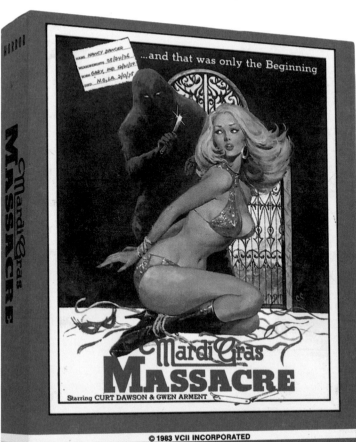

HORROR

NAME *NANCY DANCER*
MEASUREMENTS *38/24/36*
BORN *GARY, IND 12/21/58*
DIED *N.O., LA 3/01/78*

...and that was only the Beginning

MardiGras
MASSACRE

Starring CURT DAWSON & GWEN ARMENT

© 1983 VCII INCORPORATED

VC 114

THE LIFT

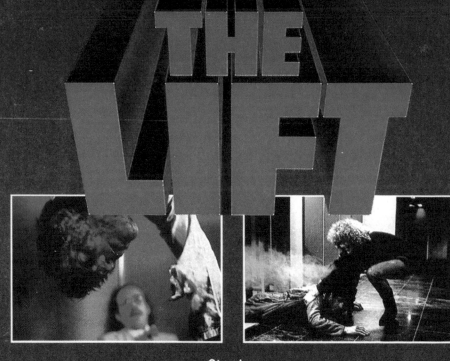

Starring

HUUB STAPEL, WILLEKE van AMMELROOY and JOSINE van DALSUM

There is something very wrong with the elevator in the Icarus office tower. The passengers never end up on the floor of their choice.

They end up dead.

When an inquisitive maintenance mechanic investigates the faulty deathtrap, he discovers that something other than malfunctioning machinery is to blame. Some dark, distorted power has gained control of the monstrous *"lift"* for its own evil design. And when his horrifying discovery is dismissed by the authorities, he alone is left to battle the unholy force.

One man against the perfect killing machine!

Color/95 Minutes/1985

Music by DICK MAAS
Produced by MATTHIJS van HEIJNINGEN
Written and Directed by DICK MAAS

R

English Language Version
Dolby and ▯▯ are trademarks of Dolby Laboratories Licensing Corporation.

MEDIA

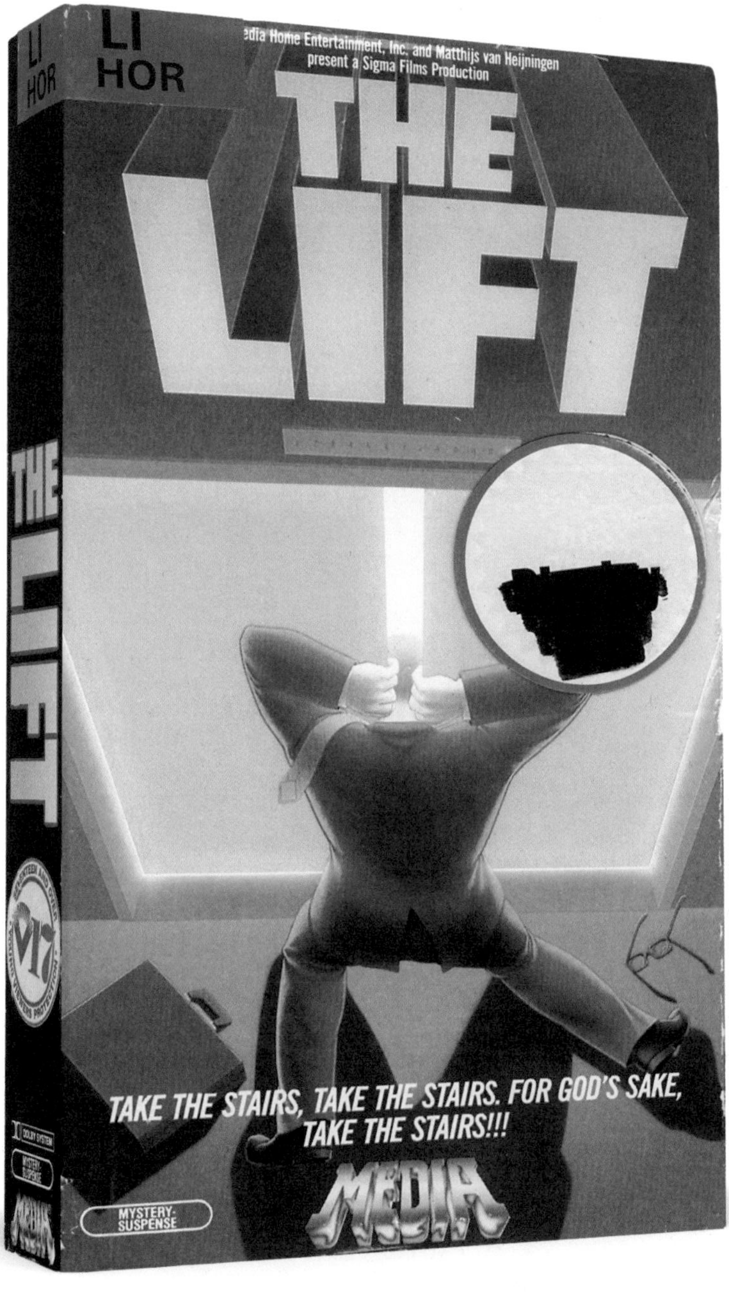
LI
HOR
LI
HOR
edia Home Entertainment, Inc. and Matthijs van Heijningen
present a Sigma Films Production
THE LIFT
TAKE THE STAIRS, TAKE THE STAIRS. FOR GOD'S SAKE,
TAKE THE STAIRS!!!
MEDIA
MYSTERY-SUSPENSE
THE LIFT
DOLBY SYSTEM
MYSTERY-SUSPENSE

NO WAITING. NO APPOINTMENT.

 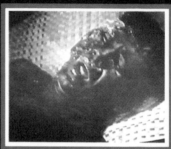

NO ESCAPE!

Paradise will never be the same. The insidious Dr. Larca uses his naive assistant as a guinea pig in plant experimentation. The project goes awry when the assistant suffers chlorophyll poisoning. The only cure is fresh red corpuscles. The once-beloved assistant becomes a green eyed monster drinking the blood of his loved ones. But then, that's what friends are for.

STARRING

JOHN ASHLEY

© 1969 Hemisphere Pictures

Running Time 110 Minutes • Color • Rated "PG"

© 1986 Magnum Entertainment—Printed in U.S.A.

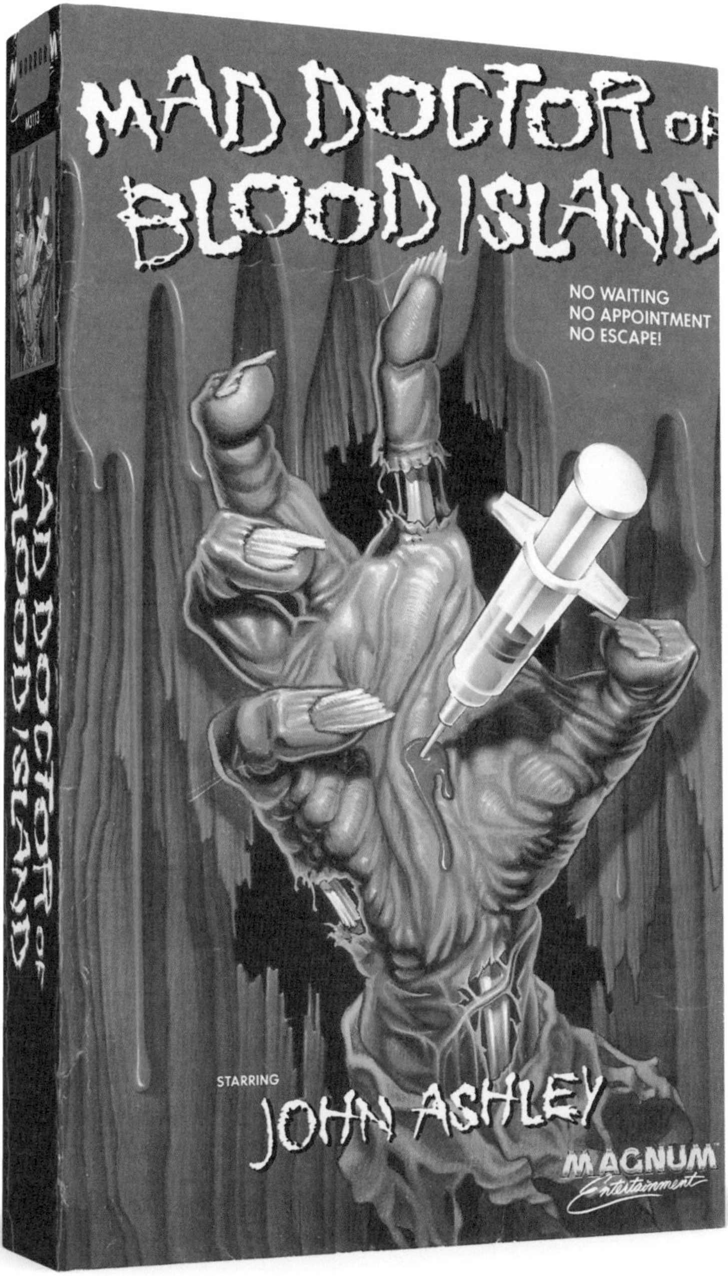
MAD DOCTOR OF BLOOD ISLAND
NO WAITING
NO APPOINTMENT
NO ESCAPE!
STARRING
JOHN ASHLEY
MAGNUM
Entertainment
MAD DOCTOR OF BLOOD ISLAND

FUNERAL HOME

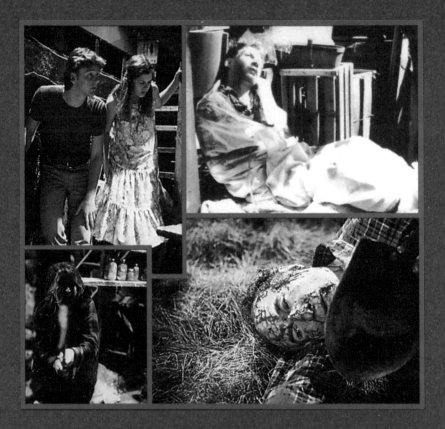

BE OUR GUEST AT GRANDMA'S...

Curious Heather, hears muffled voices in the cellar at Grandma's tourist home, formerly a funeral parlour; they say the guests aren't just slipping away quietly into the night.

RUNNING TIME: Approx. 90 Min.

R RESTRICTED
UNDER 17 REQUIRES ACCOMPANYING PARENT OR ADULT GUARDIAN

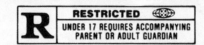

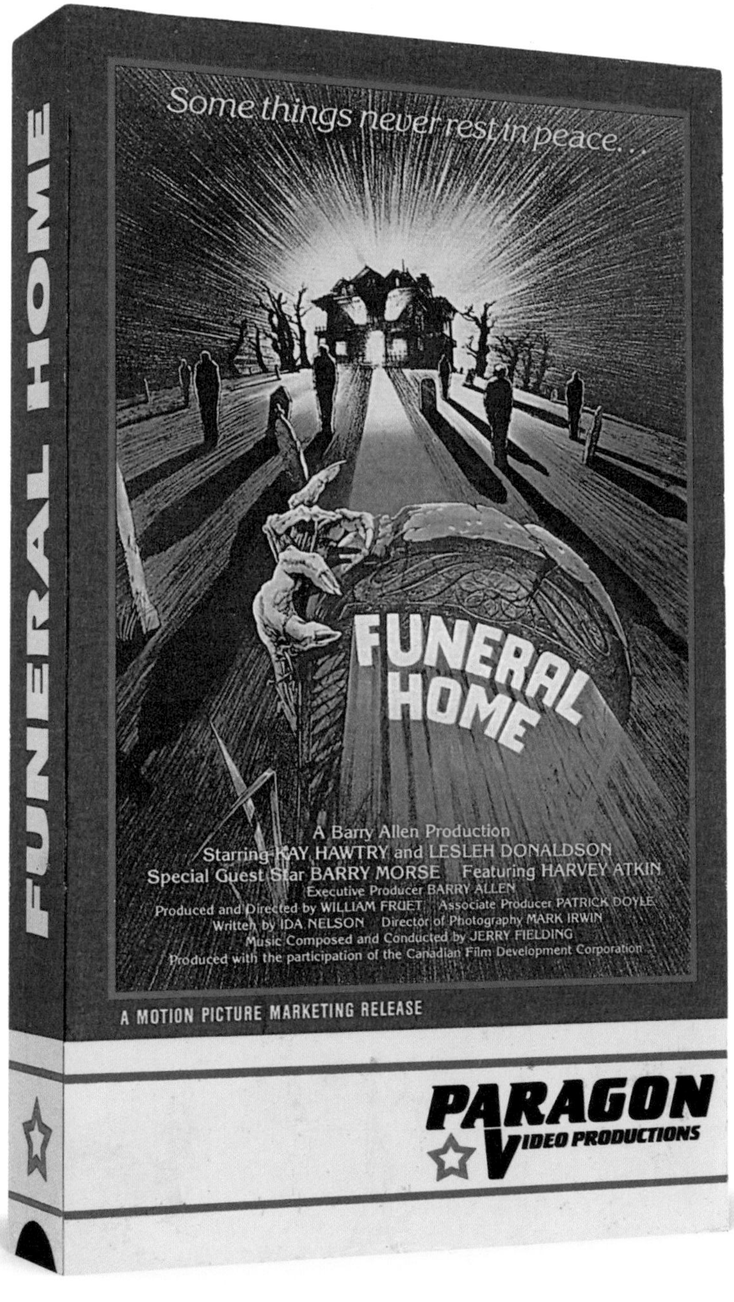

FUNERAL HOME
Some things never rest in peace. . .
FUNERAL HOME
A Barry Allen Production
Starring KAY HAWTRY and LESLEH DONALDSON
Special Guest Star BARRY MORSE Featuring HARVEY ATKIN
Executive Producer BARRY ALLEN
Produced and Directed by WILLIAM FRUET Associate Producer PATRICK DOYLE
Written by IDA NELSON Director of Photography MARK IRWIN
Music Composed and Conducted by JERRY FIELDING
Produced with the participation of the Canadian Film Development Corporation
A MOTION PICTURE MARKETING RELEASE
PARAGON VIDEO PRODUCTIONS

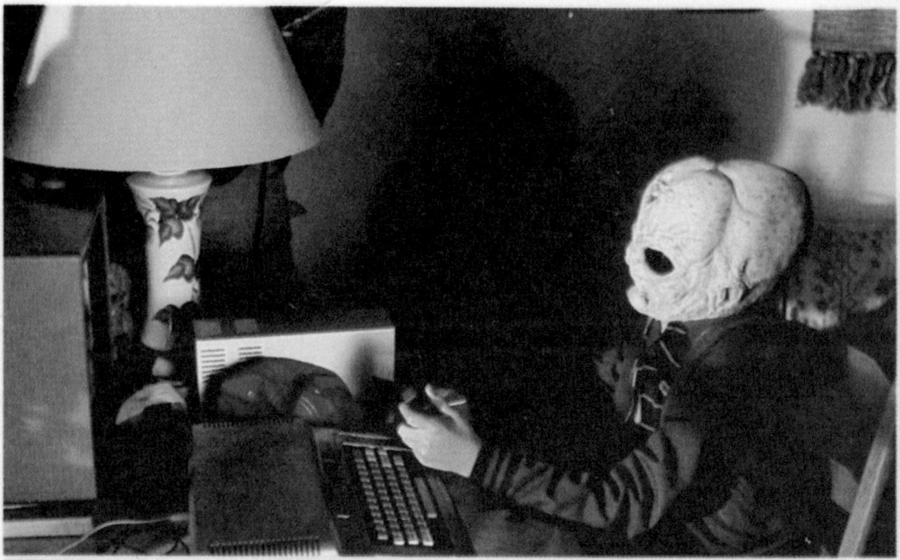

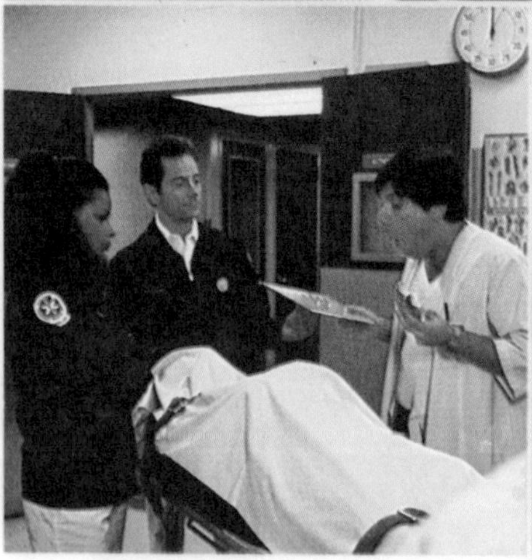

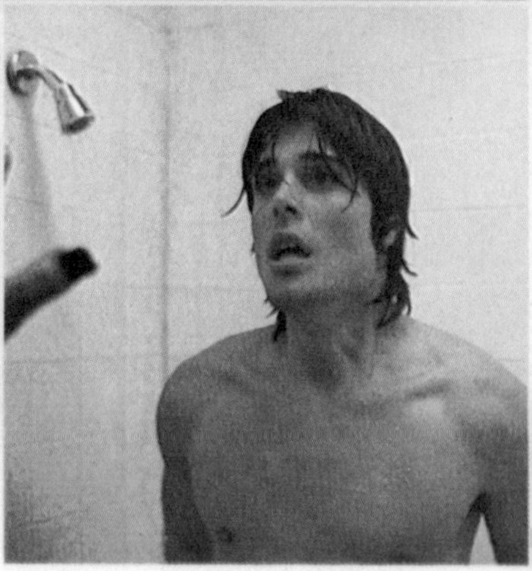

The body count continues in this vivid thriller, the fourth—and final?—story in the widely successful Friday the 13th series. Jason, Crystal Lake's least popular citizen, returns to wreak further havoc in **Friday the 13th—The Final Chapter.** After his revival in a hospital morgue, the hockey-masked murderer fixes his vengeful attention on the Jarvis family and a group of hitherto carefree teenagers. Young Tommy Jarvis is an aficionado of horror films with a special talent for masks and make-up. Has the diabolical Jason finally met his match?

R ®

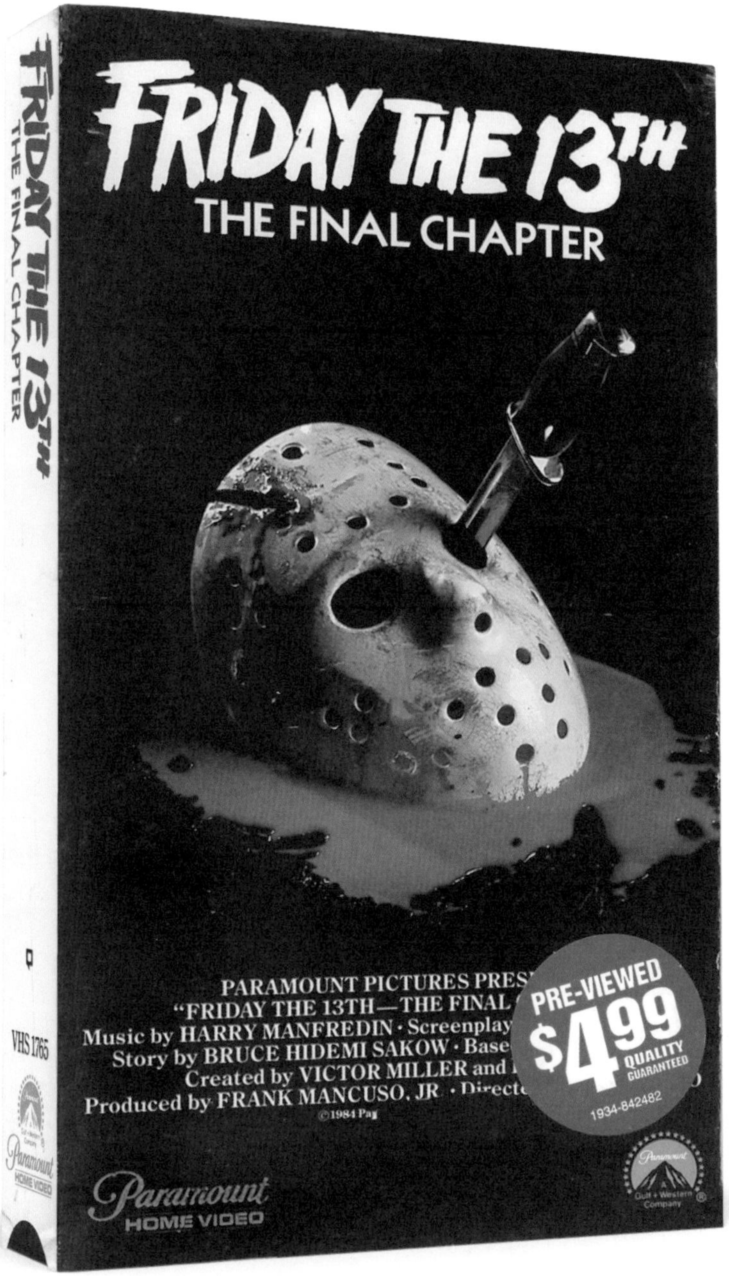
FRIDAY THE 13TH
THE FINAL CHAPTER
PARAMOUNT PICTURES PRES
"FRIDAY THE 13TH—THE FINAL
Music by HARRY MANFREDIN · Screenplay
Story by BRUCE HIDEMI SAKOW · Base
Created by VICTOR MILLER and
Produced by FRANK MANCUSO, JR · Directe
PRE-VIEWED
$4.99
QUALITY GUARANTEED
1934-842482
Paramount
HOME VIDEO
A Gulf + Western Company
VHS 1765

A TERRIFYING JOURNEY INTO THE HORROR-FILLED WORLD OF WITCHCRAFT!

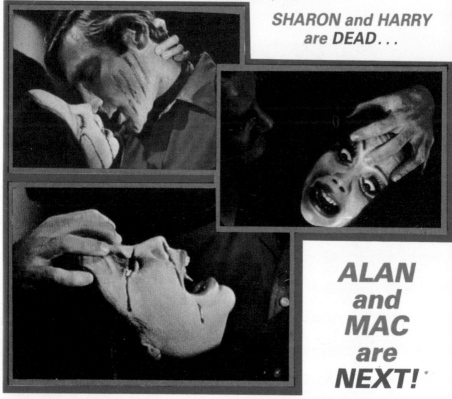

SHARON and HARRY are DEAD...

ALAN and MAC are NEXT!

MARK OF THE WITCH

AN INNOCENT CO-ED, OR BRIDE OF THE DEVIL? A COLLEGE CAMPUS IS TERRORIZED BY A KILLER WITCH... A WITCH DEAD OVER 300 YEARS! WHAT STARTS OUT AS A LIGHT-HEARTED REENACTMENT OF AN ANCIENT RITUAL BY A PSYCHOLOGY CLASS STUDYING SUPERSTITIONS THROUGHOUT THE AGES TURNS INTO A TERRIFYING JOURNEY THROUGH THE HORROR-FILLED WORLD OF WITCHCRAFT.. AND DEATH.

THE WITCH AND ALL HER COVEN WERE HANGED. NOW, OCCUPYING JILL'S BODY, SHE CALLS FORTH THE DEAD. SHE WANTS REVENGE AND, THROUGH CRUEL ACTS OF MURDER, PLANS TO RESTORE HER COVEN TO ITS FULL STRENGTH. RITUALS... A WILD ORGY... INVISIBLE DEMONS FROM THE GRAVE... COVENANTS WITH SATAN... HYPNOTIC POTIONS... CAN ANYONE DESTROY HER AND RETURN HER TO **HELL**... **WHERE SHE BELONGS.**

PRINTED IN U.S.A.

ADULTS ONLY SALE OR RENTAL TO MINORS STRICTLY PROHIBITED
ALL ACTORS & ACTRESSES ARE AT LEAST 18 YEARS OLD OR OLD

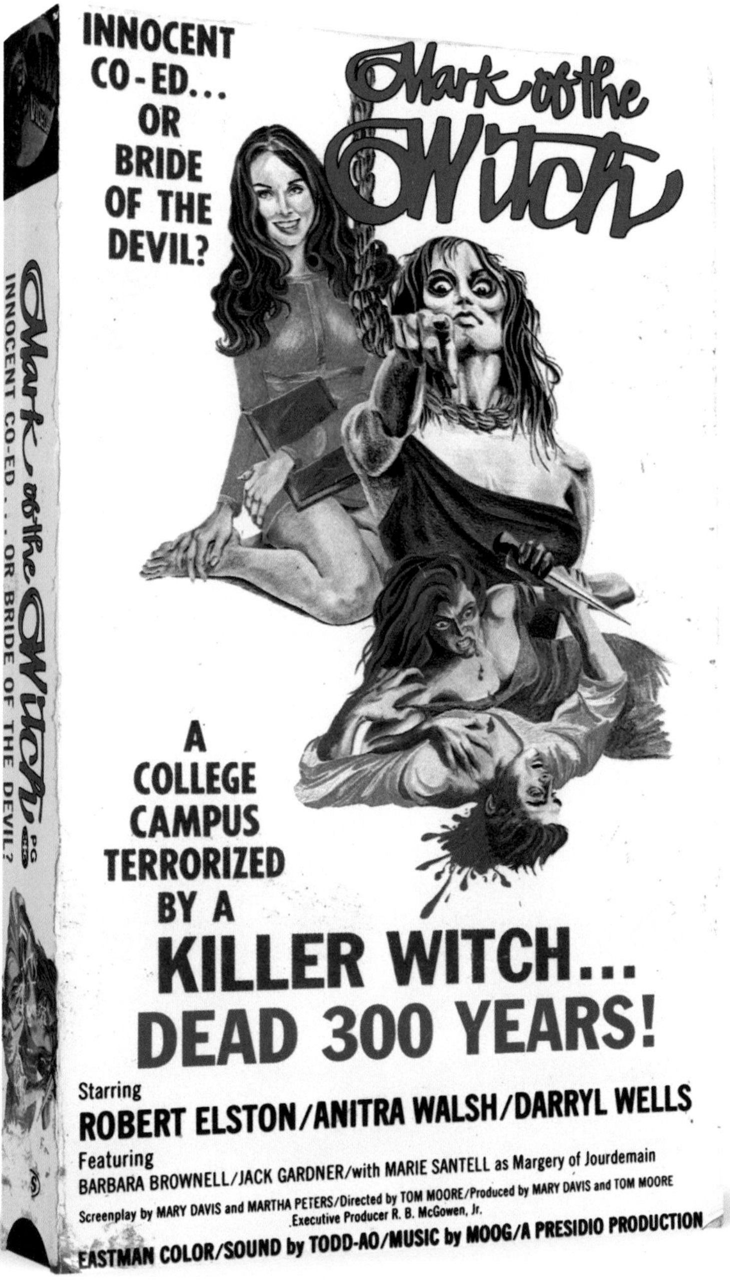
INNOCENT CO-ED... OR BRIDE OF THE DEVIL?
Mark of the Witch
A COLLEGE CAMPUS TERRORIZED BY A
KILLER WITCH... DEAD 300 YEARS!
Starring
ROBERT ELSTON/ANITRA WALSH/DARRYL WELLS
Featuring
BARBARA BROWNELL/JACK GARDNER/with MARIE SANTELL as Margery of Jourdemain
Screenplay by MARY DAVIS and MARTHA PETERS/Directed by TOM MOORE/Produced by MARY DAVIS and TOM MOORE
Executive Producer R. B. McGowen, Jr.
EASTMAN COLOR/SOUND by TODD-AO/MUSIC by MOOG/A PRESIDIO PRODUCTION
Mark of the Witch PG
INNOCENT CO-ED . . . OR BRIDE OF THE DEVIL?

kiss me kill me

WAS IT REAL
OR JUST A DREAM...

A young photographer discovers that she has befriended a witch, as an eerie succession of mysterious and diabolical events test her sanity and her sense of reality.

RUNNING TIME: APPROX. 89 MIN.

R | **RESTRICTED**
UNDER 17 REQUIRES ACCOMPANYING
PARENT OR ADULT GUARDIAN

© 1982 PARAGON • LAS VEGAS, NEVADA

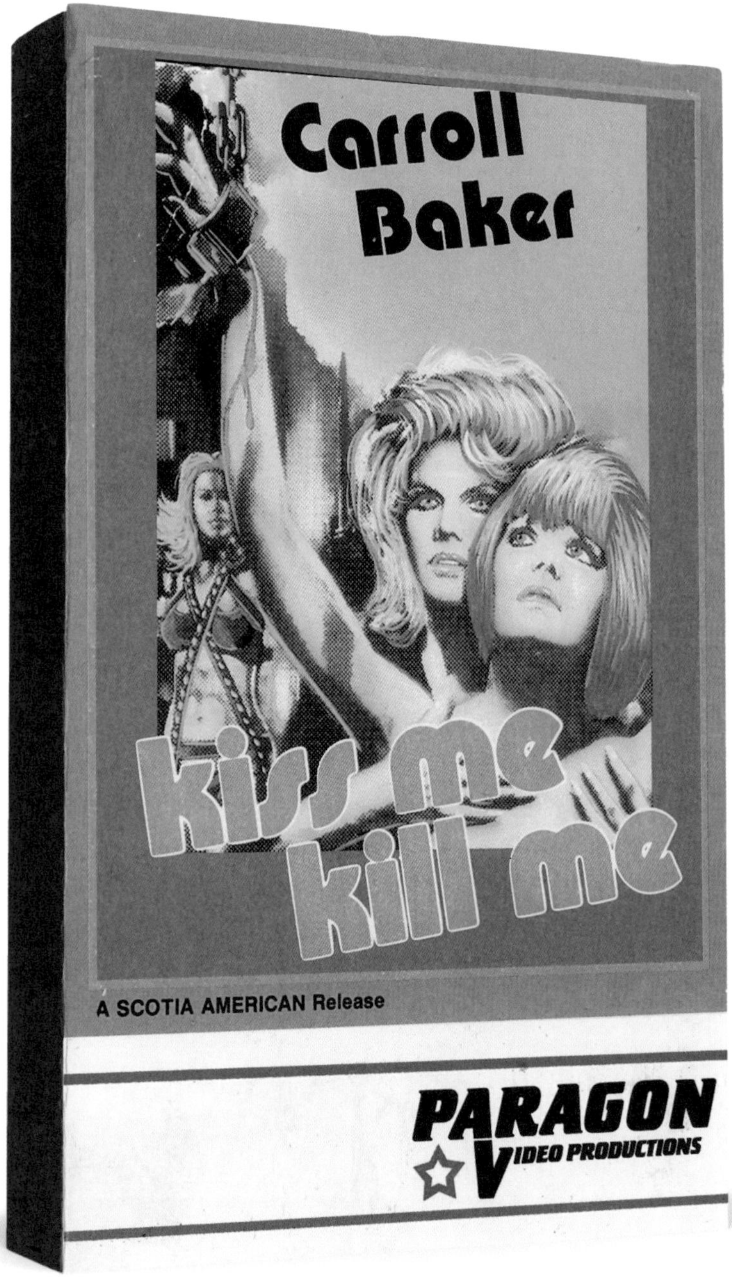
Carroll
Baker
kiss me
kill me
A SCOTIA AMERICAN Release
PARAGON
VIDEO PRODUCTIONS

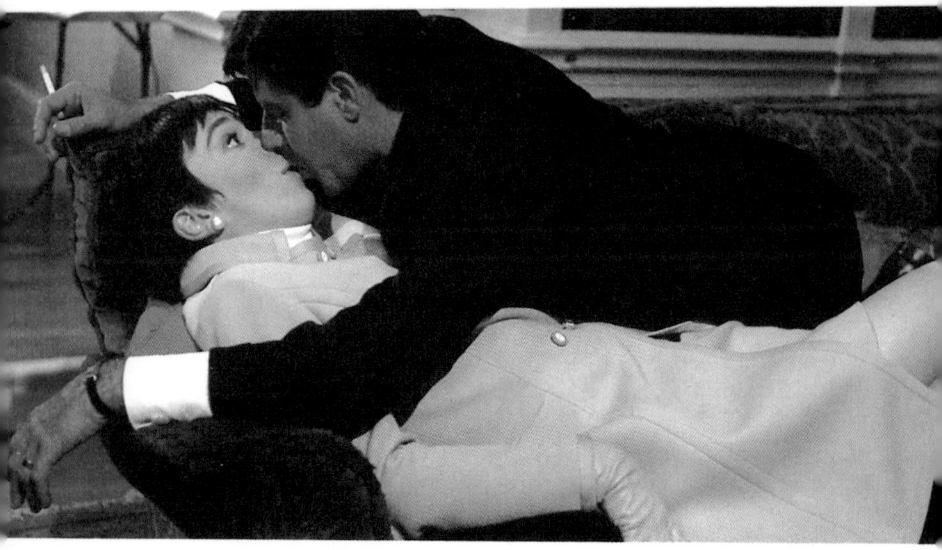

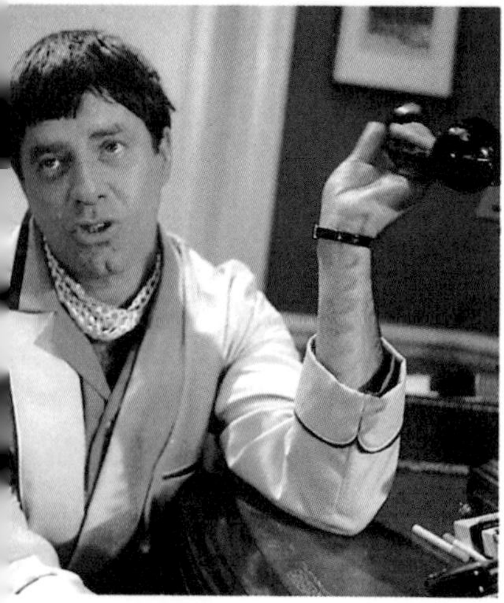

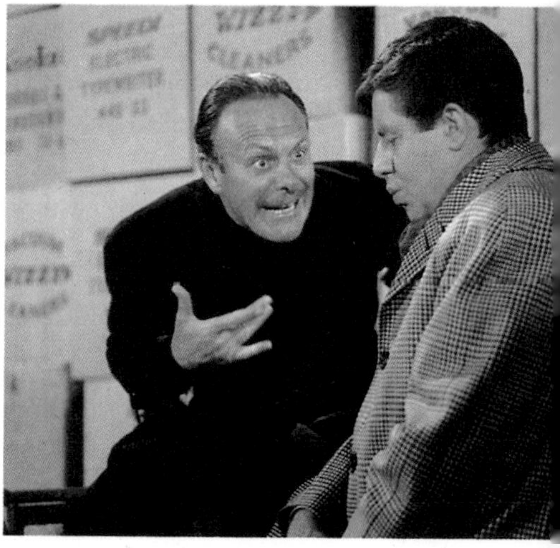

TM

Columbia Pictures Home Entertainment

A division of Columbia Pictures Industries, Inc

DON'T RAISE THE BRIDGE, LOWER THE RIVER

America's Jerry Lewis teams with Britain's Terry-Thomas.

Jerry plays a bungling, get-rich-quick con-man whose beautiful British wife Pamela (Jacqueline Pearce) rebels when he converts her ancestral home into a disco. When she demands its complete restoration, Jerry teams up with Terry, and the two decide to raise the money by selling the Arabs some phoney plans for a new electronic oil drill.

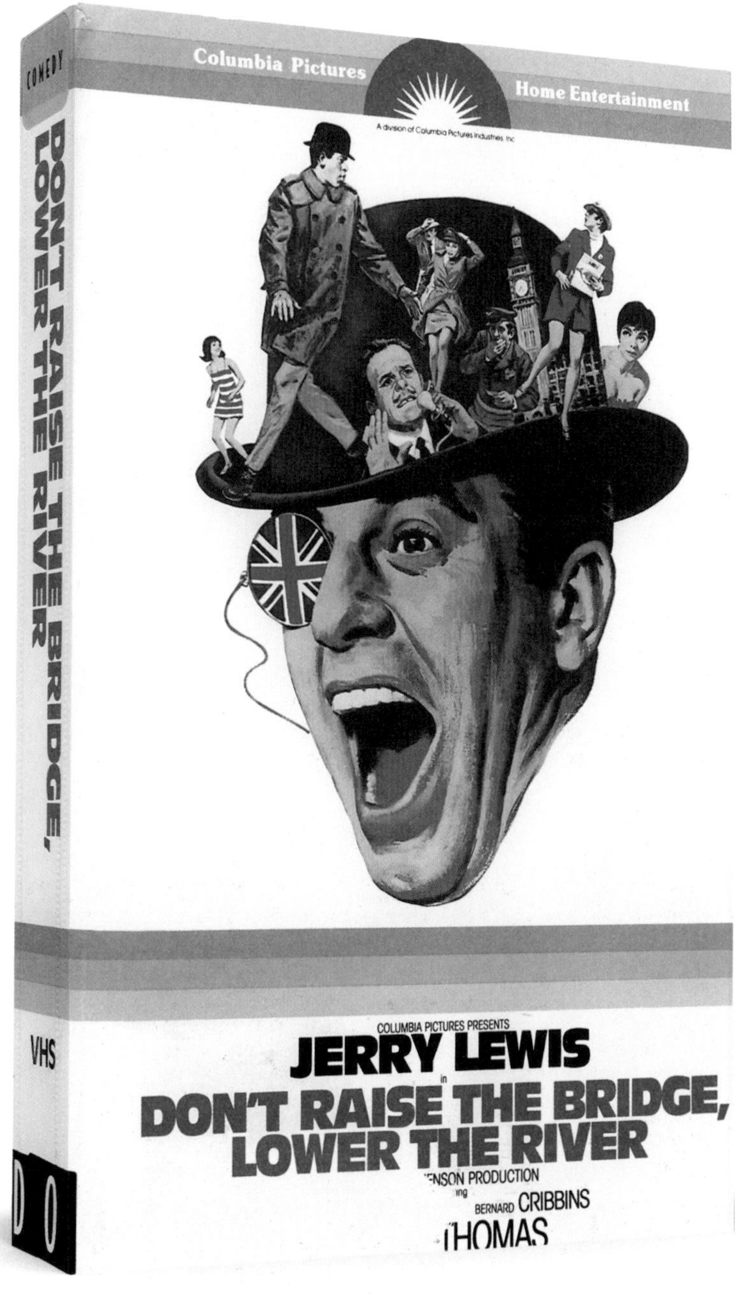
COMEDY
DON'T RAISE THE BRIDGE, LOWER THE RIVER
VHS
Columbia Pictures
Home Entertainment
A division of Columbia Pictures Industries, Inc
COLUMBIA PICTURES PRESENTS
JERRY LEWIS
in
DON'T RAISE THE BRIDGE, LOWER THE RIVER
PRODUCTION
BERNARD CRIBBINS
THOMAS

There are some things worse than death.

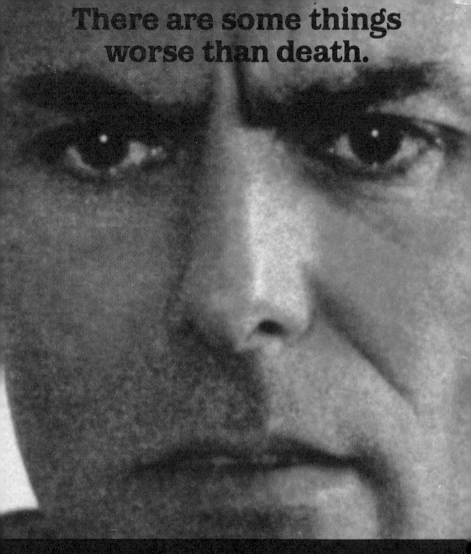

JOHN SAXON (Battle Beyond the Stars) stars in this horrific thriller of ex-GI's carrying a cannibalistic curse home to the states.

Years after the end of the Vietnam War a group of veteran are haunted by the memories of their days as prisoners of the Viet Cong. They were starved and tortured until they turned to cannibalism. Now, years later, strange nightmares, sudden blackouts and cravings for raw meat are slowly driving the same men into an insane fury that even death cannot stop.

The wicked curse is taking hold. So, if you think you've seen it all...think again.

EMONDO AMATI PRESENTS JOHN SAXON In "INVASION OF THE FLESH HUNTERS" With ELIZABETH TURNER, JOHN MORGHEN, CINDY HAMILTON. Directed by ANTHONY M. DAWSON. Produced by MAURIZIO and SANDRO AMATI. AN AIMI PICTURES RELEASE.

PROGRAM TIME: APPROX. 90 MINUTES. PROGRAM:

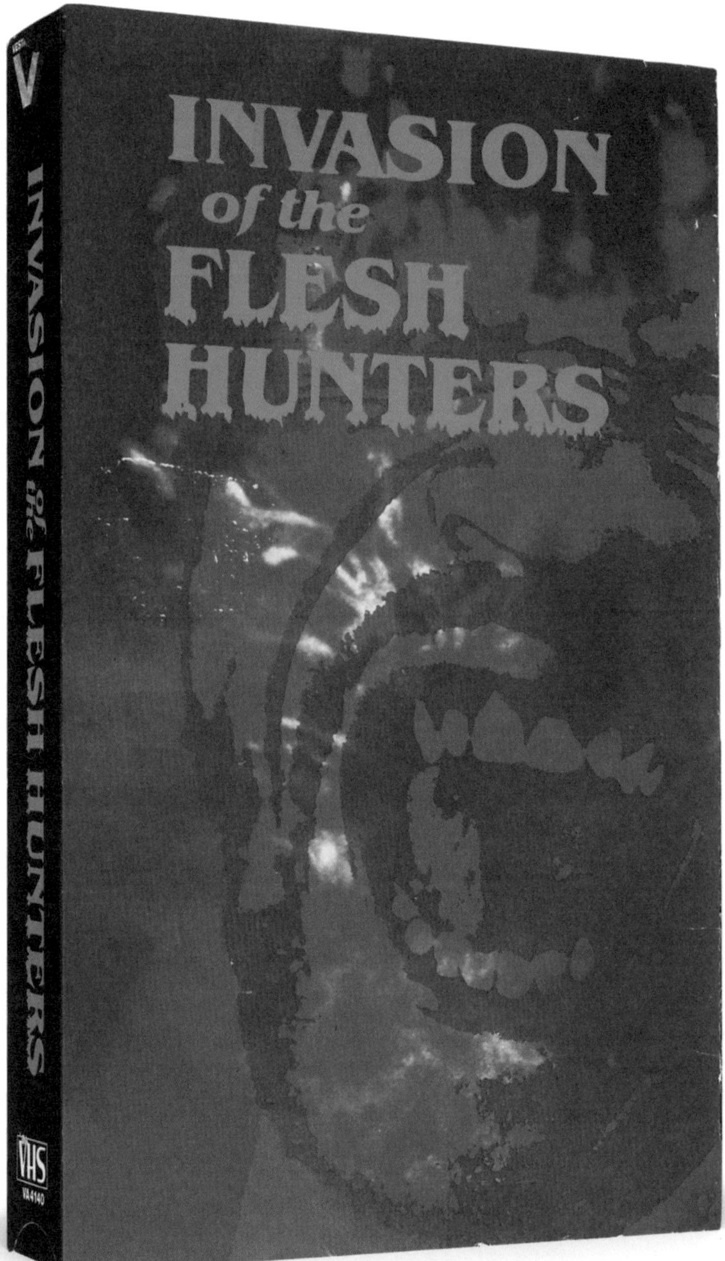
INVASION
of the
FLESH
HUNTERS
VHS
VA4140

THE INTRUDER WITHIN

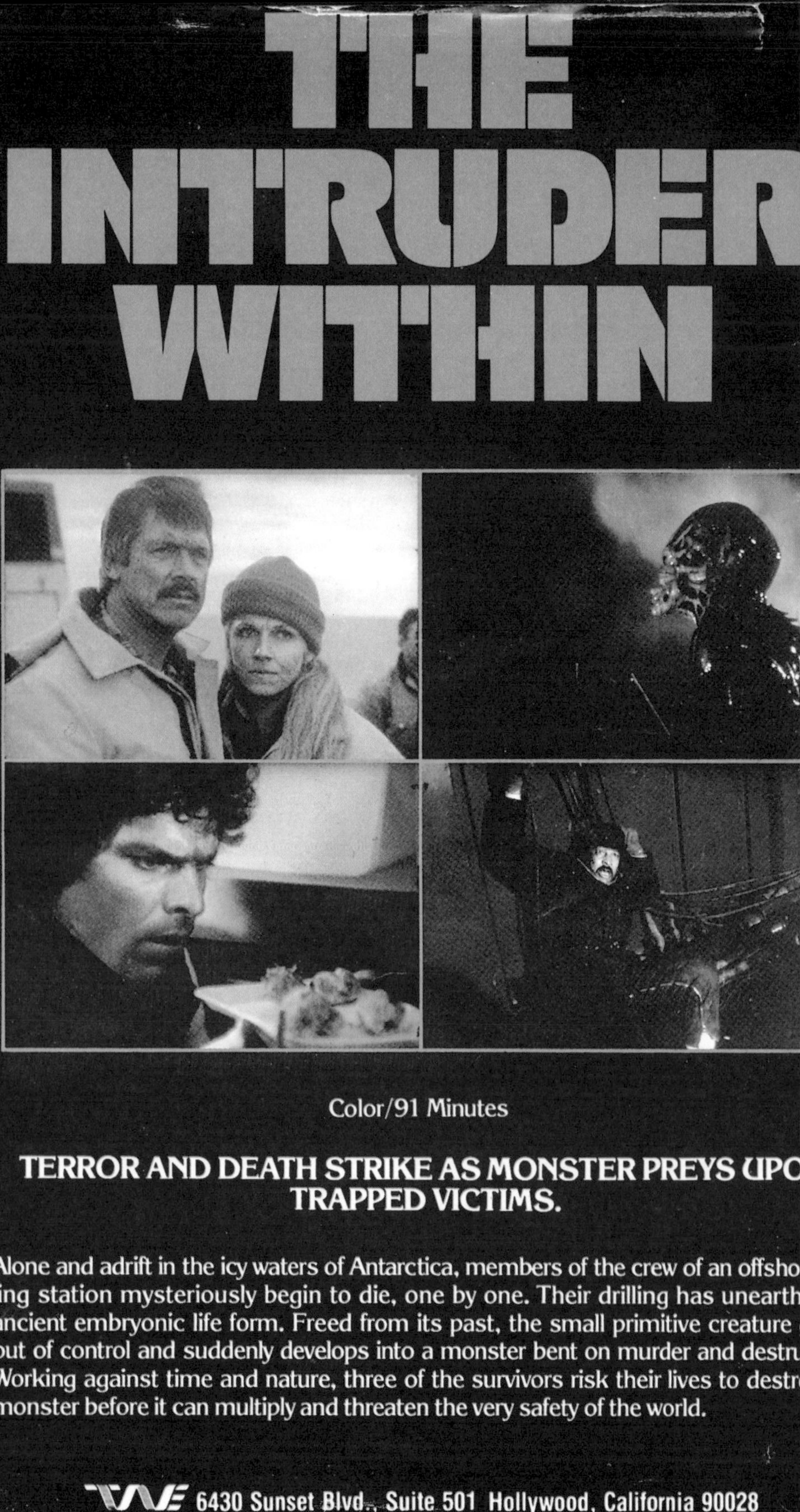

Color/91 Minutes

TERROR AND DEATH STRIKE AS MONSTER PREYS UPO TRAPPED VICTIMS.

Alone and adrift in the icy waters of Antarctica, members of the crew of an offsho ing station mysteriously begin to die, one by one. Their drilling has unearth ancient embryonic life form. Freed from its past, the small primitive creature out of control and suddenly develops into a monster bent on murder and destru Working against time and nature, three of the survivors risk their lives to destr monster before it can multiply and threaten the very safety of the world.

TWE 6430 Sunset Blvd., Suite 501 Hollywood, California 90028

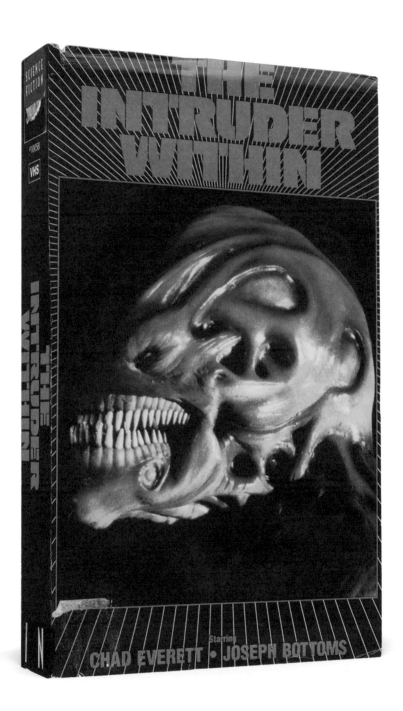

THE INTRUDER WITHIN

SCIENCE FICTION

VHS

Starring
CHAD EVERETT • JOSEPH BOTTOMS

5555 Melrose Avenue, Hollywood, California 90038
Licensed for Sale Only in U.S. and Canada.
TM & Copyright © 1992 Paramount Pictures. All Rights Reserved.

Hi-Fi playback
requires Hi-Fi VCR.

VHS hi-fi

☐☐ **DOLBY B NR**
ON LINEAR TRACKS

Dolby and the ☐☐
are trademarks of
Dolby Laboratories
Licensing Corporation.

ISBN 0-7921-0780-2

0 9736-83605-3 2

'GATOR BAIT

Louisiana's steaming bayous hide countless secrets in their
murky, snake-infested swamps. One is the beautiful Desiree,
whose animal magnetism drives men wild! Former "Playmate
of the Year" Claudia Jennings is Desiree, an untamed Cajun
poacher as savage as the alligators she traps. The corrupt
sheriff wants her in jail, but his depraved kin have more
lustful plans. Will they get her first? Will the sheriff? Or will
Desiree get them? The backwoods explode in shotgun blasts
and the roar of duelling speedboats until even the 'gators
hide in this action-packed tale that's as wild as
the swamp it was filmed in.

SEBASTIAN FILMS LIMITED INC. PRESENTS "'GATOR BAIT"
Starring CLAUDIA JENNINGS • SAM GILMAN
Co-starring DOUG DIRKSON • CLYDE VENTURA • BILL THURMAN
DON BALDWIN • JANIT BALDWIN • BEN SEBASTIAN
Introducing TRACY SEBASTIAN as "Big T"
Written, Produced and Directed by FERD and BEVERLY SEBASTIAN

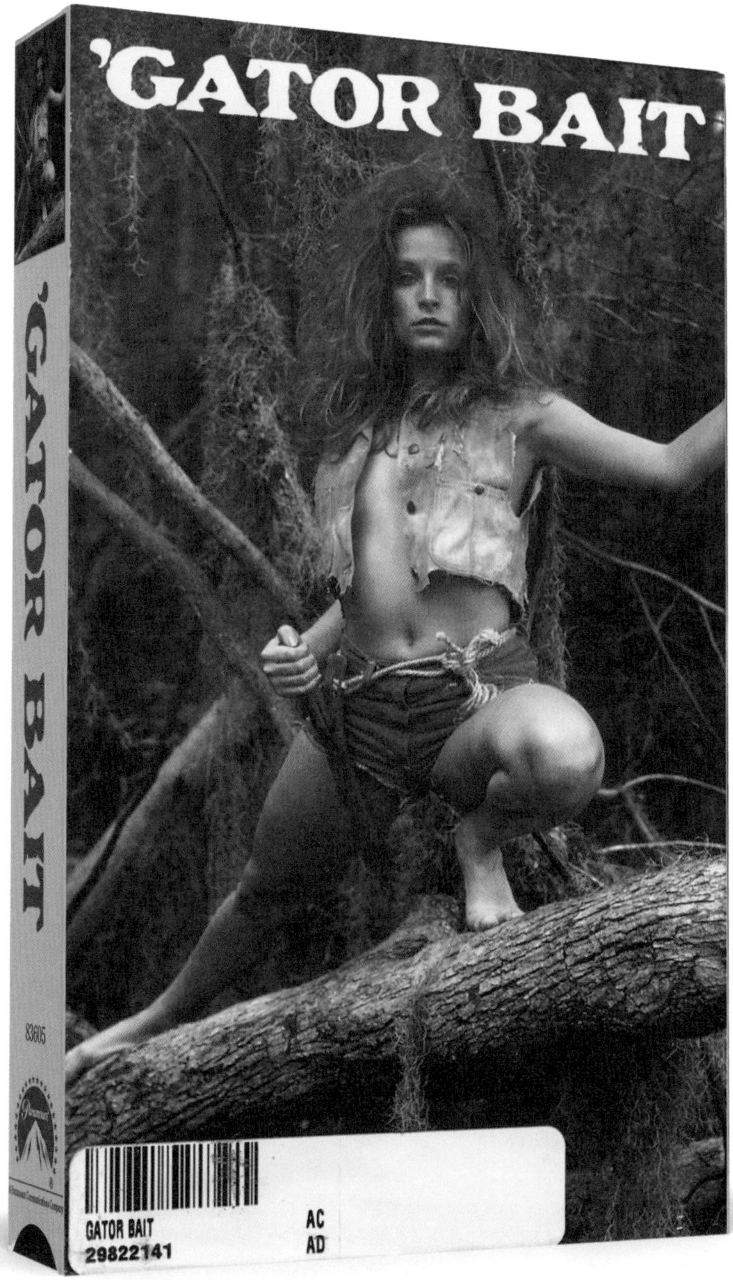
'GATOR BAIT
'GATOR BAIT
83605
GATOR BAIT
29822141
AC
AD

ISBN 1-55511-947-6
0 18713 04389 4

"Gather 'round your TV set, put on your masks...and watch..."

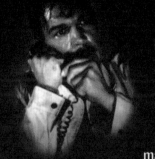

Halloween is drawing near, and all across America, children are getting ready...for what could be their last Halloween. When a crazed man wanders into Dr. Dan Chaliss' hospital, clutching a Halloween mask and raving about people trying to kill him, Dan assumes the guy is nuts. But then the man is gruesomely murdered and turned to a mysterious ash. With the man's daughter, Ellie, Dan decides to investigate the man's last days. The trail takes them to the spooky, remote town of Santa Mira, home of Silver Shamrock Novelties factory. But Silver Shamrock is anything but child's play: It is the home base of an ancient Celtic coven headed by a warlock with a diabolical plan to murder 50 million children on the devil's night. So put on your masks and get ready for a few hours of pure terror. Halloween is here again.

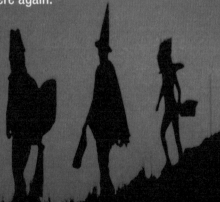

MOUSTAPHA AKKAD PRESENTS

HALLOWEEN III: SEASON OF THE WITCH

A JOHN CARPENTER / DEBRA HILL PRODUCTION

STARRING TOM ATKINS STACEY NELKIN DAN O'HERLIHY AS COCHRAN

WRITTEN AND DIRECTED BY TOMMY LEE WALLACE PRODUCED BY DEBRA HILL AND JOHN CARPENTER

EXECUTIVE PRODUCERS IRWIN YABLANS AND JOSEPH WOLF ASSOCIATE PRODUCER BARRY BERNARDI

DIRECTOR OF PHOTOGRAPHY DEAN CUNDEY MUSIC BY JOHN CARPENTER AND ALAN HOWARTH

A UNIVERSAL RELEASE

R

05-04389

COLOR

GOODTIMES® HOME VIDEO

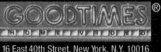

16 East 40th Street, New York, N.Y. 10016

Approximately 99 Minutes

Duplicated, Packaged and Printed in the U.S.A.

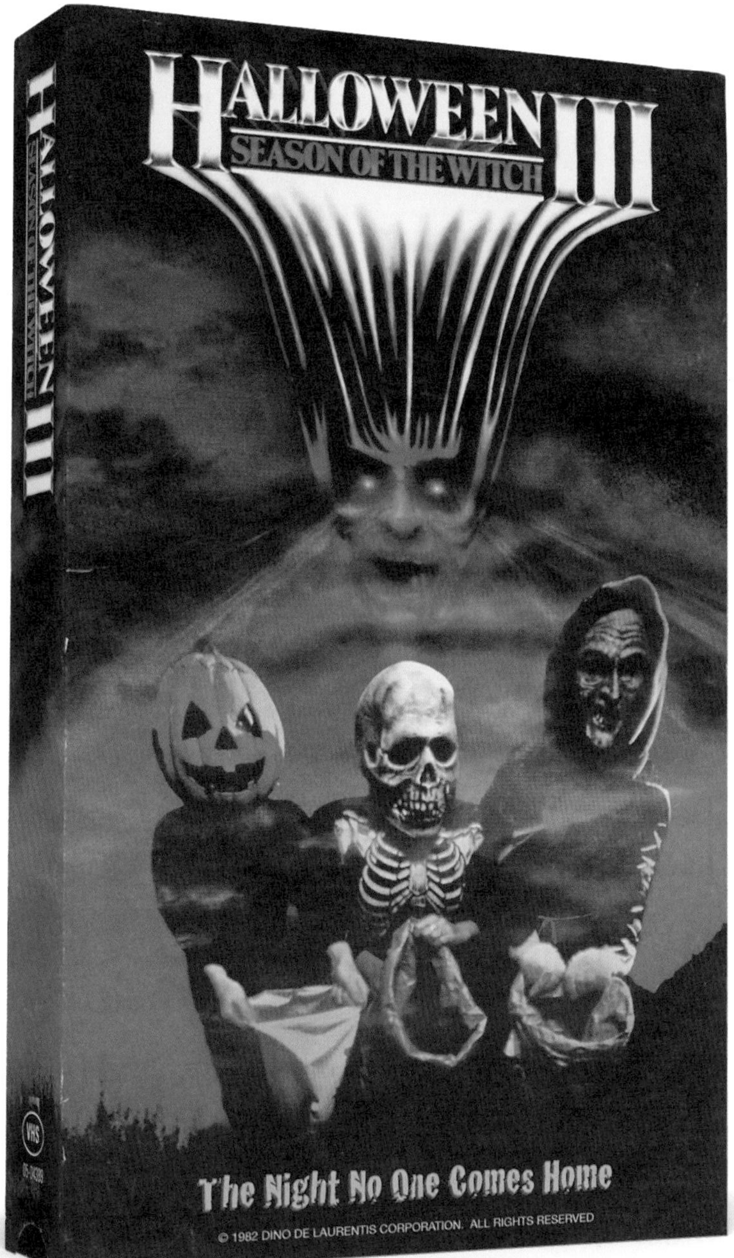
HALLOWEEN III
SEASON OF THE WITCH
HALLOWEEN III
SEASON OF THE WITCH
VHS
The Night No One Comes Home
© 1982 DINO DE LAURENTIS CORPORATION. ALL RIGHTS RESERVED

the HELTER SKELTER MURDERS

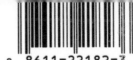

0 8611-22182-3 6

Starring DEBBIE DUFF and BRIAN KLINKNETT

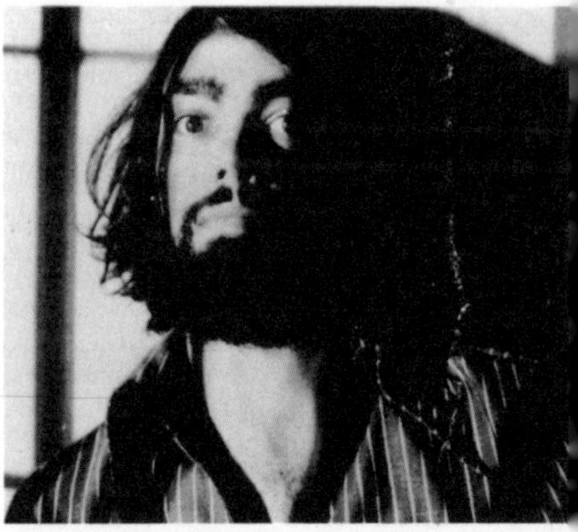

The Helter Skelter Murders is the grisly true story of one of the most notorious crimes of the century—and of the twisted mastermind behind it, Charles Manson. It's all here: drugged-out love-ins with the Manson family. Manson's crazed vision of "helter skelter," an apocalyptic era of thievery and murder from which he would emerge as the true Messiah. And the night of terror when Manson's followers slaughtered beautiful actress Sharon Tate and four friends in her luxurious Beverly Hills home.

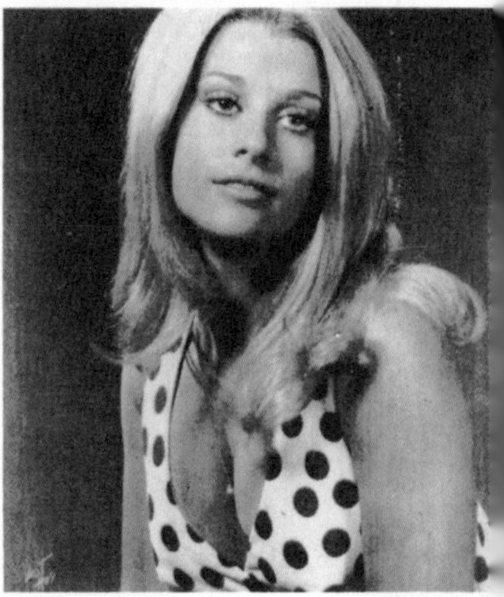

Told in riveting documentary style, *The Helter Skelter Murders* will astonish you with its vivid "you-are-there" re-creation of a time when madness reigned.

Color and Black and White/Approx. 83 Minutes R

Starring Debbie DUFF Brian KLINKNETT Phyllis ESTES Paula SHANNON Erica BIGELOW Richard KAPLAN Gary DONOVAN Linda VAN Ray PITTS

Produced by WADE WILLIAMS Screenplay by RON SHEPHERD

Directed by FRANK HOWARD An AURIC LTD. Production

Released by WADE WILLIAMS PRODUCTIONS

MEDIA

DISTRIBUTED BY MEDIA HOME ENTERTAINMENT, INC. A Heron Communications, Inc. Company

ISBN #: 1-55873-385-

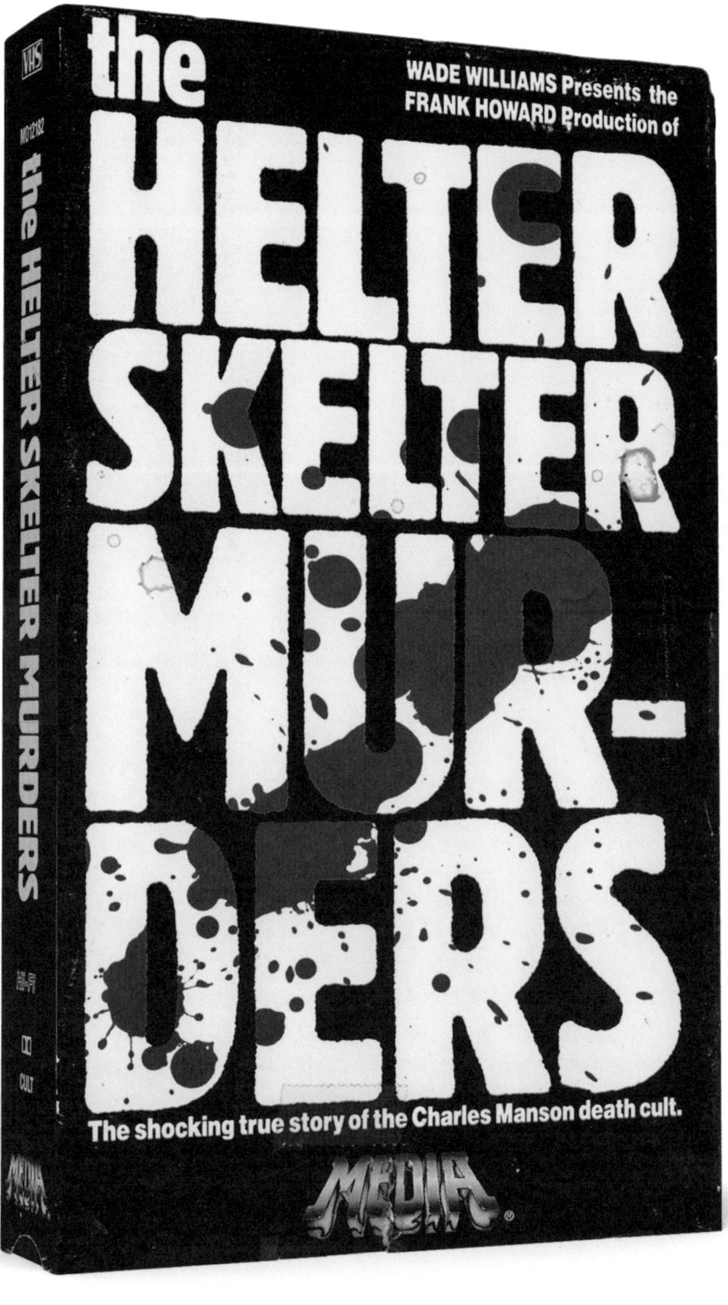
VHS
MO12182
the HELTER SKELTER MURDERS
CULT
the
WADE WILLIAMS Presents the
FRANK HOWARD Production of
HELTER
SKELTER
MUR-
DERS
The shocking true story of the Charles Manson death cult.
MEDIA

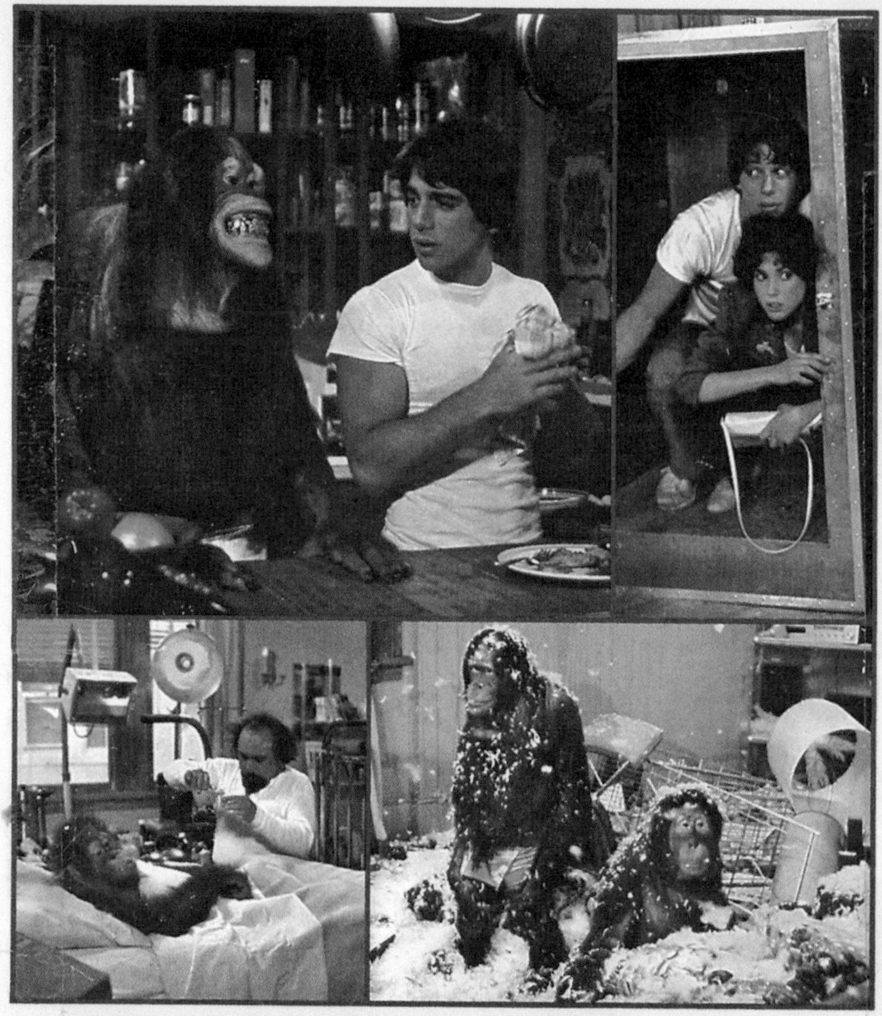

Hijinks and laughs make this a great family fun movie.

Eccentric circus owner Max Sabatini's legacy to his only son, Foster (Tony Danza) includes $5 million, with a stipulation: Foster must keep Max's three prized orangutans for at least five years. With the apes comes high-wire artist Lazlo (Danny DeVito). The four additions are too much for Foster's live-in girlfriend Cynthia (Stacey Nelkin) whose mother (Jessica Walter) encourages her to move out. Moving in is the Zoological Society, which stands to inherit if Foster fails with the apes. To ensure their success, the society dispatches mobsters to wreak havoc. Comic zaniness ensues as everyone really goes "ape."

Paramount
HOME VIDEO

Paramount
A Gulf + Western Company

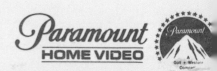

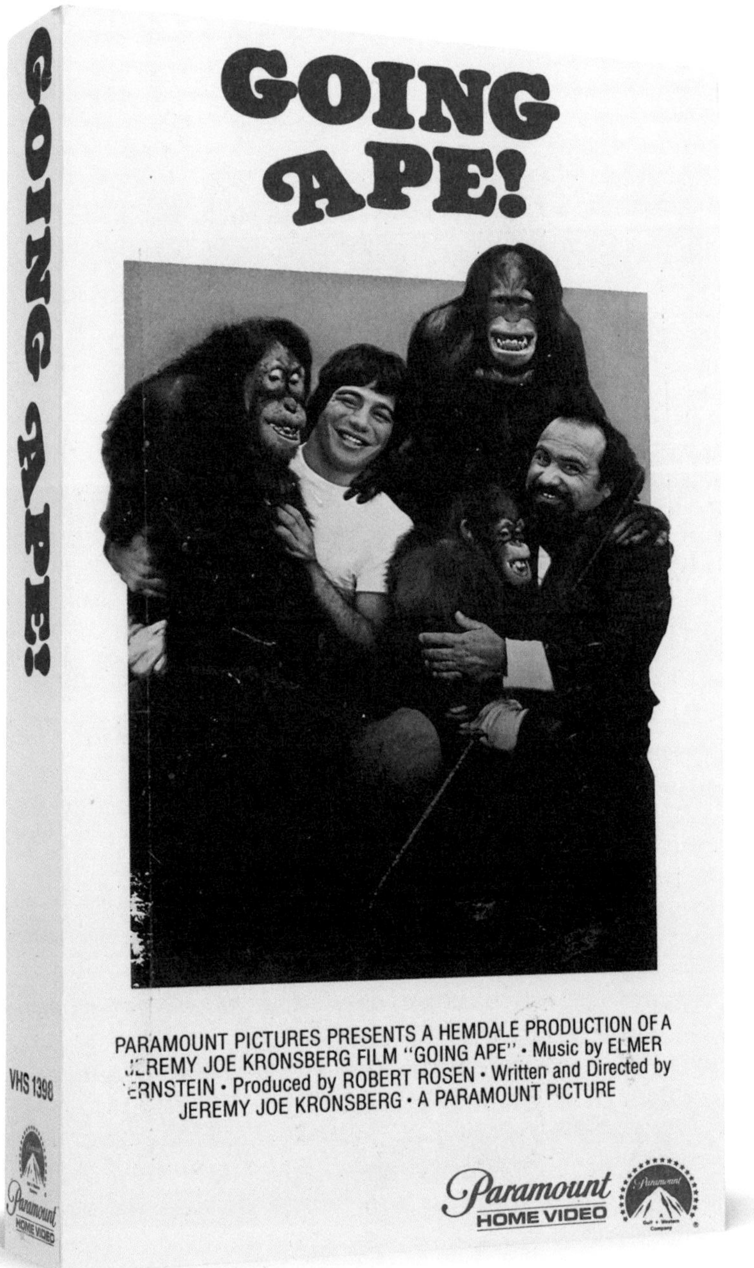
GOING APE!
GOING APE!
PARAMOUNT PICTURES PRESENTS A HEMDALE PRODUCTION OF A
JEREMY JOE KRONSBERG FILM "GOING APE" • Music by ELMER
BERNSTEIN • Produced by ROBERT ROSEN • Written and Directed by
JEREMY JOE KRONSBERG • A PARAMOUNT PICTURE
VHS 1398
Paramount
HOME VIDEO

HOODLUMS

THE ONLY THING THEY COULDN'T CONTROL WAS A WOMAN

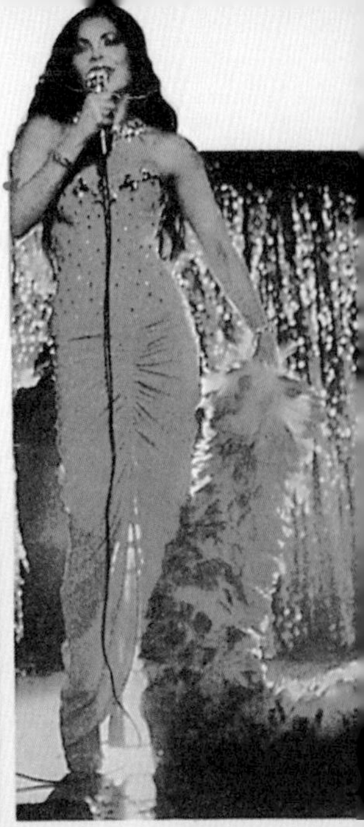

For those whose Blood Lust needs fullfilment, comes "Mac Ahiberg's" superbly directed gangster film **Hoodlums**.

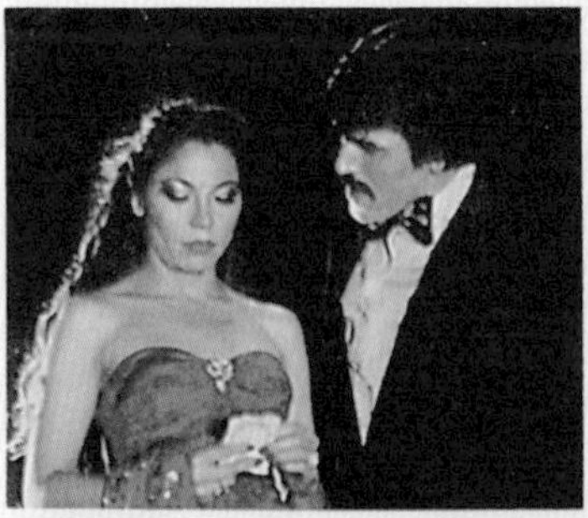

The Godfather (Michael Gazzo), the New York gangster boss (Tony Page), and the beautiful nightclub singer (Nai Bonet) spin a web of intrigue and retribution in a manner completely unexpected to the movie viewer.

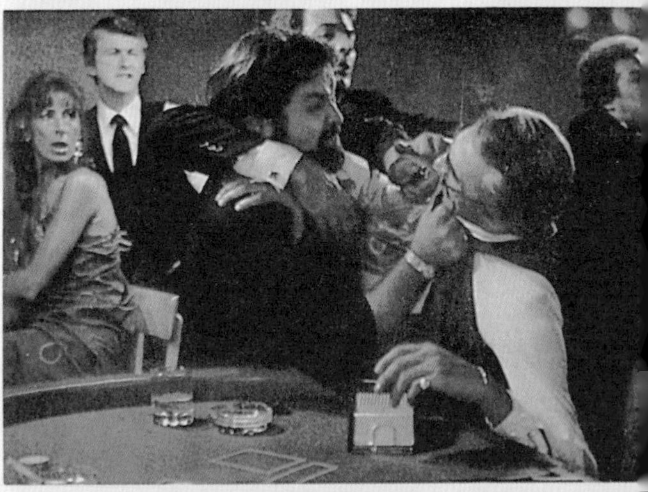

Stonefaced hitmen, beautiful women, big time gamblers and racketeers, this movie has it all!

A movie you can't afford to refuse: **Hoodlums.**

• Cast & Credits •

Nai Bonet, Michael Gazzo Tony Page, Vicki Sue Robinson, Raymond Serra Featuring Cissy Houston and Theodore 'T' Life.

Directed by
.... **Mac Ahlberg**
Screenplay by
..... **Edith E. Colegrave**
Story by
Nai Bonet & Bill Tasgal
Music by
Joe Delia & Tom Bernfeld
Edited by
.... **Ian Maitland**
Produced by
.... **Bill Tasgal**
Executive Producer
.... **Nai Bonet**

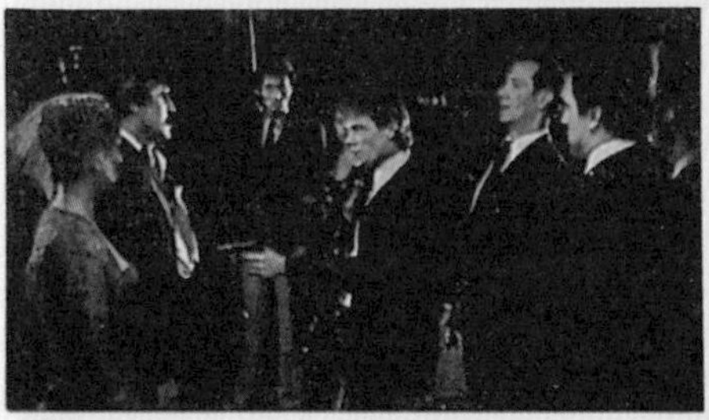

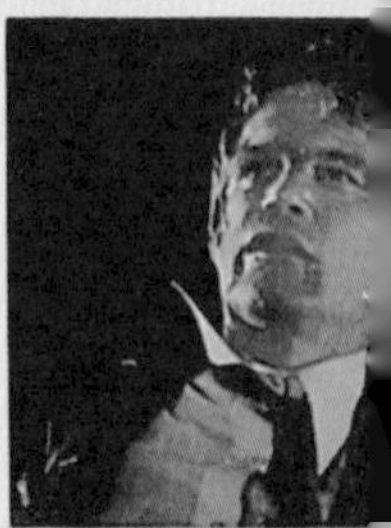

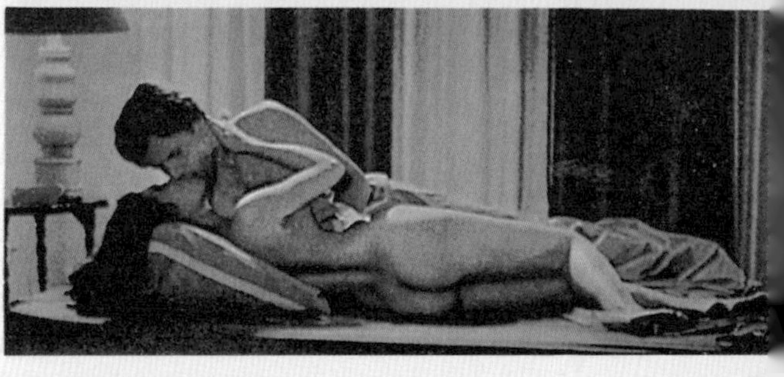

This program is marketed under licence by Twilight Home Entertainment Ltd.

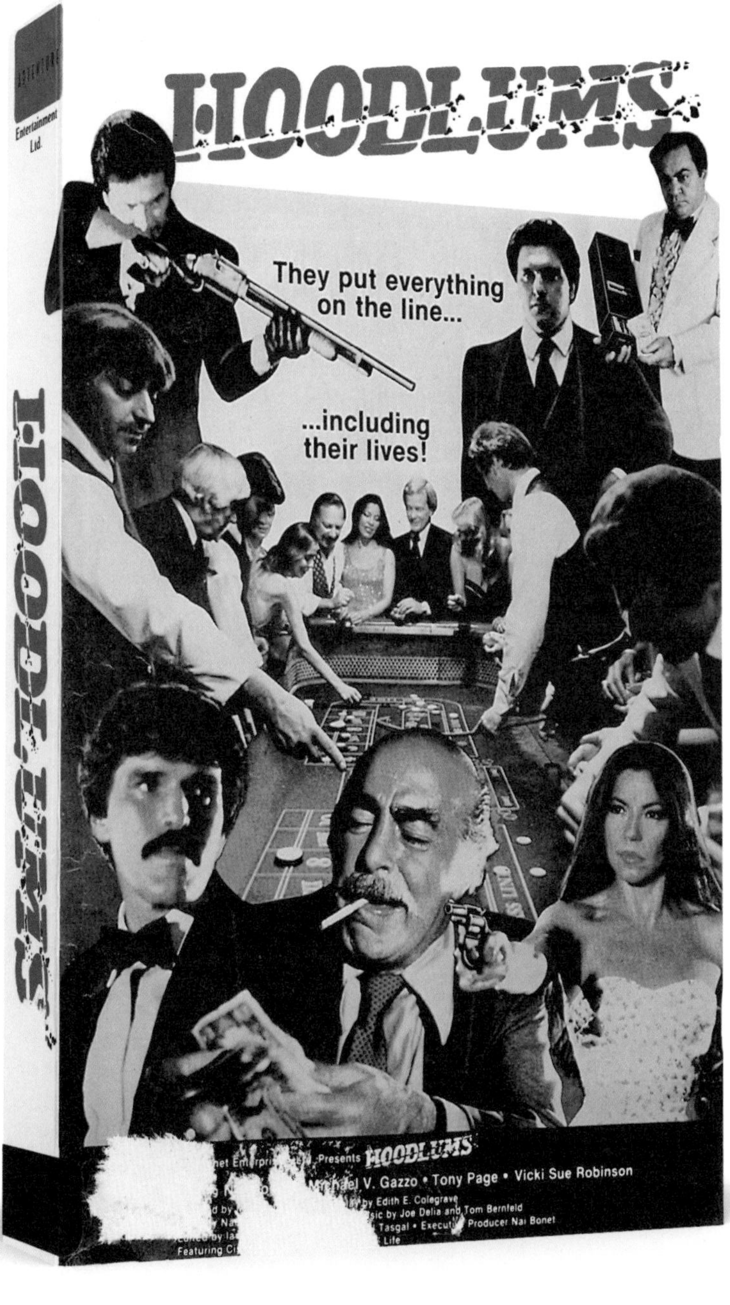
Entertainment Ltd.
HOODLUMS
They put everything on the line...
...including their lives!
HOODLUMS
Presents HOODLUMS
Michael V. Gazzo • Tony Page • Vicki Sue Robinson
by Edith E. Colegrave
Joe Delia and Tom Bernfeld
Producer Nai Bonet

ILSA Harem Keeper of the Oil Sheiks

The place ... an oil rich sheikdom in Arabia. The time ... Now. ILSA, the SHE WOLF OF THE S.S. is back, more vicious and brutal than ever. This time she is the harem keeper to the insatiable lusts of Sheik Hakim, known as the El Sharif, a wealthy and chillingly cruel oil lord. ILSA with her two black assistants, Satin and Velvet, arrange and execute the kidnappings of well known international beauties for use in his private harem. Here she is the teacher and vicious taskmaster of the kidnapped girls. Here with the threat of torture she forces the terrified girls to obey and submit to the erotic desires of her brutal employer.

CREDITS

ILSA	Dyanne Thorne
ADAM	Mike Thayer
EL SHARIF	Victor Alexander
SATIN	Tanya Boyd
VELVET	Marilyn Joy
KAISER	Wolfgang Roehm
Director	Don Edmonds
Producer	William J. Brody
Scenario	Langton Stafford

VIDEATRICS

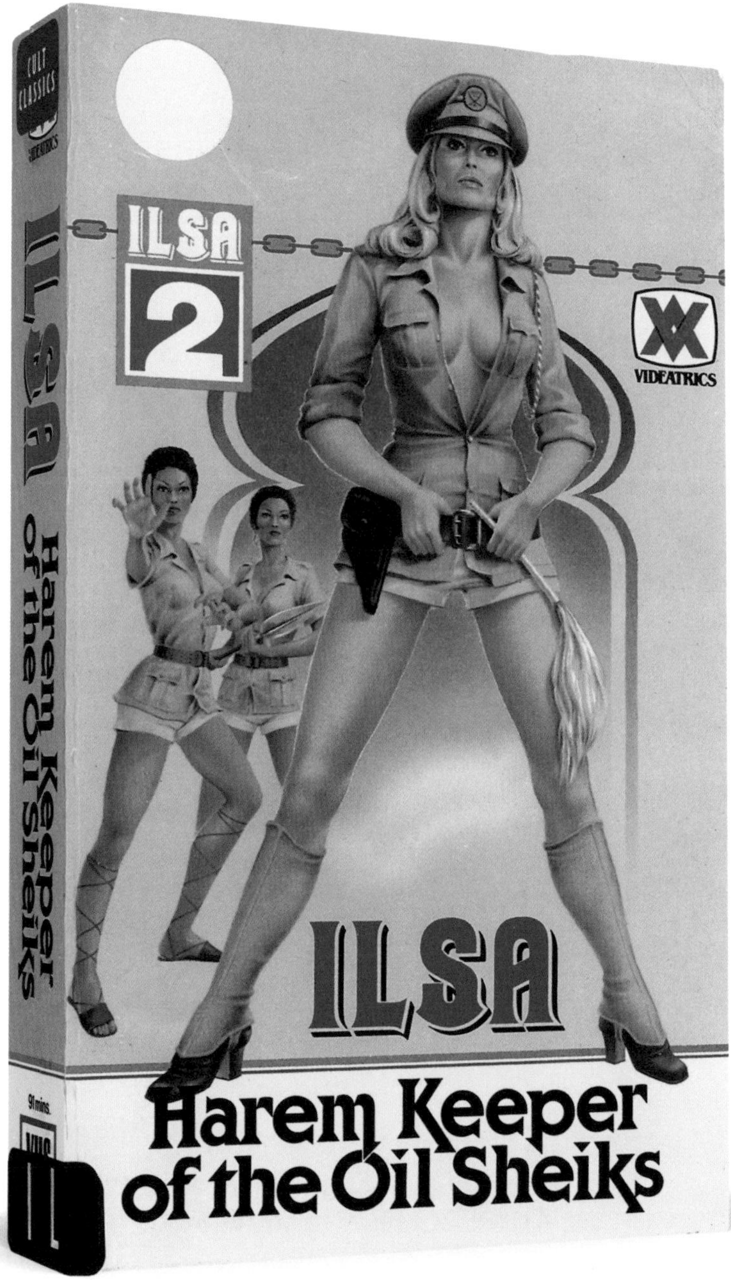
CULT CLASSICS
VIDEATRICS
ILSA
Harem Keeper of the Oil Sheiks
91mins.
ILSA
2
VIDEATRICS
ILSA
Harem Keeper of the Oil Sheiks

ILSA She Wolf of the SS

She was the most dreaded Nazi of them all. With her·'Black Widows' she committed crimes so terrible — even the SS feared her. Until an American POW uses his sexual prowess to combat her insatiable appetite and bring her to her knees.

CREDITS

Ilsa	DYANNE THORNE
Wolf	GREG KNOPH
Ingrid	SANDI RICHMAN
Margrit	JOJO DE VILLE
The General	WOLFGANG ROEHM

Director DON EDMONDS   Producer HERMAN TRAEGER
An AETAS FILM production

CINEPIX
USA., INC.

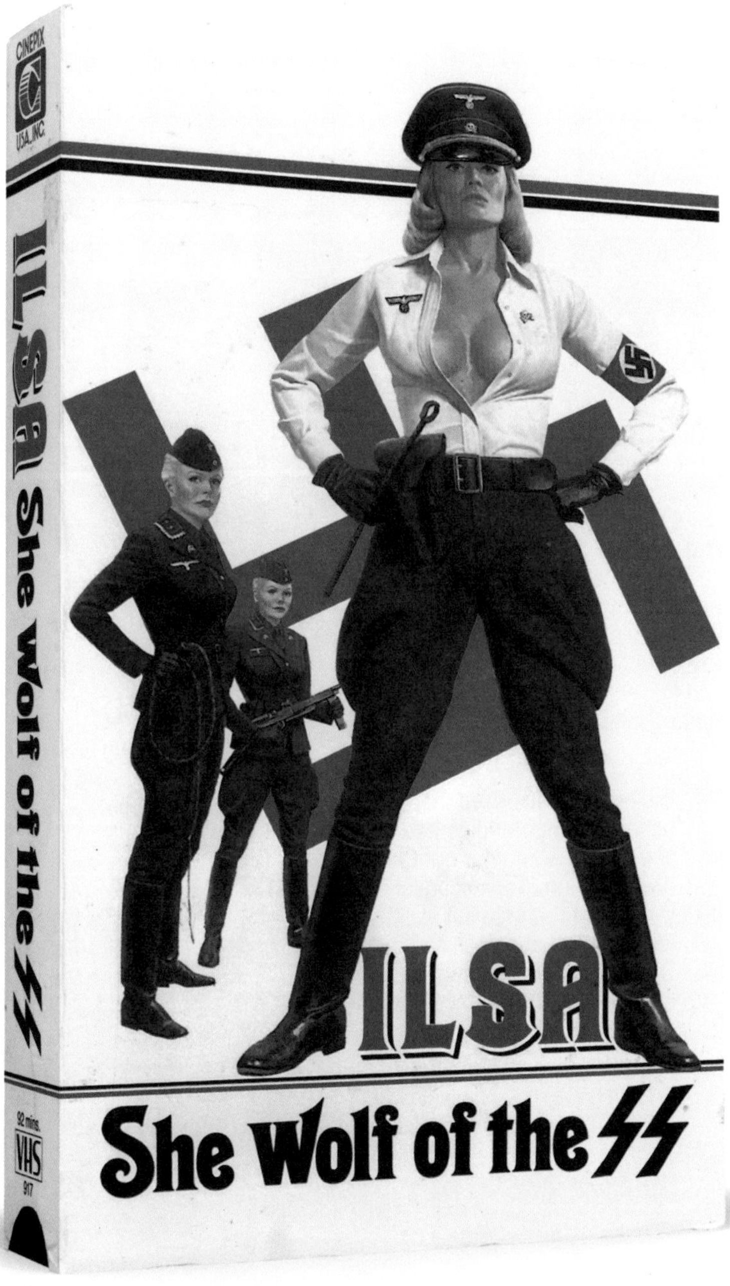
CINEPIX
USA_INC.
ILSA She Wolf of the SS
92 mins.
VHS
917
ILSA
She Wolf of the SS

Hospital of Terror

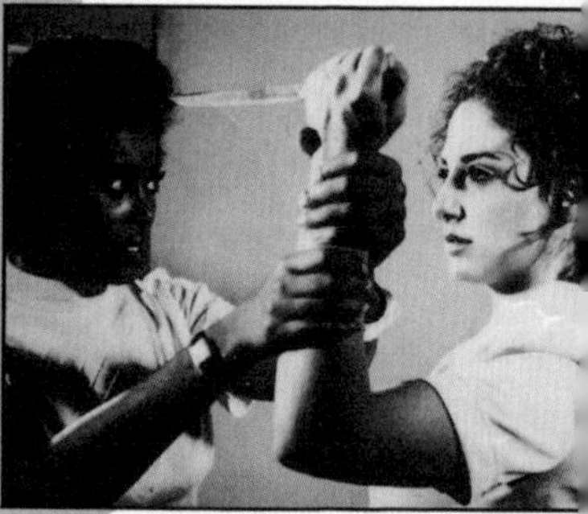

Con man Thomas Reanhauer is the leader of a phony religious sect. His bizarre powers go berserk during a mock exorcism and he suffers a massive heart attack. He's rushed to the hospital where doctors perform surgery against his wishes. He dies on the operating table, but gets revenge by transferring his evil spirit into the soul of a young innocent nurse.

The nurse, possessed by his raging fury, terrorizes the entire hospital using needles and knives. Her bloody slaughter continues day and night. One victim is thrown into a huge vat of scalding molten steel. Only her boyfriend, Dr. Desmond, lives long enough to solve the mystery of the demonic nightmare.

Color
Running time
90 minutes

NTSC/USA Manufactured in U.S.A.
Package design and artwork
© MCMLXXXV/SUPER VIDEO INC.
All rights reserved.

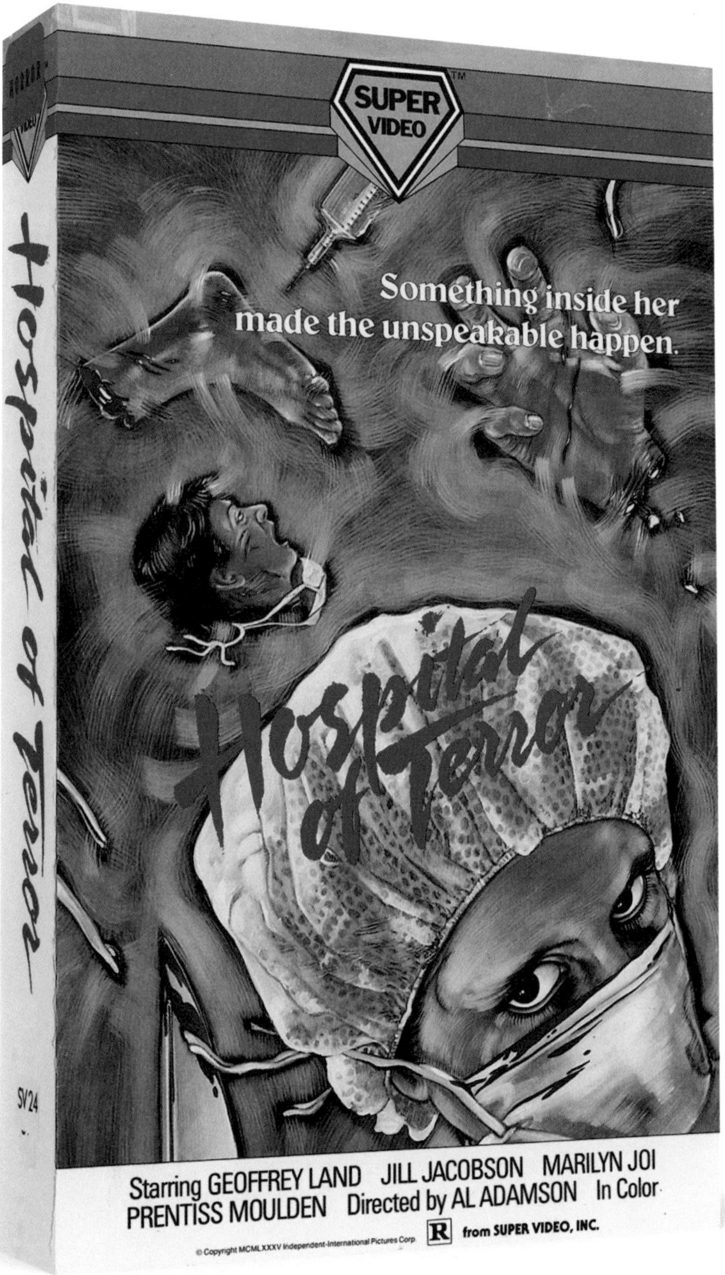
SUPER VIDEO
Something inside her made the unspeakable happen.
Hospital of Terror
Starring GEOFFREY LAND JILL JACOBSON MARILYN JOI PRENTISS MOULDEN Directed by AL ADAMSON In Color
R from SUPER VIDEO, INC.
© Copyright MCMLXXXV Independent-International Pictures Corp.
Hospital of Terror
SV24

A TOTALLY OUTRAGEOUS COMEDY!

HOG WILD is a sensational comedy-adventure about a gang of nasty bikers called the "Rustlers" who provoke a group of nerdy high school kids into getting the ultimate revenge! Sexy PATTI D'ARBANVILLE plays total macho man TONY ROSATO'S biker girl until high school heartthrob MICHAEL BIEHN steps in and wins her heart!

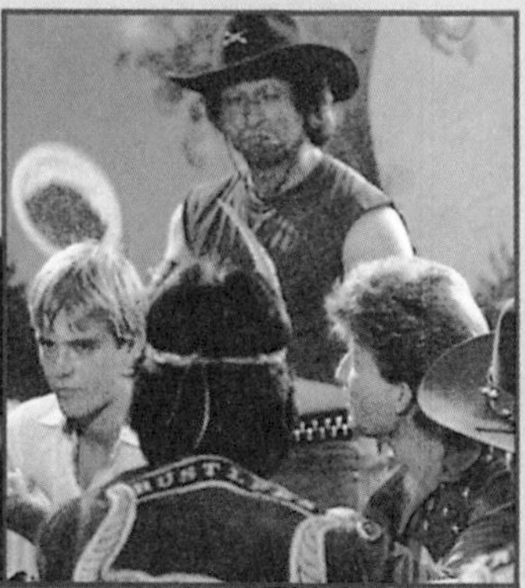

So get set for the ride of your life! It's an outrageous comedy-adventure that's going to drive you absolutely HOG WILD!

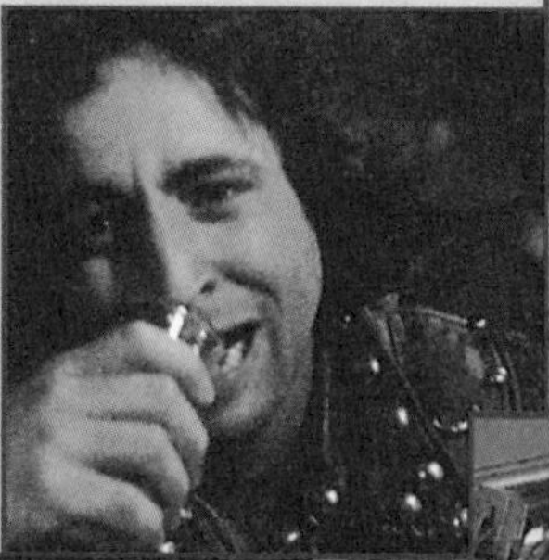

Color, 97 minutes, Comedy/ Adventure

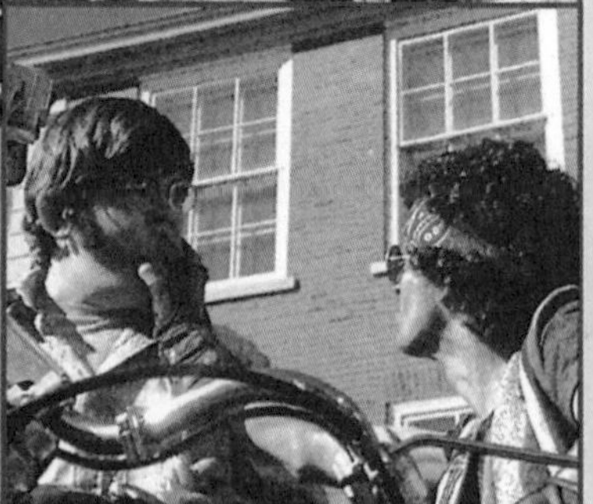

hi-fi
MONO

PG

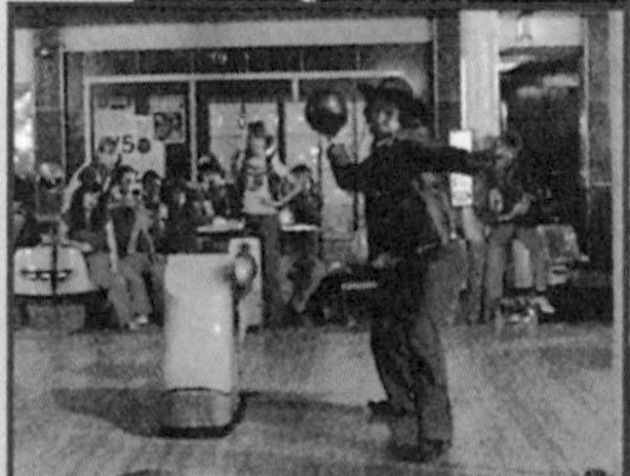

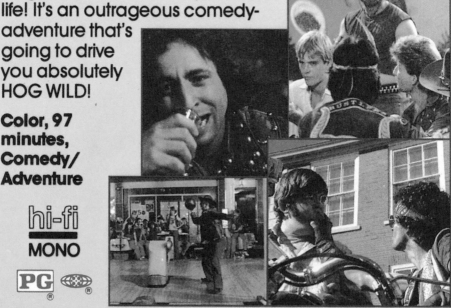

PIERRE DAVID and VICTOR SOLNICKI Present HOG WILD
Starring PATTI D'ARBANVILLE MICHAEL BIEHN TONY ROSATO
Directed by LES ROSE Written by ANDREW PETER MARIN
Executive Producers PIERRE DAVID VICTOR SOLNICKI STEPHEN MILLER
Produced by CLAUDE HEROUX A FILMPLAN INTERNATIONAL Production
in Association With REINDEER FILM and
The Canadian Film Development Corp.
AVCO EMBASSY PICTURES Release

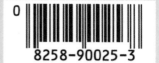

0 8258-90025-3

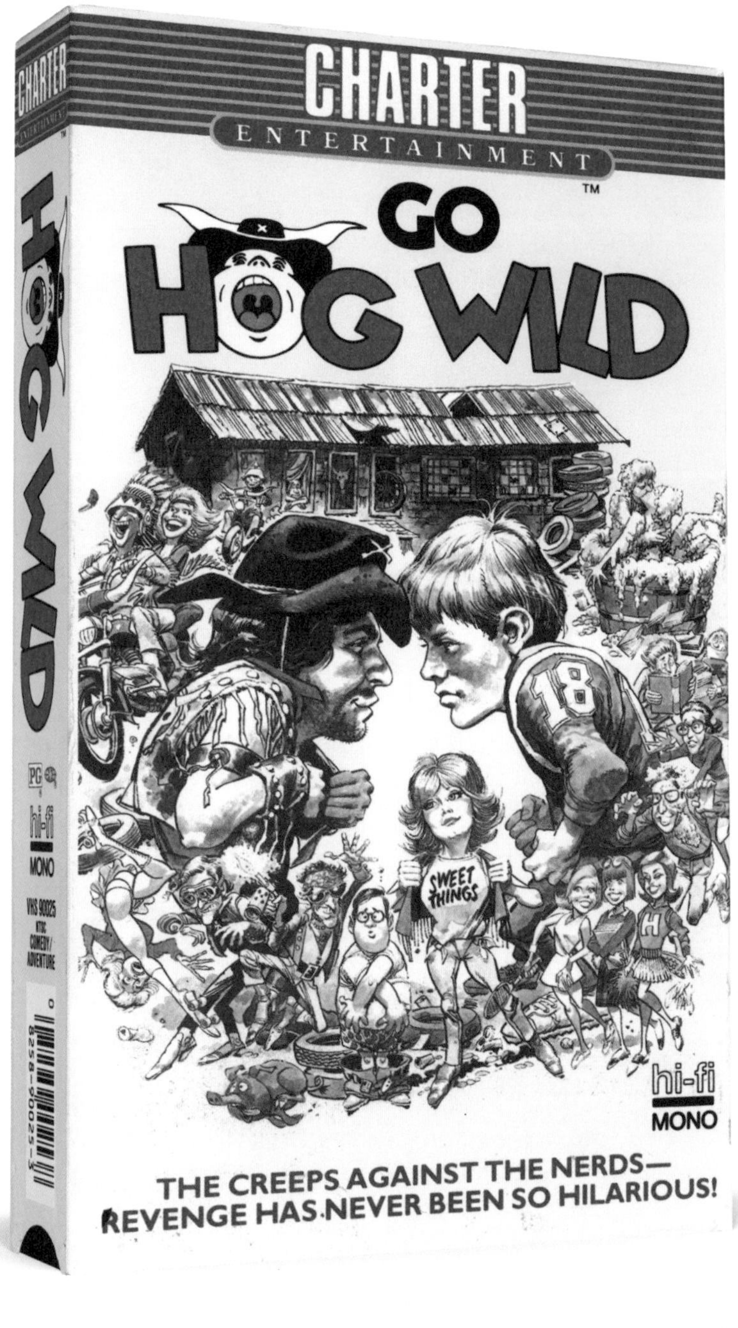
CHARTER
ENTERTAINMENT
GO HOG WILD
TM
SWEET THINGS
18
hi-fi
MONO
THE CREEPS AGAINST THE NERDS—
REVENGE HAS NEVER BEEN SO HILARIOUS!
VHS 90025

Leave your sanity on the door step!

(Color, 1973) It sits there, shrouded in mist and mystery, a nesting place for living evil and terror from the dead. It's Hell House. Roddy McDowall heads the cast of this exciting chiller about four psychic investigators and the dark, brooding mansion they themselves call "the Mt. Everest of haunted houses." It's already destroyed one team of researchers. Now this brave quartet ventures in for another try at unraveling its secret. But before they succeed, they must suffer through madness, murder and everything else the spirits that dwell here have in store for them. Yet learning the truth just might drive them all insane. An ingeniously-devised ghost story, THE LEGEND OF HELL HOUSE will thrill and delight veteran horror fans from the first creaking door to the very last slithering shadow.
94 Minutes

PG

☐ **CLOSED CAPTIONED** by National Captioning
®Institute. Used with Permission.

Recorded in Hi-Fi.

 Only factory sealed packages contain this mark on wrapper.

CBS/FOX VIDEO
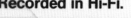
Industrial Park Drive

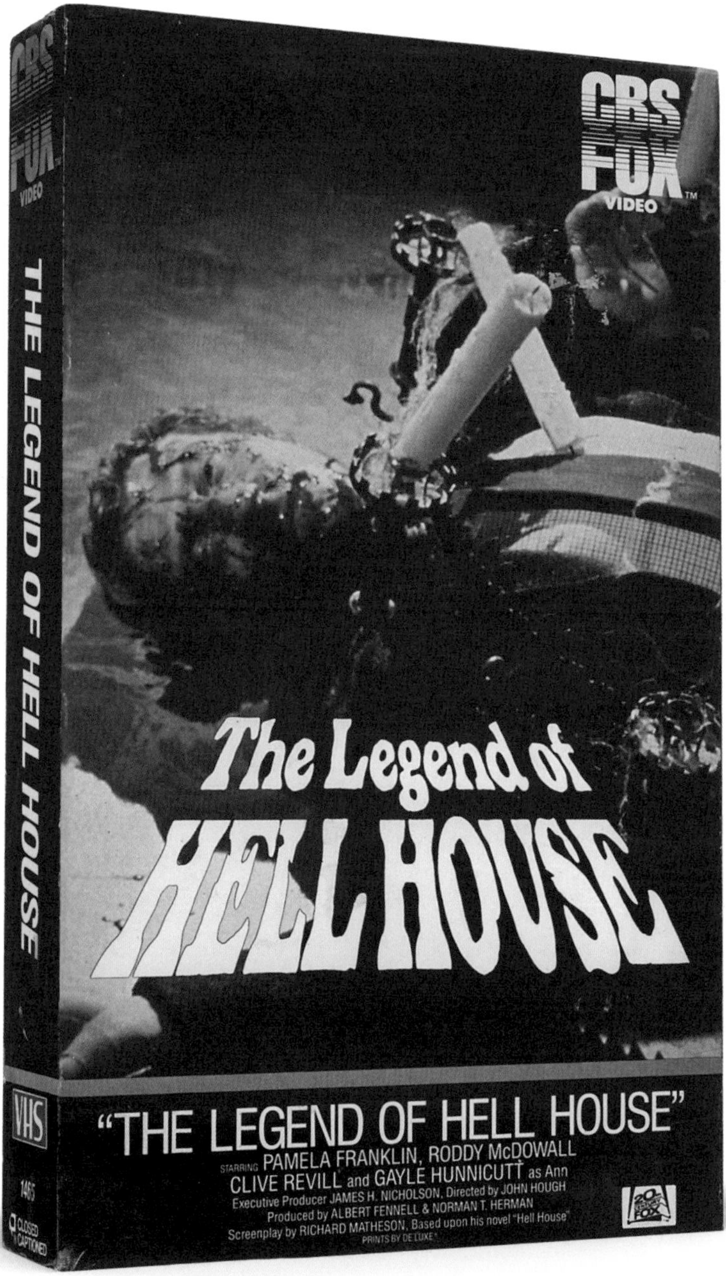
CBS
FOX
VIDEO
THE LEGEND OF HELL HOUSE
CBS
FOX
VIDEO
The Legend of
HELL HOUSE
VHS
"THE LEGEND OF HELL HOUSE"
STARRING PAMELA FRANKLIN, RODDY McDOWALL
CLIVE REVILL and GAYLE HUNNICUTT as Ann
Executive Producer JAMES H. NICHOLSON, Directed by JOHN HOUGH
Produced by ALBERT FENNELL & NORMAN T. HERMAN
Screenplay by RICHARD MATHESON, Based upon his novel "Hell House"
PRINTS BY DE LUXE
1465
CLOSED CAPTIONED

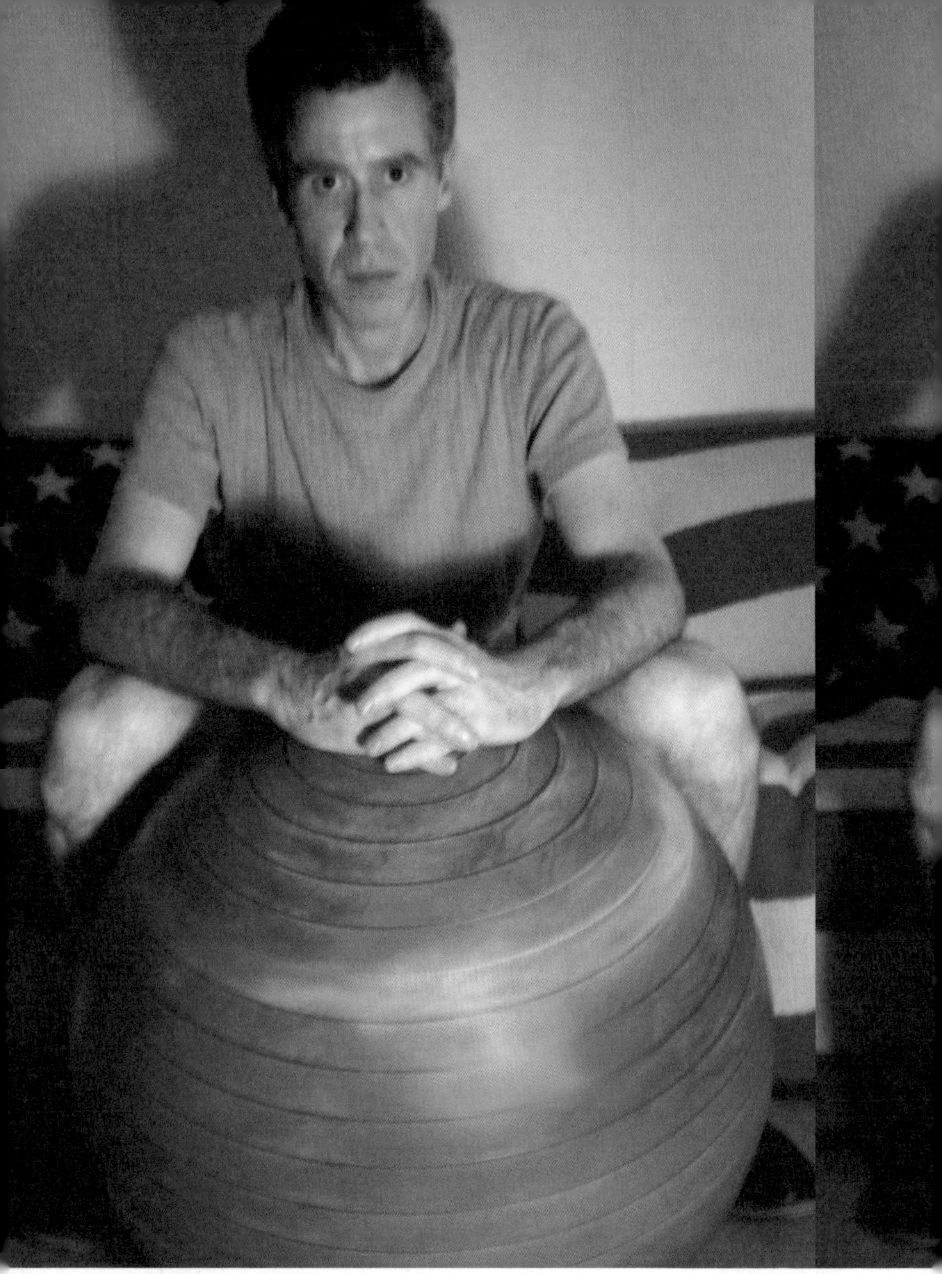

Formerly San Franciscan by way of Chicago, Jacques Boyreau is now based in Portland and Eugene, Oregon. He is a fastidious werewolf and atheist who opposes Satan. Past jobs include movie production (*Hippy Porn; Mod Fuck Xplosion; In; Planet Manson; Candy Von Dewd*); vinyl production (*The Peter Fonda Album; Night of the Living Dead Vinyl; Bruce Lee, Heroin, and The Punk Scene*); book production (*Trash: The Graphic Genius of Xploitation Movie Poster Art; The Male Mystique*). Between 1994-2006 he organized a commune/nightclub in California called The Werepad. His current work includes 35mm film programming and art curation, notably the "SuperTrash" series beginning October 2009 at The Andy Warhol Museum. In his spare time, he is a marketing specialist for Ninkasi beer.